Gender Justice and Development: Vulnerability and Empowerment

T0316046

Vulnerability associated with human interdependence is a wellspring of values in care ethics. Vulnerability resulting from social problems, by contrast, demands remedy. Empowerment is frequently the just form of remedy, and so empowerment finds its place in contemporary development theory. Development planners and global aid providers now focus upon improving the wellbeing of the most vulnerable – especially women – by empowering them economically, socially and politically.

Eight ethical theorists consider vulnerability and empowerment in this volume. Jay Drydyk argues that empowerment is necessarily relational, not simply a matter of expanding choices. Christine Koggel reviews Drydyk's discussion through the lens of feminist relational theory, considering how norms and institutions shape, delimit, and promote empowerment. Gail Presbey examines East African women's empowerment through the writings and biography of Wangari Maathai. Stacy Kosko considers indigenous self-governance and indigenous participation in shared governance. Serene Khader reflects upon postcolonial feminist criticism of the concept of adaptive preference. Vida Panitch discusses economic vulnerability that attends the global market in surrogate birth. Anupam Pandey reviews third world ecofeminist activism and literature. Ann Cudd envisions international humanitarian intervention to support women's autonomy against oppressive state and social institutions.

This book was originally published as a special issue of the *Journal of Global Ethics*.

Eric Palmer is Professor of Philosophy at Allegheny College, Pennsylvania, USA. His recent research in development ethics concerns multinational corporate responsibility in for-profit credit and payment schemes directed towards the poor through microfinance, e-payment systems, credit cards and payday lending. He is co-editor of the *Journal of Global Ethics*.

Gender Justice and Development: Vulnerability and Empowerment

Volume II

Edited by
Eric Palmer

Routledge
Taylor & Francis Group

LONDON AND NEW YORK

First published 2015 by Routledge

2 Park Square, Milton Park, Abingdon, Oxon OX14 4RN
711 Third Avenue, New York, NY 10017, USA

Routledge is an imprint of the Taylor & Francis Group, an informa business

First issued in paperback 2017

British Library Cataloguing in Publication Data
A catalogue record for this book is available from the British Library

ISBN 13: 978-1-138-85259-4 (hbk)
ISBN 13: 978-1-138-06026-5 (pbk)

Typeset in Times New Roman
by RefineCatch Limited, Bungay, Suffolk

Publisher's Note
The publisher accepts responsibility for any inconsistencies that may have
arisen during the conversion of this book from journal articles to book chapters,
namely the possible inclusion of journal terminology.

Disclaimer
Every effort has been made to contact copyright holders for their permission to
reprint material in this book. The publishers would be grateful to hear from any
copyright holder who is not here acknowledged and will undertake to rectify
any errors or omissions in future editions of this book.

Contents

Citation Information

The following chapters were originally published in the *Journal of Global Ethics*, volume 9, issue 3 (2013). When citing this material, please use the original page numbering for each article, as follows:

Chapter 7

Global surrogacy: exploitation to empowerment
Vida Panitch
Journal of Global Ethics, volume 9, issue 3 (2013) pp. 329–343

Chapter 8

Globalization and ecofeminism in the South: keeping the 'Third World' alive
Anupam Pandey
Journal of Global Ethics, volume 9, issue 3 (2013) pp. 345–358

Chapter 9

Truly humanitarian intervention: considering just causes and methods in a feminist cosmopolitan frame
Ann E. Cudd
Journal of Global Ethics, volume 9, issue 3 (2013) pp. 359–375

Please direct any queries you may have about the citations to
clsuk.permissions@cengage.com

Notes on Contributors

Cynthia Bisman is Professor Emeritus of the Graduate School of Social Work and Social Research at Bryn Mawr College, Pennsylvania, USA. Her most recent book, *Social Work: Value-Guided Practice for a Global Society* (2014) provides a framework to promote social justice inclusive of geography and culture. Bisman presents and publishes widely on the moral core of social work, has been the associate editor (North America) for the journal *Ethics and Social Welfare*, and provides a range of editorial functions for journals in the United States and the United Kingdom.

Ann E. Cudd is University Distinguished Professor of Philosophy at the University of Kansas. She is the author of *Analyzing Oppression* (Oxford, 2006) and co-author of *Capitalism, For and Against: A Feminist Debate* (Cambridge, 2011). Her work explores how economic and feminist ideas illuminate ethical and political issues, including intervention in interpersonal and international contexts.

Jay Drydyk is Professor of Philosophy at Carleton University, Ottawa, Canada. He is a Fellow of the Human Development and Capability Association and Past President of the International Development Ethics Association. He is co-author of *Displacement by Development: Ethics, Rights, and Responsibilities* (Cambridge, 2011) as well as articles on ethics and development, the capabilities approach, social and global justice, human rights, and global ethics.

Serene J. Khader is Jay Newman Chair in Philosophy of Culture and Associate Professor of Philosophy at Brooklyn College, City University of New York, USA. She has written extensively on the concept of adaptive preferences and is the author of *Adaptive Preferences and Women's Empowerment* (2011). Most of her work is in the area of global feminist ethics, but she also publishes more broadly in the areas of ethics, political philosophy, and feminist philosophy.

Christine M. Koggel is Professor of Philosophy at Carleton University, Ottawa, Canada and Harvey Wexler Chair in Philosophy, Bryn Mawr College, USA. Her book, *Perspectives on Equality: Constructing a Relational Theory*, shapes the foundation for her research interests in the areas of moral theory, practical ethics, social and political theory, and feminism. She is the editor of *Moral Issues in Global Perspective*; co-editor of *Contemporary Moral Issues and Care Ethics: New Theories and Applications*; and author of numerous journal articles and chapters in edited collections. Her current research in development ethics explores concepts and issues relevant to a global context.

Stacy J. Kosko is the Assistant Director of the Minor in International Development and Conflict Management, and a Research Associate in the Center for International Development and Conflict Management, at the University of Maryland, where she previously served as Associate

Director of the College Park Scholars Public Leadership program. She has consulted for the World Bank and several human rights organizations in Eastern Europe and now serves on the Executive Board of the International Development Ethics Association and is co-Coordinator of the HDCA Human Rights Thematic Group. Prior to joining UMD, she was Deputy Director of The Advocacy Project. She holds a PhD in Policy Studies and international development from UMD and an MS in Foreign Service from Georgetown University.

Eric Palmer is Professor of Philosophy at Allegheny College, Pennsylvania, USA. His recent research in development ethics concerns multinational corporate responsibility in developing nations, particularly in cases of resource extraction. He also focuses upon vulnerability and finance, inquiring into for-profit credit schemes directed towards the poor in less developed nations (through microfinance) and in more developed nations (through credit cards and payday lending). He argues that corporate responsibility in each of these areas of business, when viewed through the lens of the capability approach to development, implies specific duties for multinational corporations and for finance capital.

Anupam Pandey studied Political Science and International Relations at Jawaharlal Nehru University, New Delhi, and completed her PhD on Ecofeminism and International Relations Theory at Carleton University, Ottawa, Canada. Since 2008, she has been teaching at the Political Science and International Development Studies departments in Saint Mary's University and Dalhousie University, Halifax, Canada. Her research and teaching interests are gender and ecological justice issues in development theory and practice, and globalization and its impact on the Third World, with special reference to South Asia. Her recent publications on ecofeminism are included in *Sustainable Development* (2010) and *Capitalism and Confrontation*, Red Quill Books (2013).

Vida Panitch is an Assistant Professor of Philosophy at Carleton University in Ottawa, Canada. Her research interests lie at the intersection of bioethics, feminist philosophy, and distributive justice. Her work engages the concepts of justice, exploitation, and commodification as normative guides to the distribution of health-related goods and services both domestically and internationally, and to the assessment of emerging global health practices.

Gail M. Presbey is Professor of Philosophy at the University of Detroit Mercy, USA. Her areas of expertise are social and political philosophy, philosophy of nonviolence, and African philosophy. She has done research in Kenya, South Africa, Ghana, and India, having received two J. William Fulbright grants. She has had three edited books and over 50 articles and book chapters published, including republications and translations in German, French, Italian, and Spanish. She also teaches African history and politics, and philosophy of feminism. She has been Executive Director and then President of Concerned Philosophers for Peace (2002–2010). Her home page can be seen at http://presbegm.faculty.udmercy.edu/.

Preface

Christine M. Koggel, Cynthia Bisman and Eric Palmer

This is a two volume publication in the Routledge Special Issues as Books (SPIB) series. The two volumes are connected by the common title of *Gender Justice and Development*. The full title for Volume I is *Gender Justice and Development: Local and Global* and for Volume II it is *Gender Justice and Development: Vulnerability and Empowerment*. Each volume began as a special issue: Volume I, edited by Cynthia Bisman and Christine M. Koggel, was published as Volume 6, Number 3 of *Ethics and Social Welfare* in 2012 and Volume II, edited by Eric Palmer, was published as Volume 9, Number 3 of the *Journal of Global Ethics* in 2013.

The special issues emerged from papers that were given at the Ninth International Development Ethics Association (IDEA) conference at Bryn Mawr College, Pennsylvania, USA in June 2011. Because the College has a long history of educating and empowering women from around the world, Bryn Mawr was selected by IDEA to host its first international conference in the U.S. with the theme, 'Gender Justice and Development: Local and Global.' About 100 participants from around the world presented papers reflecting a diverse range of theoretical, conceptual, empirical, practical, and activist perspectives from work that included philosophy and the humanities, social sciences, social work, development studies, policy studies, policy making, and local and global organizing. In addition to the papers that were selected for the special issues, now re-published in this two volume set, Volume 10, Number 2 of the online journal, *Ethics & Economics/Ethique & Economique* edited by Mario Solis and Jay Drydyk collected several additional papers. This special issue, with papers available in PDF format, can be found at: http://ethique-economique. net/Volume-10-Numero-2.html

The time was right then, as it continues to be now, to explore gender at local, national, and global levels as a key factor in devising policies for addressing inequalities of all kinds and for alleviating poverty and promoting social, economic, and political justice. As the papers in both volumes show, there is no single definition of gender justice and much disagreement among local, national, and international power-holders and those subjected to power about what constitutes gender injustice and how to alleviate or eliminate it. That said, changes envisioned by measures such as improving health care for women and children, recognizing care as work vital to the survival and flourishing of any society, and increasing women's access to education, property, and work outside the home reflect agreement on the key role that women can play when gender is taken seriously in development theory and policy. Among other things, a commitment to implementing these policies can help to remove discrimination on the basis of gender and to alleviate the inequalities and injustices that discriminatory practices and traditions produce. Despite positive changes on a number of fronts, women across the world, in rich as well as poor countries, continue to suffer for lack of power, agency and voice; continue to be vulnerable to ill-health, early morbidity, the effects of climate change, and violence; and continue to endure inequalities of various kinds. To give content to one example, sexual violence is pervasive in war-torn and post-conflict contexts, has been ignored in the armed forces, organized sports, and college campuses in the U.S. and beyond, is evident in Nigeria with the kidnapping and enslaving of young girls, and is seen in the north of England where officials condoned sexual abuse of girls. These cases gaining public attention in 2014 indicate the need to continue placing gender at the forefront of moral, social, and political theory and action. Given these ongoing conditions in the contemporary context, we believe that reaching a wider readership through the re-publication of these two volumes on *Gender Justice and Development* is imperative. We also believe that exposure to and awareness of IDEA's focus on development ethics can help to devise the theory, the policy, and the social activism needed for addressing these conditions.

The International Development Ethics Association (IDEA) is a cross-cultural group of philosophers, social scientists, and practitioners who apply ethical reflection to global development goals and strategies, to North/South relations, and to human and social development in general. Its goals are to promote discussion of the nature of ethically desirable development, of ethical means for achieving development, and of ethical dilemmas arising in the practice of development. IDEA's international conferences aim to share and apply ethical reflection to development goals and strategies and to relations between the 'North' and 'South'; to effect ethically sound development policies, institutions, and practices; and to promote solidarity, mutual support, and interchange among development theorists and practitioners throughout the world.

On this understanding of its goals, it is clear that IDEA views development as needing to identify and address injustices at local, national, and global levels and to understand the intersections of these. Such concerns were promoted in David A. Crocker's seminar on 'Ethics and Third World Development' at the 1984 World Federation of Future Studies meetings at the University of Costa Rica, an event that fostered a Development Ethics Working Group. The organization's more familiar name was introduced at its First International Conference on Ethics and Development, held in 1987 at the same university, and led by Crocker, who held the IDEA Presidency until 2002.[1] The development ethics approach has continued through the history of IDEA, and its concerns are evident in the thematic titles of its later conferences: 'Economic Crisis, Ethics, and Development Alternatives' (Merida, Mexico,1989); 'The Ethics of Ecodevelopment: Culture, the Environment, and Dependency' (Tegucigalpa, Honduras,1992); 'The New Economic Order and Development: Ethical Challenges for the 21st Century' (Santiago, Chile,1995); 'Globalization, Self-determination, and Justice in Development,' (Madras, India,1997); 'Poverty, Corruption, and Human Rights: Ethics of Citizenship and Public Service' (Zamorano, Honduras, 2002); 'Accountability, Responsibility and Integrity in Development: The Ethical Challenges in Sub-Saharan Africa and Beyond' (Kampala, Uganda, 2006); 'Ética del desarrollo humano y justicia global' (Ethics of Human Development and Global Justice) (Valencia, Spain, 2009); and 'Gender Justice and Development: Local and Global' (Bryn Mawr, USA, 2011).

In July 2014, IDEA held its tenth international conference, a 30th Anniversary celebration, in its place of birth, San Jose, Costa Rica, with the theme 'Contribuciones desde la ética del desarrollo para un futuro social sostenible' (Development Ethics Contributions for a Socially Sustainable Future). IDEA is committed to ensuring that the best of the papers from its conferences are collected and published, as these volumes show. Similar work is planned as an outcome of the Costa Rica event. We are grateful to Routledge and especially to Kimberley Smith and Emily Ross for recognizing the timeliness and importance of *Gender Justice and Development* and giving these papers new life in this two volume set of the SPIB series.

---

1 Consult Lori Keleher, "International Development Ethics Association (IDEA)," in Deen K. Chatterjee, ed. *Encyclopedia of Global Justice*, Springer, 2011 and "History of IDEA" at the organization's website, http://developmentethics.org/about–2/.

Introduction: Vulnerability and Empowerment

This issue of *Journal of Global Ethics* draws together a thematic collection on the paired topics of human vulnerability and human empowerment. A selection of papers has been developed following presentations at "Gender Justice and Development: Local and Global," a conference of the International Development Ethics Association, hosted at Bryn Mawr College in Pennsylvania, USA, in June 2011. Two papers that also serve to highlight these themes have been selected from among those received by the journal, and a brief essay that develops them within a recent political context completes the issue.

Vulnerability and empowerment are central concepts for ethics in development and in development cooperation. Many development programmes now focus on improving the wellbeing of the most vulnerable by empowering them economically, socially and politically. As Stacy Kosko reminds us in this issue, vulnerability is a term that means susceptibility to wounding. It certainly does not appear to be a promising condition in that regard. Philosophers will nevertheless accept vulnerability as central to the human condition (consider Thomas Hobbes, for one), and some will value it positively, as an element of an ethic of care (Carol Gilligan, citing Erik Erikson). Denis Goulet, in *The Cruel Choice*, has proposed that those in positions of relative invulnerability should choose to adopt vulnerabilities for the sake of re-humanizing their relations with others. Goulet seeks to undermine differences in power, the recognition of which he takes to be the very source of underdevelopment. Just this year, Joan Tronto, in *Caring Democracy*, takes the acknowledgement of vulnerability as central to a citizen's role. The condition that Hobbes would control by all means necessary has undergone a restoration, as the papers within this issue of *Journal of Global Ethics* further attest.

Vulnerability has returned as a philosophically pertinent category, but the specific dimensions of vulnerability require further ethical appraisal. Infrequently, a shared and voluntary vulnerability can be a positive aspect of group identification (as may currently be seen in the condition of avowed Chicago White Sox baseball fans, who have seen the worst season in forty years). Misery loves company, and builds community, at least on occasion. More frequently, the recognition of wounds and of specific vulnerabilities is followed by calls for remedy and for empowerment as a just form of remedy.

Empowerment is the primary focus of two theoretical papers that open this issue. Jay Drydyk's contribution argues that empowerment must be carefully distinguished from agency, since agency, even as a technical term in development ethics, is too thin a concept to support consideration of the relational aspect of power, and of power's effects on well-being. If dominance and subjection are characteristics found within a society, then an increase in agency for nearly all (say, in the abundant opportunity that arises with the spread of the internet) may nevertheless also reduce the power of some, and perhaps also reduce their well-being freedom (for some may become subject to more thorough monitoring and perhaps also to debilitating fear, as a consequence). Drydyk argues that some individuals and groups are "asymmetrically vulnerable," since

1

their well-being may not be advanced alongside an increase in their agency under conditions of dominance by others. He presents a collection of brief cases in development contexts that illustrate changes producing different realizations of empowerment, one of which has parallels to the technological example above, and one of which considers the role of solidarity as an option that reduces vulnerability.

Christine Koggel continues Drydyk's discussion of the connections of freedom, well-being and empowerment by viewing these concepts as well as Drydyk's own discussion of them through the lens of feminist relational theory. Koggel notes five dimensions of inquiry that the relational approach promotes as she considers "the power residing in dominant norms, structures and institutions" that shape, delimit, and forward women's empowerment. She considers institutions and relations discussed in the World Bank's *World Development Report 2012: Gender Equality and Development*, which itself features explicit discussion of gender norms and a theoretical orientation that invokes Sen's *Development as Freedom*. Koggel also examines the relational focus in a background paper for the 2013 *World Development Report* by Patti Petesch. Petesch discusses gender dynamics and new opportunities for women's economic activity in conflict and post-conflict situations in Liberia, Sudan, Afghanistan and West Bank and Gaza.

Gail Presbey also presents a study of change and empowerment in women's lives within a biographical essay that considers Wangari Maathai and covers Maathai's own thoughts. Presbey enriches her discussion of Maathai by introducing parallel themes and relevant analysis from other East African authors. She extends her account of Maathai's life to the arc of Kenyan women's lives more generally, bringing news of women's increasing presence in Kenyan politics and their increasing independence from men as heads of households and landholders in the eyes of the law. Presbey notes particular progress for women following constitutional reforms of 2010.

The articles that follow these turn more directly to focus upon vulnerability itself, both how it is characterized and how empowerment and participation can reduce it. Stacy Kosko considers the self-determination of indigenous groups, including the conditions under which they choose to participate in shared governance. Developing a line of thought from Denis Goulet and David Crocker, Kosko presents a scale of political participation and self-determination that serves as a framework for evaluating non-elite participation in governance. Serene Khader continues work she commenced in *Adaptive Preferences and Women's Empowerment* (Oxford 2011), developing a nuanced response to postcolonial feminist critics who argue that adaptive preference is a misconception born of a misunderstanding of oppression. Khader does allow that "the range of applicability of the concept of adaptive preference is smaller than typically thought" and she introduces a more fine-grained account of value distortion that notes cases of limited distortion, cases of choices made as tradeoffs to gain some of what is valued, cases of misperception of facts by the agent, and cases of misunderstanding that arises on the part of the interpreter.

Vida Panitch presents a particular case of economic vulnerability in a study of the global commerce in surrogacy. The gap in wealth between prospective parents and surrogate produces a failure of both justice and consent as these are taken to be conditions of just exchange in Alan Wertheimer's characterization of mutually advantageous exploitation. Panitch argues that the relation counts as coercion because bargaining power on the part of the surrogate is lacking due to her limited economic options. Panitch argues that this suggests a negative right of the surrogate against the state, rather than a right against the prospective parents: a right not to be in such a position of limited options. Panitch suggests that empowerment may be achieved in this situation not by banning surrogacy; instead, a "significant portion of the state revenue from commercial surrogacy in India ought to be invested in female empowerment goals ... [through] investment in women's education, literacy, health, employment options, and general resource shares ... as necessitated by the reproductive rights of its female citizens."

Two articles from writing recently accepted at the journal appear to particularly complement these discussions of vulnerability and empowerment, and so they have been included in this special issue. Anupam Pandey provides an extensive review of "third world" ecofeminist activism and literature. Like Presbey, Pandey visits the case of Maathai, but she focuses more particularly on Maathai's place as activist in a global social movement, indicating parallels between Maathai's own Green Belt Movement and the Garhwal (India) Chipko Movement and Maiti Movement of Nepal. Drawing from both activist and theoretical sources, Pandey theorizes a "southern materialist ecofeminism" as a political project explicitly directed against globalization and grounded in "a bonding between nature and women based on the labor of women." Ann Cudd presents an argument of a very different character, considering norms for international humanitarian intervention in support of women's autonomy and against oppressive state and social institutions. Cudd's argument amounts to a reflection upon the balance between cosmopolitan responsibility and state sovereignty that is informed both by a women's rights perspective and by the emerging international norm of "Responsibility to Protect."

Thanks to many who provided advice and refereeing for the special issue. Amrita Banerjee, Sirkku Hellsten, Will Kymlicka and Andie Palmer contributed helpful referee work and criticism, as did several of these authors, for the benefit of each other. The Denis Goulet Memorial Prize in Development Ethics was awarded to two papers presented at the Bryn Mawr conference by Shalini Iyengar and Stacy Kosko. A revised version of Iyengar's paper appears in *Révue Ethique et Economique* 10:2 as "A Tangled Web? Asking the Gender Question in the Multilateral Development Banks' Law and Justice Policies in India," and a revised version of Stacy Kosko's paper appears in this issue of JGE. Thanks goes to the Goulet Prize committee for its work: to Nigel Dower, Workineh Kelbessa and Lori Keleher, as well as to Asuncion St. Clair, President of IDEA, and past President Jay Drydyk. Thanks go especially to Christine Koggel, the primary organizer of the IDEA 2011 conference, and to Cynthia Bisman and Jay Drydyk for their aid in its development. A distinct selection of papers from the conference, many of which are of relevance to themes of this issue, may be found in a special issue of *Ethics and Social Welfare* edited by Cynthia Bisman and Christine Koggel (6:3, September 2012).

Thanks also to to the editors of *Journal of Global Ethics* for allowing this special issue to take form.

Eric Palmer
Allegheny College, USA

3

Empowerment, agency, and power

Jay Drydyk

Department of Philosophy, Carleton University, Ottawa, Ontario, Canada

As 'empowerment' and 'agency' have received wider usage within development research and policy, ambiguities and variant meanings have proliferated. Amidst this conceptual drift, there has also been a tendency to assimilate the two concepts. This tendency is problematic in a number of ways. First, 'agency' has various meanings, and the weakest of these captures little of the concept of empowerment. Second, empowerment has a conceptual link with well-being that agency cannot have. Third, when empowerment is assimilated with expanded agency, that agency is not considered in a relational way: the focus is on how the agency of a group or individual becomes greater than it was, not on the degree to which their agency is dependent on or dominated by the agency of others. If 'empowerment' no longer refers to social relations, it loses its direct relevance to the transformation of those relations and, as some critics have claimed, it ceases to be a 'transformative' concept. After showing that there are cases of empowerment that cannot be captured by conceptions of empowerment that 'take power out', I draw upon the capability approach to propose relational conceptions of agency and empowerment that 'bring power back in'.

Introduction

It is nearly customary by now to begin a conceptual article on empowerment by lamenting how confused the concept has become over the last decade. Keleher has shown, for instance, how the meaning of 'empowerment' for economic-growth conceptions of development diverges from its meaning for the capability approach (2007, 2008). But confusion about the meaning of 'empowerment' is evident even within the human development approach. In *Human Development Report 2000, Human Rights and Human Development* (UNDP 2000) one encounters 'empowering' everywhere, but with various meanings and no discussion of what they have in common. In the chapter titled 'Rights Empowering People in the Fight Against Poverty', 'empower' is used as a synonym either for 'enable' or for 'enable and motivate'. Other uses are more specific: the Gender Empowerment Measure, for instance, pertains to 'whether women are able to actively participate in social and economic life' (18).[1]

A similar misfortune seems to be overtaking the concept of agency. After ages of philosophical debate about the meaning of 'agency', development scholars are now joining in. Sabina Alkire, who earlier reported 30 different definitions of 'empowerment' (Ibrahim and Alkire 2007, 380–403), has observed a similar tendency for 'agency' (Alkire 2008). Of course, it could be argued that this is not such a misfortune, but rather a sign of progress, indicating that both concepts are now being fitted and adapted in a more nuanced way to the real world of development.

In addition to this conceptual drift, there is also a tendency to assimilate the two concepts. Alkire, for instance, sometimes switches from one to the other in mid-sentence, on one occasion noting that they are 'related but often differently defined' (2008, 2). Before this process of semantic assimilation continues, we must wonder whether anything will be lost if 'expanded agency' and 'empowerment' are eventually regarded as synonyms. Both terms are clearly important to the human development approach, of which the central aim is to 'put people back into development'. Indeed, Haq listed empowerment as one of the four central ideals of the human development approach (1995, 16). Will this be watered down somehow if 'empowerment' is taken to mean nothing more than 'expanded agency'?

One concern arises from reflection on how the meaning of 'empowerment of women' has changed since it was endorsed in 1995 at the Fourth World Conference on Women, held in Beijing. There its connotations included *transformation* of gender *relations* (Eyben and Napier-Moore 2009, 287) and other power relations with which they are linked (Batliwala 2007, 559). That was often how activists, too, understood 'empowerment'. In 1992, when Batliwala led an Asia-wide study of how empowerment was understood by civil society organisations that made women's empowerment their stated objective, she found that they 'defined empowerment as a process, and the results of a process, of transforming the relations of power between individuals and social groups' (1993, 2007, 560). Within 10 years, however, the relational conception had fallen out of use in development institutions, replaced by the expanded-choice conception. According to a recent study of OECD Development Assistance Committee, the UK Department for International Development, the Swedish International Development Agency, the United Nations Development Programme and the World Bank, 'Today, most frequently, empowerment is about choice, decision-making, realising opportunities and potential, and community action' (Eyben and Napier-Moore 2009, 291). The new idea of empowerment as choice-expansion is neither relational nor transformative; it has no connotations referring to gender relations or other power relations; nor does it imply any transformation of social relations. Thus, to advocate empowerment in this new sense is no longer to advocate transformation of gender relations. This has provoked various reactions from people whose conceptions of empowerment are relational: Batliwala holds that, if it is the overly diluted idea of empowerment as choice-expansion that prevails in development discourse, it is better to give up on 'empowerment' and seek another vocabulary for advocating transformation of gender relations (2007, 564), while others contend that 'empowerment' should not be abandoned, that it is better to resist the expanded-choice conception and struggle for wider acceptance of a relational, transformative conception. These concerns apply directly to agency conceptions of empowerment, since thinking of empowerment as expanded agency is a specific way to think of empowerment as expanded choice.

Before addressing the power issue, I will consider other conceptual gaps between empowerment and agency, along with attempts that have been made to bridge them. This analysis will show that, while empowerment entails expanded agency, it is not reducible to expanded agency, because empowerment has a conceptual link with well-being that agency cannot have. As far as this goes, empowerment can be described metaphorically as becoming better able to shape one's life for the better – to modify Narayan's phrase (2005, 4). I continue by considering whether the political objections to this and other choice-based conceptions of empowerment can also be supported by sound conceptual argument, and, if so, whether relational dimensions can be added, to bring power back in.

Empowerment as expanded scope for agency

The recent flurry of effort to measure empowerment has already distorted the meaning of the term somewhat by focusing attention ever more on the means of empowerment – such as education, community organisation, the political culture, and openness of institutions (Narayan 2005). The reason for this focus is understandable: the comparative presence or absence of these means is more readily measurable than the degree to which people have been empowered by them. Still, an exclusive focus on the means of empowerment could give many false-positive readings of empowerment. For instance, literacy is an important means of empowerment; illiteracy can be disempowering to women (among others), but literacy does not empower women in all cases, since other factors such as tradition, family structure, or development itself (Boserup 1970) may keep them disempowered. For this reason, it is crucial to keep in focus the meaning of 'empowerment' as a result or outcome. Elsewhere I have given a detailed analysis of 'empowerment' as a result or outcome (Drydyk 2008, 2010), but I will not presuppose it here.

To speak of empowerment as a result or outcome presupposes a process of change to produce it. So 'empowerment' evidently refers not simply to a state of affairs but to a process of change with a specific kind of outcome. In this respect it differs already from 'agency', which refers either to a given person's degree of involvement in a course of action or to the scope of actions that a person could be involved in bringing about. Thus an initial difference appears: 'agency' refers to a state of affairs while 'empowerment' refers to a process of change. Moreover, 'empowered' and 'empowering' are scalar: one person can be more empowered than another or one development project can be more empowering than other. Superficially, though, it would seem that these gaps can be crossed easily by phrases like 'expanded agency' which also reference change and are scalar. To see whether there are any more substantive differences between the two concepts, we should attend more closely to the concept of agency, especially as it has been developed recently within the capability approach.

Sen introduced an idea of agency into the capability approach as an evaluative space contrasting with capability (1992, 39–72, 1993). The valuable functionings that a person has reason to value, and actually manages to achieve, comprise that person's well-being achievement. The alternative combinations of functionings that a person *can* achieve comprise that person's capability or well-being freedom. The property of increasing a person's well-being freedom is a good-making property: for instance, what makes some drugs good or advantageous is that they can be used to expand our well-being freedom, specifically by enabling us to stay healthy, or indeed to stay alive. Agency, by contrast, is conceived in terms of achieving goals that people happen to value, rather than functioning in ways that they have reason to value. Such goals may be other-regarding or in other ways unrelated to the person's own well-being. This too is a source of advantage or disadvantage, defining an evaluative space. So some drugs may also be advantageous to athletes by enabling them to win competitions, even if some health risks are involved. 'Agency' in this sense refers to a person's scope for achieving that person's valued goals.

The role of 'agency' in this sense, within the capability approach, has been to supplement well-being freedom as an evaluative space exhibiting the inequalities that should matter for social policy and social justice. It was thought to be a necessary supplement because the important inequalities may not just be about individuals' own well-being; people have other causes and concerns, some altruistic, and unequal freedom to successfully pursue these causes and concerns can also be a significant inequality.

However, this concept of agency has a serious defect compared with the idea of well-being freedom: it is unavoidably subjective. Hence it is subject to the problem of adaptive preferences: if grinding poverty causes people to give up on their hopes and aspirations, they have as a result fewer unachieved goals. Has their agency thereby expanded? There is another puzzle about asceticism: the man who gives away his fortune to become a *sadhu* has thereby given up a great many goals that he might have achieved with his fortune, but he has gained a goal that he now values more, a simple meditative life. Has his agency been reduced or increased?

Another defect in this conception of agency is that it might underemphasise the aspect of active decision-making. 'Agency freedom' might refer simply to the extent to which a person's valued goals can be achieved, whereas 'agency achievement' might refer simply to the extent to which a person's valued goals are actually achieved. But here we must ask, 'achieved by whom, exactly?' To require that agency achievements include only those valued outcomes brought about by the agent, and no one else, would be quite unrealistic, since little can be brought about in the world without the cooperation (or at least the non-interference) of others. This requirement is also too individualistic, excluding achievements brought about through collective action. Moreover, short of agency achievement there is a range of unsuccessful agency attempts, for which we must also leave conceptual space. On the other hand, we do not want to include cases like the following as cases of agency achievement:

> Sire – over what do you rule?
> 'Over everything', said the king, with magnificent simplicity.
> Over everything?
> The king made a gesture, which took in his planet, the other planets, and all the stars.
> . . . And the stars obey you?
> 'Certainly they do', the king said. 'They obey instantly. I do not permit insubordination.'
> . . . I should like to see a sunset . . . Do me that kindness . . . Order the sun to set . . .
> . . . You shall have your sunset. I shall command it. But, according to my science of government, I shall wait until conditions are favorable.
> 'When will that be?' inquired the little prince.
> 'Hum! Hum!' replied the king; and before saying anything else he considered a bulky almanac.
> 'Hum! Hum! That will be about – about – that will be this evening about twenty minutes to eight. And you will see how well I am obeyed!'
> The little prince yawned. He regretted his lost sunset. And then, too, he was already beginning to be a little bored. (de Saint-Exupéry 1943, 38)

Active decision-making

The potential weaknesses of this conception of agency have been known to capability theorists for some time, and so they began to focus more on the degree of active involvement that people have in achievement of their goals. In Sen's contribution to the Beijing Conference, he stressed that what is essential to the concept of women's agency is to have an 'active role in pursuing whatever goals she has reasons to support and promote' (1995, 104). From this and other work by Sen, David Crocker has reconstructed what he calls Sen's 'ideal of agency' (Crocker 2008, 157). At the bottom, agency is presented as a scalar property: some people manage to exercise, in what they do, a greater degree of agency than others, and a person or group may at some times exercise a greater degree of agency than they do at other times. The degree to which agency is exercised varies according to the degree to which four conditions are met. Agency is exercised (a) insofar as a person either performs an activity or plays a role in performing it, (b) insofar as this activity has an impact on the world, (c) insofar as the activity was chosen by the person (d) for reasons of their own (in individual or group deliberation). Presenting the four dimensions in this order is, I think, highly suggestive of what the core idea is really about, namely, the degree to which one's activities are one's own, or, so to speak, the 'ownership' of one's activities. A contrary of 'agency' in this sense would perhaps be 'alienation'. Acting for reasons 'of one's own' might also vary by degree of autonomy versus heteronomy. In her discussion of the measurement of agency, Alkire suggests employing self-determination theory for this purpose, to distinguish between actions that are chosen under coercion or social pressure versus those supported by people's own values and views of their own lives (2008, 22).

I have argued elsewhere (Drydyk 2008, 2010) that something like this is one essential component of empowerment (I referred to it simply as 'active decision-making'). What I will argue here is that this is just one component of empowerment which, while essential, is far from exhaustive of empowerment.

Recall that the idea of empowerment is scalar. In one direction we can distinguish changes that are more empowering than others; in the other direction we can distinguish changes that are more disempowering than others. There are multiple criteria for making these comparisons. Intuitively, one criterion ought to be the weight or importance of what it is that people are empowered to do. If the captain of the Titanic tells the passengers that they are now permitted to arrange the deck chairs in any way they wish, this would perhaps expand their agency freedom, but it would not be especially empowering. A patriarchal society that relaxed customary rules of dress and behaviour for women would thereby expand their agency freedom somewhat, but it would be far more empowering if these women gained control over major life-decisions about education, employment, marriage, childbearing, and household division of labour. These, too, would be additional expansions of agency, but the idea of agency lacks any criterion for recognising these as *weightier* expansions of agency. For the capability approach, surely impact on well-being freedom should serve as the criterion. But this is external to the concept of agency. Agency, as we are now considering it, is a concept of autonomous personal involvement in activities; it is not about the consequences of those activities on a person's life. Simply put, the idea of agency sorts actions by what goes into them, not by what comes out. The fact that one type of action is more consequential than another cannot, by itself, endow that type of action with greater agency.

There is, however, an objection to this line of argument. Arguably agency is gauged in part by the consequences of an activity, in that greater agency would be attributed to an activity with greater effective power (Alkire 2008, 14ff.; Alsop, Bertelsen, and Holland 2006, 16). If effective power took into account the significance of an activity's effects, and impact on well-being freedom counts towards significance, then greater agency should be attributed to activities with greater impact on well-being freedom.

The response is that, while effective power is important to agency, and effective power could be estimated in this way, it would be unwise to do so, especially for the capability approach. The reason is that this would erode the distinction between agency freedom and well-being freedom. The purpose of this distinction is to acknowledge that not everything that people do is devoted to their own well-being, and that well-being freedom is not the only touchstone of value and advantage. Other things we do and have and encounter are advantageous to us just because our interaction with them is *ours,* issuing from our own autonomous decision-making.[2] This distinction is lost if agency is conceived consequentially in terms of well-being rather than in terms of autonomy.

The following distinction stands, then: we conceive of empowerment as *greater* insofar as it has *greater impact on well-being freedom,* but the idea of agency should not be linked to well-being freedom in this way.

Let me draw together some of the results that seem to have emerged so far. Agency is one essential element of empowerment. Yet well-being freedom cannot be included as an internal criterion for expansion of agency. On the other hand, impact on well-being freedom does (among other factors) gauge the extent to which people have been empowered. This suggests a working relationship between the two. Empowerment is concerned with agency, but not reducible to it. Restricted agency means a reduction in the degree to which people's activities are autonomously or deliberatively chosen. This is one way in which people can be disempowered. But they are also disempowered if there are barriers blocking such autonomous/deliberative activity from having an impact on well-being freedom. When agency is disconnected from well-being freedom in this way, it is reduced in some cases to the freedom to choose which pathway or sidewalk to sleep on, or which bridge to sleep under. Therefore, from a capability perspective, empowerment must be concerned not only with expanding agency but also with removing the gaps and barriers between people's agency and the expansion of their well-being freedom.

Empowerment and power

Even for this revised conception of empowerment, the idea of power remains somewhat difficult to digest. Being empowered is not reducible to gaining power, and, if all that 'empowerment' means is becoming better able to shape one's life for the better, some cases of empowerment will not involve power gains at all. Therefore, on one hand, 'empowerment' cannot be defined by considerations of power alone. On the other hand, the use of 'empowerment' in development research and policy generally expresses concerns about power. So while power is a concern of 'empowerment', it does not work easily into its definition. In this section I review the difficulties and propose a solution.

Arguably empowerment differs from agency in that 'empowerment' means an expansion of power. Indeed, among the meanings reported by *OED Online* the only one relevant to our context is: 'To bestow power upon, make powerful' (s.v. 'empower', 2b). However, there are two reasons for treating the link between these ideas with greater circumspection.

First, in our context, the idea of being better able to shape one's life is essential. If we imagine a case where the disenfranchisement of women ends, surely we would want to say that they have made some gain in power or that their power is less severely restricted. Yet we should be reluctant to say they have been empowered unless they were able to use this new political power to shape their own lives. Or, if there are two such cases, and women managed only in one case to use the vote to shape their own lives, we would want to say that these women achieved greater empowerment than the others. Therefore, while it is clear that depriving people of power can be disempowering, it is not always the case that gaining power is empowering. Consequently, it is *not* inconsistent either to say that someone has been empowered without gaining power or to say that someone has gained power without being empowered in our sense.

Second, while gaining power can be an important means of empowerment, it is important to avoid defining outcomes in terms of their causes. To see this point, consider a parallel case. Exposure to sunlight is at present the only known cause of melanoma (skin cancer), but we do not define skin cancer in terms of sunlight exposure. Why not? If we did, then it would be inconsistent to claim that a case of skin cancer could be caused by anything else. If, rather than letting the link between the two be regarded as a factual claim, open to being supported or disputed by evidence, we defined 'skin cancer' in terms of sunlight exposure, we would not only be making this evidence irrelevant, but we would be blocking the path of inquiry into other possible causes – because we are defining 'skin cancer' so as to imply it could not possibly have any other cause. Similarly, to define 'empowerment' as becoming better able to shape one's life *by means of gains in power* would imply that it could not possibly have any other causes; however, we know that in some cases people can be empowered by simple expansion of agency, without any further gains in power. So this approach to defining 'empowerment' is fraught with inconsistencies.

These caveats notwithstanding, we may still be able to articulate power gains as one dimension of empowerment, and we can do this if we take a relational approach to agency. Let me begin with a hypothetical example.

I have argued elsewhere (Drydyk 2008) that empowerment does imply power in at least one way. If a group became better able to shape their lives by, for instance, forming a producers' cooperative, and if this were at first supported by one government and then undermined by the government elected in its place, how empowered were they? We would want to say: they would have become more empowered if they had been able to sustain their cooperative against the attacks of the new government. It is *durable* empowerment that is worth having, and so it is legitimate to include this idea of durability within the concept of empowerment. Durability in this example required power. For these reasons, some reference to power must be made in an adequate definition of empowerment.

What I want to propose now is that this reference to power can be articulated as a reference to relationships between the agency and choice of one group and the agency and choice of another group. Whether the producers *have* the choice of operating their cooperative depends on choices that the politicians *make*. And the choices available to the politicians are not reciprocally limited by any choices that the producers might make. On this issue, then – the continued existence of the cooperative – the politicians are predominantly decision-makers while the producers are predominantly decision-takers.

In the next section I will argue that there are three independent aspects of empowerment and none of them is reducible to either or both of the others. First, however, I want to attend to some analytical details.

I will attempt to sidestep debates about the nature of choosing. I will simply work with the view that choosing is deciding what to do, which normally leads to carrying out that action, or at least trying. Similarly, I would bracket those meanings of 'having a choice' that would commit us directly, one way or another, on the topic of free will and determinism. For present purposes, we can say that a person has result R as a choice when R is a goal that the person values and when this person is capable of seeing to it that R results. Two implications might be noted. First, having a choice is more than being capable of making a choice, since it is possible to make choices that are futile or highly unlikely to succeed, as for instance when 'fringe' candidates run for offices that they are unlikely to win. They decide to run, they try to win, but winning was not a choice that they realistically had. Second, by limiting the choices we have to those that we value, I am excluding unwanted choices. This focuses the meaning of 'choices we have' on a less sprawling set of choices that is more relevant to people and the relationships that matter to them. For instance: a thief is less interested in having the mere choice of taking something from me than in having the choice of taking something from me and getting away with it.

Power is sometimes an asymmetry in which the choices that one group *makes* shape or determine the choices that another group *has*, undeterred by choices that the second group might make. But it can also be a more subtle asymmetry, in which the more powerful group does not need to do or choose anything. Law enforcement does not normally require that law enforcers actually use all of the coercive choices that they have. It is sufficient for the population to simply be aware of what choices the law enforcers have to know that disturbing peace and public order, and getting away with it, is not a choice that most people realistically have.

Power, then, can be understood as an asymmetry involving agency. I am not claiming that this is the only way to understand power. In terms of the many distinctions between 'power-over', 'power-to', 'power-with', and 'power-within',[3] the asymmetry I have identified defines 'power-over' primarily. However, the others can also be defined in agency terms – though possibly imperfectly. 'Power-to' would be defined simply as having an effective choice to achieve some valuable outcome; thus it closely resembles the concept of agency freedom. 'Power-within' could refer to conditions for recognising choices that one has and being ready to make them. 'Power-with' might turn out to be ambiguous in a way that is not discussed in the literature: choices made by a group might either restrict or expand the choices that its members have. Thus power-with might be either repressive or transformative.

Relational dimensions of empowerment

It can be shown by clear hypothetical examples that these relational ideas do capture one aspect of what 'empowerment' means. If this aspect is not captured by the ideas of empowerment as simple expansion of choice or as becoming better able to shape one's life, then we may conclude that the relational ideas comprise an irreducible element of the concept of empowerment.

Case 1. Conquerors expanding the choices of subjects. Imagine that Earth has been captured by Martians, who send each adult human being, every day, a list of tasks they must accomplish. The relationship is not reciprocal: humans cannot prescribe tasks for Martians. Now imagine that the Martians change their procedure: instead of sending down tasks for each individual, they send down tasks for each household, leaving it to household members to decide by whom each task will be done. With this change, human choice and agency are expanded. But no one would say that this change is especially empowering, since the asymmetrical relationship between humans and Martians remains unchanged.

Case 2. Vulnerability of minorities. A similar problem arises if we think of empowerment as *becoming better able to shape our own lives*. Imagine a resource-poor province, occupied by an ethnic minority, within a resource-rich state that is ruled by the majority. The state decides to devolve development decisions down to the provinces; however, this is accompanied in the first year by equalization payments to share revenues with poorer provinces. However, as time goes on, these payments become very unpopular in the rich provinces, since lost provincial revenues need to be replaced through taxation. Even with this tax increase, citizens of the rich provinces are much better able to shape their lives for the better than are citizens of the poor provinces. How empowering is this new scheme for citizens of the poor provinces? Under it, they will be somewhat better able to shape their own lives, but whether this will continue depends on political choices by citizens of rich provinces. Moreover, these rich-province citizens remain much *comparatively* better able to shape their own lives for the better. Is the new scheme empowering? Yes and no. While it is somewhat empowering, it is not as empowering as it might have been: it is insecure, rather than durable, and the citizens of the poor provinces are ultimately less able to shape their own lives than are citizens in the rich provinces. Because the former are a minority, the relationship is not reciprocal: choices in rich provinces affect empowerment in the poor provinces far more than choices in the poor provinces affect empowerment in the rich ones.

From cases like these – of which many more can be found not just in imagination but in fact – we should conclude that empowerment does have relational aspects, and these can be neglected both by the choice conception of empowerment and by the idea of being better able to shape one's own life. In the remainder of this section I will formulate these aspects abstractly, and in the following section I will take up concrete cases.

To capture some elemental relations between the choices of different people, let us begin with individuals and work up to groups. There are endless cases in which the choices that one person has depend on choices that another has, or makes. Sometimes this dependency is a good thing. For instance, one person does not have the choice of being the friend of another unless the other chooses to accept and reciprocate; so too with any fully voluntary transaction. When each party's having a choice (to become friends or to make this transaction) depends on a choice by the other party, we can call the relation *mutually dependent* or *reciprocal*. These can be contrasted with cases in which one person's having a choice depends on choices that the other person makes or has, without reciprocation. Sometimes this asymmetry is a good thing: for instance, if someone wishes to rob and assault me, but I have the choice of calling for protection (and assuming this choice will evidently be an effective one), then the robber/assailant does not have the choice of robbing/assaulting me and getting away with it. My choice of calling for protection is not dependent on any choices made by the robber/assailant.[4] In asymmetrical cases like these, we might say that one person's choices are *subject to* choices (made or had) by the other.

We can also step back from particular choice relations between individuals to recognise larger-scale choice relations between and within groups.

Choice relations between groups. Consider the scope of choice that members of a group have: the set of goals that they have reason to value and that they are individually able to accomplish. If the scope of choice for members of group B is subject to the choices which members of group A make or have, we might say that members of B are in a position of *asymmetrical group subjection.* In some cases, this may be a good thing, for instance if the groups are children and adults. For other groups, such as women and men: not so good. This might be contrasted with a society governed by rights, in which the scope of choice for any group is limited by the rights of others and subject to decisions by any others to exercise those rights; this we might call *reciprocal subjection.*

Choice relations within groups. Now consider groups as collective decision-makers, where decisions are made on actions to be taken by the group. Here the question concerns what influence any individuals or subgroups might exercise on the group's decisions. Let us say that *dominance* prevails to the extent that some group members *consistently* have influence over group decisions that is independent of any choices made or had by others – who we will characterise as *subjected* to that dominance. As in the case of group subjection, dominance can be unacceptable along some lines (gender, race, class) yet acceptable along others (adulthood).[5]

Vulnerability. Suppose that, by reducing the goals that group members can accomplish, group subjection also reduces their ability to achieve well-being. That is to say, in this case group subjection reduces their well-being freedom, compared with other groups. Or, suppose that, within a group, the dominance of a subgroup has a similar effect on others, reducing their freedom to live equally well. In these cases, when the well-being freedom of a group or subgroup is constrained either by their group subjection or by the dominance of others, we may say that they are *asymmetrically vulnerable.*

This conceptual sketch cannot be expected to capture many of the nuances and complexities that characterise actual power relations. I put it forward only as a first step towards showing in greater detail what the relational dimensions of empowerment might involve. In the meantime, until this can be fleshed out, let us describe these dimensions by saying that a group is *empowered* when its asymmetrical group subjection and subjection to dominance are reduced, particularly when their asymmetric vulnerability is reduced as a result.

Empowerment in development contexts

Consider now what these ideas may tell us about empowerment and disempowerment as they actually occur in development contexts.

> *E-choupals.* In India more than 2 million farmers are now connecting to markets through village-based computer stations called e-choupals. ... This innovation came from an Indian private sector company, ITC, which has annual revenues of $2.6 billion and a large, diversified, and growing involvement in agribusiness trade. ... *Choupal* is the Hindi word for the village square, a place where elders meet. E-Choupals use information technology to bring about virtual meetings between farmers, buyers, and suppliers. ITC installs each Internet access kiosk, powered by solar-charged batteries, in the house of a farmer who is trained to operate it. Local farmers use the computer to access information free of charge. After checking prices, they can choose to buy or sell through ITC or go to local markets instead. ... Efficiency improvements in buying and selling have led to increased revenues for farmers and for ITC. (Narayan 2005, 14)

Introduction of this system is presented in *Measuring Empowerment* as a straightforward case of empowerment. However, when all dimensions of empowerment are taken into account, it turns out to exemplify weak empowerment at best. Better access to market information and the option to sell directly to ITC do give the farmers more choices, so their agency has been expanded. Moreover, their reason for taking up these options is to get better prices for their products, which, other things being equal, could put them in at least a slightly better position to enhance their well-being; hence the new system makes them better able to shape their lives for the better. However, the farmers remain vulnerable to markets, and their expanded agency through expanded access to information is subject to the choice of a single corporation. By comparison, public availability of market information, not subject to the choice of any particular players within the market, would have been more empowering.

> *The Self Employed Women's Association.* SEWA was born in 1972 as a trade union of self employed women. It grew out of the Textile Labour Association, TLA, India's oldest and largest union of textile workers founded in 1920 by a woman, Anasuya Sarabhai. The inspiration for the union came from Mahatma Gandhi, who led a successful strike of textile workers in 1917. . . . the ideological base provided by Mahatma Gandhi and the feminist seeds planted by Anasuya Sarabhai led to the creation by the TLA of their Women's Wing in 1954. Its original purpose was to assist women belonging to households of mill workers and its work was focussed largely on training and welfare activities. . . . .
>
> In 1971, . . . on an appeal from women [cart-pullers, head-loaders, and used garment dealers] and at the initiative of the leader of the Women's Wing, Ela Bhatt, and the president of the TLA, Arvind Buch, the Self-Employed Women's Association (SEWA) was born . . . . (SEWA 2008a)
>
> SEWA's main goals are to organise women workers for full employment. Full employment means employment whereby workers obtain work security, income security, food security and social security (at least health care, child care and shelter). SEWA organises women to ensure that every family obtains full employment. By self-reliance we mean that women should be autonomous and self-reliant, individually and collectively, both economically and in terms of their decision-making ability. (SEWA 2008b)

As a case of empowerment, the SEWA story has a number of distinctive features that are captured well by the relational dimensions of empowerment. Women workers and Textile Labour Association (TLA) leaders combined to create a new organisation within the TLA; one initial objective was to strengthen the women's bargaining power against the small business owners who bought their services – a goal of reducing their group subjection. A further perceived barrier to achieving this was subjection to dominance by other groups within the TLA. Consequently, the SEWA strategy aimed both to escape the dominance they experience within the TLA and to reduce their subjection to purchasers; in our terms, both were sought in order to reduce the asymmetric vulnerability of these women workers.

  This case also offers a further important lesson about how to think of power. In the previous case, farmers empowered themselves by interacting with an actor (ITC) and entities (the commodity markets) in relation to which they were dependent and vulnerable. Yet it would be a mistake to infer that in order to be empowered people must always and only engage with more powerful agents and entities. We see in other cases that empowerment can involve engagement with and among people with comparatively little power. Principal among these are engagements of solidarity, exemplified not only by SEWA but also by trade unions such as the one from which it emerged, and other membership-based organisations aiming to make their members more powerful collectively than they can be individually. One lesson to draw from this is that when we discuss the social environment and say that empowerment involves engaging with the powerful actors and features of that environment, we cannot have in mind just those who are more powerful actors, but we must include all who can have any effect, including those who at a given moment may be less powerful actually, for the moment, than they may be potentially, for the future. Another lesson to draw is that steps taken to reduce dependency/vulnerability overall may carry risks of creating other kinds of dependency/vulnerability. The TLA was formed to reduce its members' vulnerability to employers and purchasers. For male members, choice and control were symmetrical: members' control over means to their well-being and agency goals depended on collective choices of the union as executed by the leadership, yet those in turn depended on choices made by the members. However, asymmetric subjection and vulnerability were still experienced by women members. SEWA reduced the women's vulnerability both to employers and to the TLA.

In the next case, a group experiences disempowerment, which they struggle to reverse.

Jamuna bridge. The Jamuna is one of the great rivers of Bangladesh, creating a geographic barrier separating the western half of the country from the east; the bridge in question was completed in 1998. The Jamuna Multi-Purpose Bridge Authority (JMBA) contracted out its social impact survey to the Bangladesh Rural Advancement Committee (BRAC), a large and established NGO. Based on this survey, JMBA prepared a 'Revised Resettlement Action Plan' that recognized the entitlement of 15,000 households to compensation (JMBA, n.d.). These plans, however, ignored more than 75,000 inhabitants of the sandy islands known as *chars*. In order to shorten the span of the bridge and stabilize the riverbed beneath it, the river was channelized, beginning in 1994, by reinforcing its banks. The effect was to shift and quicken river currents, which in turn made downstream erosion more rapid and less predictable. *Chars* that had been stable for decades were washed away in a matter of days (Schmuck 2000, 14), and some families had to make multiple moves as their new homes met the same fate as their previous dwellings (Sarker, Huque, and Alam 2003, 76). The *char* dwellers' cause was taken up by an NGO that had been working in the area, the Jamuna Char Integrated Development Project (JCDP), which first tried to raise the issue with the developer, JMBA, and the World Bank, one of the project financiers. When these attempts at dialogue failed, JCDP filed a claim with the Inspection Panel of the World Bank (Dulu 2003, 93–113). This claim presented evidence of *char* erosion and displacement that had already been caused by the channelized river and a grim projection of displacement yet to come, rendering as many as four to five thousand families homeless and without any source of earning (JCDP 1996, 16).

In this case, the *char* dwellers needed to be recognised as persons displaced by the bridge project who deserved to be compensated, resettled, and assisted in restoring or improving their former living standards (as required by World Bank resettlement policy). Their choices were subject to the choices of at least six other actors: Jamuna Multi-Purpose Bridge Authority (JMBA), the Government of Bangladesh, Bangladesh Rural Advancement Committee (BRAC), the Jamuna Char Integrated Development Project (JCDP), the World Bank, and its Inspection Panel. The work of the JCDP gave the *char* dwellers more choices and mitigated their subjection and vulnerability to the other five actors. The aim of their interaction with JMBA, the Government of Bangladesh, BRAC, and the World Bank was to influence their behaviour and to gain recognition and compensation. As a result of the interaction, some people did receive compensation packages. It would perhaps be cruel to say that they thereby became better able to shape their lives. While they remained vulnerable to decisions taken by the developer, the government, and the World Bank, their vulnerability was constrained insofar as their political and legal action limited the choices that the developer had.

On the other hand, it is not just governments, developers, NGOs, and trade unions that can be disempowering or empowering. Naila Kabeer has observed that entrenched practices and values can also be disempowering, even in cases where agency may expand:

> *Disempowering contexts of choice.* The need to bear the approved number of children in order to secure social status and family approval takes its toll on women's bodies and on their lives as they bear children beyond their capacity. Furthermore, status considerations in cultures of

son-preference require women to give birth to a certain number of sons; to favour their sons over their daughters in ways that reinforce social discrimination against women; and to bring their daughters up to devalue themselves, thereby acting as agents in the transmission of gender discrimination over generations. (Kabeer 1999, 40)

It is common to explain group subjection of women in terms of male dominance within families. However, this example requires a different explanation, since it questions what would happen if male dominance within family decision-making were not a factor: might women continue to support son-preference because they thought that this is what good women must do? The group subjection in this case is subjection to choices of a cultural group, including women among its members. Naturally, it remains to be seen whether women participate reciprocally either in cultural choice or in family decisions. However, this case reveals an important strength of the framework of choice relations that I have presented: it allows for understanding culture as involving relations of subjection.

Conclusions

A capability approach to empowerment should neither overrate nor underrate the importance of agency. Rather, the concept of empowerment contextualises agency in two ways: in relation to well-being freedom and in the relational contexts of power. Or, to put this in another way, empowerment has three distinct but related dimensions: agency, well-being freedom, and power. Development that is defective in any one of these dimensions is less empowering than it might have been, or, arguably, than it ought to be.

One consequence of this is that empowerment is not reducible to any one of the three. Sen drew attention to this in his contribution to the Beijing Conference by welcoming the greater attention to women's agency, over and above concern for women's well-being, that was being demanded of development thinking in that period (Sen 1995, 104–105). And he also recognised the relational aspects, though perhaps not explicitly enough, in identifying family decision-making as an important nexus between women's contributions to a household and their share in division of goods and benefits (Sen 1995, 105–106). There is precedent, then, for recognising the *multidimensionality* of empowerment, in the capability approach.

It may be helpful to keep the intuitive arguments for this multidimensionality in mind. Well-being and even rudimentary forms of well-being freedom can be enhanced without significantly expanding agency: an illustration might be improving nutrition for prisoners. But it is obviously more empowering if people play a greater role in enhancing their own well-being, and this is captured by the idea that people are empowered insofar as they are better able to shape their own lives. This shows that expanded agency is an essential dimension of empowerment. However, conversely, agency expansion by itself is not as empowering as agency expansion that links with well-being freedom, enabling people to better shape their lives *for the better*, as illustrated by the contrast between being allowed to arrange the deck chairs on a sinking vessel versus being allowed to do something more relevant to saving lives. Nor is agency expansion as empowering as it might be (even if it does enhance well-being freedom) as long as group subjection or intra-group dominance remain. For as long as those conditions remain, people remain asymmetrically vulnerable.

What, then, is the value added by the concept of empowerment? It seems to lie in recognising how large and how varied the gaps and barriers can be between these three dimensions. The human development approach has always insisted that autonomous personal involvement is essential to human development, both as an end and as a means. Yet little will result from this if capability theorists have nothing to contribute about *how* and *under what conditions* agency can be an effective means – effective specifically in expanding people's substantive freedom to live in ways that they have reason to value. Ultimately the policy potential of such an approach will seriously underperform if it comes to little more than recommending 'add agency and stir' to development policies. The contributions required are case studies and analyses of the enormously varied types of interaction, influence, solidarity, control, and transformations that are needed in practice to connect the dots between agency, well-being, and power. The concept of empowerment is a place-marker for just that sort of research.

In that research, taking a relational approach is essential. This is not to say that measuring gains or losses in people's agency, choice, or ability to shape their own lives is unimportant. But it is to say that capturing these gains and losses is not sufficient, unless the fragility or durability of those gains and losses are also captured. To capture this, it is necessary to understand changes in group subjection, intra-group dominance, and vulnerability. In doing so, we bring power back into our understanding of empowerment.

Acknowledgements

I learned much from discussion of an earlier version of this article, 'How to Distinguish Empowerment from Agency', at the 2008 Conference of the Human Development and Capabilities Association in New Delhi and from comments by Desmond McNeill on a previous article, 'Durable Empowerment'. I am grateful for continuing conversations that I have had with Christine Koggel and, most recently, for editorial suggestions by Eric Palmer.

Notes

1. Some usages are mystifying, such as: 'Since the process of human development often involves great struggle, the empowerment involved in the language of claims can be of great practical importance' (UNDP 2000, 22).
2. What I am saying here is that, according to the capability approach, things and events are advantageous to a person because of the role they play in activities arising from that person's autonomous agency. The capability approach also holds that things and events are advantageous to a person because of their contribution to that person's well-being freedom. For example, health care is advantageous because it enhances our capability to live a longer and healthier life. Although it acknowledges both as evaluative spaces, the capability approach insists that the second is superior for purposes of social policy in revealing the inequalities that matter most.
3. For a good survey of this complex literature, see Allen (2011).
4. Notice that this asymmetry might not hold in a case of domestic assault if the assailant can threaten retaliation for calling in protection.
5. I readily admit that 'subjection' and 'dominance' sound harsh as applied to children. But the fact is children are subject to choices of their parents, who are also dominant in family decisions, even when these relations are loosened over time to provide for the children's growth and the expansion of their agency.

References

Alkire, Sabina. 2008. *Concepts and Measures of Agency*. OPHI Working Paper Series, Working Paper No. 9. Oxford: Oxford Poverty and Human Development Initiative.
Allen, Amy. 2011. "Feminist Perspectives on Power." In *The Stanford Encyclopedia of Philosophy*, edited by Edward N. Zalta, Spring. Accessed December 30, 2012. http://plato.stanford.edu/archives/spr2011/entries/feminist-power/

Alsop, Ruth, Mette Bertelsen, and Jeremy Holland. 2006. *Empowerment in Practice: From Analysis to Implementation*. Washington, DC: World Bank.

Batliwala, Srilatha. 1993. *Women's Empowerment in South Asia: Concepts and Practices*. New Delhi: ASPBAE/FAO (United Nations Food and Agriculture Organization, Asia South Pacific Bureau of Adult Education).

Batliwala, Srilatha. 2007. "Taking the Power Out of Empowerment – An Experiential Account." *Development in Practice* 17 (4–5): 557–565.

Boserup, Ester. 1970. *Women's Role in Economic Development*. London: George Allen and Unwin.

Crocker, David. 2008. *Ethics of Global Development; Agency, Capability, and Deliberative Democracy*. New York: Cambridge University Press.

Drydyk, Jay. 2008. "Durable Empowerment." *Journal of Global Ethics* 4 (3): 231–245.

Drydyk, Jay. 2010. "Participation, Empowerment, and Democracy: Three Fickle Friends." In *New Directions in Development Ethics: Essays in Honor of Denis Goulet*, edited by Amitava Dutt and Charles Wilber, 333–356. Notre Dame, IN: University of Notre Dame Press.

Dulu, Majibul H. 2003. "The Experience of Jamuna Bridge: Issues and Perspectives." In *Demanding Accountability; Civil-Society Claims and the World Bank Inspection Panel*, edited by Dana Clark, Jonathan Fox and Kay Treakle, 93–113. Lanham, MD: Rowman & Littlefield.

Eyben, Rosalind, and Rebecca Napier-Moore. 2009. "Choosing Words with Care? Shifting Meanings of Women's Empowerment in International Development." *Third World Quarterly* 30 (2): 285–300.

Haq, Mahbub ul. 1995. *Reflections on Human Development*. New York: Oxford University Press.

Ibrahim, Solava, and Sabina Alkire. 2007. "Agency and Empowerment: A Proposal for Internationally Comparable Indicators." *Oxford Development Studies* 35 (4): 380–403.

JCDP (Jamuna Char Integrated Development Project). 1996. *Submission to Inspection Panel: A Request for Inspection on the Effect of Jamuna Multi-purpose Bridge on the Jamuna Char Inhabitants*. Dhaka.

JMBA (Jamuna Multi-Purpose Bridge Authority). n.d. "JMBA Completed Works." In *JMBA*. Accessed November 10, 2005. http://www.jmba.gov.bd/completed.html

Kabeer, Naila. 1999. *The Conditions and Consequences of Choice: Reflections on the Measurement of Women's Empowerment*. UNRISD Discussion Paper 108. Geneva: United Nations Research Institute for Social Development.

Keleher, Loretta Wills. 2007. "Empowerment and International Development." PhD diss., University of Maryland. http://hdl.handle.net/1903/75844

Keleher, Lori. 2008. "Growth, Capabilities, and Empowerment: A Comparison of the Concept and Role of Empowerment Within the Economic Growth Approach and the Capability Approach." Human Development and Capability Association 2008 conference, New Delhi, September 13.

Narayan, Deepa. 2005. *Measuring Empowerment: Cross-disciplinary Perspectives*. Washington, DC: World Bank.

de Saint-Exupéry, Antoine. 1943. *The Little Prince*. Translated by Katherine Woods. New York: Harcourt, Brace & World.

Sarker, Maminul H., Iffat Huque, and Mustafa Alam. 2003. "Rivers, *Chars* and *Char* Dwellers of Bangladesh." *International Journal of River Basin Management* 1 (1): 61–80.

Schmuck, Hanna. 2000. *The Char-People and the Jamuna Bridge in Bangladesh: An Independent Study on the Project for Compensating Erosion and Flood Affected Persons (EFAP)*. Dhaka: Jamuna Char Integrated Development Project.

Sen, Amartya. 1992. *Inequality Reexamined*. Cambridge, MA: Harvard University Press.

Sen, Amartya. 1993. "Capability and Well-Being." In *The Quality of Life*, edited by Martha C. Nussbaum and Amartya Sen, 30–50. Oxford: Clarendon Press.

Sen, Amartya. 1995. "Agency and Well-Being: The Development Agenda." In *A Commitment to the World's Women: Perspectives on Development for Beijing and Beyond*, edited by Noeleen Heyzer, Sushma Kapoor and Joanne Sandler, 103–112. New York: UNIFEM (United Nations Development Fund for Women).

SEWA. 2008a. "History." In *Self Employed Women's Association*. Ahmedabad, India, July 28, 2008. www.sewa.org/aboutus/history.asp

SEWA. 2008b. "Introduction." In *Self Employed Women's Association*. Ahmedabad, India, July 28, 2008. www.sewa.org/aboutus/index.asp

UNDP (United Nations Development Programme). 2000. *Human Development Report 2000: Human Rights and Human Development*. New York: Oxford University Press.

A critical analysis of recent work on empowerment: implications for gender

Christine M. Koggel

Harvey Wexler Chair in Philosophy, Bryn Mawr College, Bryn Mawr, PA, USA

A flurry of publications on empowerment by institutions such as the World Bank that emerged from about 2000–2005 was followed by critiques and then a seeming lull in the popularity of and work on empowerment. However, the concept has reappeared recently in what I take to be an important new development that highlights the relational feature of empowerment. In this paper, I begin with the capabilities approach as delineated by Amartya Sen and, specifically, his application of it to gender. This shapes the background against which I highlight how recent work on empowerment by Jay Drydyk, the *World Development Report 2012, Gender Equality and Development*, and Patti Petesch utilizes but also departs from Sen. I then argue that insights from this recent research can be developed further through a feminist relational framework. With its focus on relationships, relational theory can better capture possibilities for empowering women in and through an analysis of the relationships they are in.

A flurry of publications on empowerment by institutions such as the World Bank that emerged from about 2000–2005 was followed by initial critical analysis and then a lull in the use of empowerment as a conceptual and analytic tool for addressing poverty and inequalities more generally. However, the concept seems to have acquired new life in significant work that is now being done by various international bodies and research programs, many of which refer to or have been influenced by the work of Amartya Sen and the capabilities approach more generally. The capabilities approach focuses on what people are able to be and to do and not merely on indicators such as levels of income or wealth. On Sen's account, for example, poverty is best understood as a deprivation of capabilities. As is well-known, Sen pays particular attention to deprivations suffered by women and makes the strong claim that

> [t]he extensive reach of women's agency is one of the more neglected areas of development studies, and most urgently in need of correction. Nothing, arguably, is as important today in the political economy of development as an adequate recognition of political, economic and social participation and leadership of women. (1999, 109)

For Sen, addressing gender inequalities is important not only because it limits what women can be and do but also because attending to deprivations in women's health, education, work opportunities, and political participation is integrally connected to removing inequalities of various sorts for women, their children, and families. Crucial for Sen, however, is his rejection of the idea that it is merely a matter of providing resources to women. This is treating them like 'passive recipients of cunning development programs' (11) or of 'governmental handouts' (178). Instead the focus needs to be on opening opportunities that allow women to 'effectively shape their own destiny and help each other' (11). This is the thrust, importance, and purpose of agency for Sen and for capability theorists more generally. Yet how agency is conceptualized needs to be unpacked. This is precisely what recent theorists attempt to do in delineating kinds of freedom and differentiating agency from empowerment in ways that are relevant to addressing gender inequalities.

I begin the paper with a discussion of the capabilities approach as delineated by Sen, one that I take to be a powerful challenge to the dominant view that poverty, and development more generally, can be understood in terms of economic processes alone. I argue that Sen's account is important for making the interconnectedness of kinds of inequalities clear and convincing, but that it fails, in the end, to account for inequalities in power and the effects of power in institutional, national, and global contexts. I show that recent work by Jay Drydyk (2013) moves in the right direction by distinguishing agency from empowerment and reconnecting the meaning of the latter with relations of power and the need to engage with and challenge them. I then highlight relational features as they apply to gender in the World Bank's *World Development Report 2012, Gender Equality and Development* and Patti Petesch's background paper for the *World Development Report 2013* and critically assess these in light of Drydyk's account of empowerment. A central question will be whether this recent turn to a relational dimension in an account of empowerment can address the sorts of disempowering factors that emerge from gender norms embedded in relationships of power. I will argue that feminist relational theory with its direct attention to issues of power in relationships of all kinds and at all levels can provide better tools for revealing and analyzing the force of gender norms and the implications of this for empowering women. To anticipate my central argument, we need an account of the role of power to reveal its embeddedness in relationships, to examine how power is connected with institutional norms and structures that are assumed and taken-for-granted, to assess what needs to be done to address women's vulnerabilities to disempowering factors in particular contexts; and to draw out the full promise of the relational and interactional dimensions of empowerment.

Sen's account of the capabilities approach

In general terms, the capabilities approach describes human functionings, and what human beings need to function as, as a base from which to examine and evaluate whether individuals have the capabilities to function in ways that matter to what they can do and be. Sen provides examples of

> capabilities like being able to avoid such deprivations as starvation, undernourishment, escapable morbidity and premature mortality, as well as the freedoms that are associated with being literate and numerate, enjoying political participation and uncensored speech and so on. In this constitutive perspective, development involves expansion of these and other basic freedoms. Development, in this view, is the process of expanding human freedoms, and the assessment of development has to be informed by this consideration. (1999, 36)

Sen's account, thus, allows an examination into whether people in particular contexts and under specific conditions have the freedom to function in ways that matter to themselves (agency freedom) and their well-being (well-being freedom). For Sen the two kinds of freedom are integrally connected: addressing deprivations in well-being through the provision of political, economic, and social resources opens up opportunities and choices that in turn can expand the agency one has to determine one's own path and be in control of the choices one makes. And enhancing one's agency can in turn strengthen one's voice in public debates and contribute to the expansion of rights and resources. As Sen puts it,

> Social and economic factors such as basic education, elementary health care, and secure employment are important not only on their own, but also for the role they can play in giving people the opportunity to approach the world with courage and freedom. These considerations require a broader informational base, focusing particularly on people's capability to choose the lives they have *reason to value*. (63, my emphasis)

Sen's defense of the need for a broad informational base is also a demand for context specific attention to people's lives. The breadth of information relevant to the analysis is apparent in the examples he provides of the diversities of people and contexts: 'The respective roles of personal heterogeneities, environmental diversities, variations in social climate, differences in relational perspectives and distributions within the family have to receive the serious attention they deserve for the making of public policy' (109). Couple this with Sen's account of the interconnectedness of kinds of freedoms that can enhance agency and well-being and we have the makings for understanding why attention to the diversity of people, contexts, structures, and conditions will matter for theory and policy. To give but one example provided by Sen and relevant to this paper, female deprivation in many parts of the world cannot be captured by an account of income levels alone. This measure can mask gender inequalities in undernourishment, mortality, illiteracy, security and safety as well as inequalities in women's access to family income, property, and work. And these factors will vary depending on the conditions, history, norms, values, and institutional structures present in specific contexts. In other words, the details will matter to assessing deprivations and shaping policies that can remove particular sorts of unfreedoms.

It is not surprising, then, that Sen rejects the idea that theorists need to articulate an 'ideal', whether of development, justice, or equality, toward which all people and all nations should aim.[1] Sen is explicit about this in *The Idea of Justice*, where he argues that we do not need to articulate or defend an ideal or transcendental *theory* or provide a *definitive list* of values or principles to make judgments about what is just or unjust. We can evaluate and judge conditions or institutions as unjust in specific contexts without having a fully-established ideal or transcendental theory of justice ready at hand. Most importantly for Sen, the bulk of the evaluative work rests on the crucial role played by participation and deliberation: 'When we try to determine how justice can be advanced, there is a basic need for public reasoning, involving arguments coming from different quarters and divergent perspectives' (2009, 392). Here again agency, in the sense of a person's ability to 'effectively shape their own destiny' (1999, 11), is central to being able to participate in debates, deliberate about injustices, and make decisions about policies to address specific kinds of injustices. Crucial to Sen's account as well is the idea that the making of public policy should happen in and through the participation of those who reason about and are affected by conditions, practices, and values *in their own contexts*:

> public participation in these valuational debates – in explicit or implicit forms – is a crucial part of the exercise of democracy and responsible social choice. In matters of public judgment, there is no escape from the evaluative need for public discussion. (1999, 110)

To summarize Sen on theory and policy, the central role given to public reasoning means that judgments about what is of value and about what policies will remove unfreedoms and enhance agency can be made in and through democratic processes that emphasize the importance of the 'exercise of public reasoning;' that focus on implementing policies applicable to specific contexts and conditions; and that can provide justifications through reasoned debate for why some processes or policies are better than others for addressing injustices or for achieving better or more justice in particular contexts that manifest specific injustices.

All this said in support of Sen's account of the capabilities approach as complex, contextual, and multifaceted, I want to argue that it does not go far enough. Its focus is still too exclusively on individuals and on the goal of enhancing their agency so that they can live lives they value or have reason to value. It does not delve sufficiently deep to question the actual relationships assumed by and embedded in institutions and structures or how these can entrench inequalities at various levels that are difficult to understand and to remove. What is missing in Sen is an analysis of how political, economic, and social institutions embed norms, structures, and practices that stand in the way of removing some inequalities and of having some people participate in debates about those inequalities. To return to the example from above, nowhere is this more evident than in the case of inequalities assumed by and emerging from norms that shape expectations about women's proper role and function. What women are able to do and be is often tied to gender norms that are entrenched in relationships and institutions that shape perceptions and self-perceptions of what women are like, what they deserve, and what they *ought* to do and be. In much of my research that makes use of feminist relational theory, I argue that we need an account that puts relationships rather than individuals at the center of the analysis. This direction is now being taken by recent research on empowerment by Jay Drydyk (2013) that reconceptualizes agency, differentiates it from empowerment, and puts an analysis of relations of power back into empowerment. The question for this paper will be whether this turn to relationality goes far enough – particularly as it applies to the range of injustices that get in the way of enhancing women's agency, well-being, and empowerment opportunities.

Putting power back into empowerment

Jay Drydyk (2013) does useful conceptual analysis in differentiating agency from empowerment and having the latter do work with respect to theory and policy that it has not thus far. For Drydyk, agency is individualist, autonomous, deliberative, and has a subjective component:

> Agency is exercised insofar as (a) a person either performs an activity or plays a role in performing it, (b) this activity has an impact on the world, (c) the activity was chosen by the person (d) for reasons of their own (in individual or group deliberation). (page this volume).

Drydyk credits the capabilities approach for giving agency a role that is a needed supplement to well-being accounts that focus on providing resources (and thereby treating people as passive recipients rather than active agents). As can be gleaned from the discussion of Sen above, an account of well-being is objective in the sense of identifying the kinds of unfreedoms or deprivations (what a person has 'reason to value') that should matter for theory and policy. Agency, however, captures the idea that over and above what will advance well-being is the importance of people being able to reason and decide what is of value *to them*. For Drydyk, agency is fundamental but also 'unavoidably subjective'. He argues, therefore, that focusing on agency alone makes what people choose susceptible to charges of adaptive preferences – an agent who adapts what is of value to them to the norms and conditions that shape those values for that person. I take Sen to avoid this objection because he connects well-being freedom and agency freedom and defends the need to assess each in the context of people's lives and conditions. Yet Drydyk's point is that agency conceived as individual control and involvement with respect to a person's ability to decide and act is justifiably distinguishable from well-being: the latter assesses the consequences or outcomes of decision and action to making a person's life *better* in ways that the former does not. Here is where Drydyk's account of empowerment starts to do some important work.

In describing the 'flurry' of efforts to measure empowerment in the years 2005–2009, Drydyk notes that attention was indeed placed on the outcomes or means for empowering people (objective or well-being factors). Yet this was to the exclusion of an examination of other less visible factors such as tradition and family structures that so often interfere with possibilities for empowering some people. Therefore, for example, women could be viewed as being empowered when literacy rates were improved or when work opportunities opened up. Drydyk argues that while agency can be tied to well-being through an account of expanded agency (as is the case with Sen's reference to the importance of the 'extensive reach of women's agency'), this is still not sufficient for capturing the many and varied ways in which agency is thwarted or hindered even when attention is paid to resources and institutions (well-being factors) that can enhance agency. Drydyk uses the phrase 'empowerment as expanded scope for agency' to connect the concepts of agency and empowerment and to take the examination of these beyond what the literature has done thus far.

Drydyk identifies several features of empowerment that both make use of and depart from agency as such. Empowerment is (1) already conceptually linked to well-being in a way that agency is not (though this can be teased out in an account of expanded agency); (2) a *process of change* whereas agency is about a *state of affairs* of 'autonomous personal involvement in activities' (page this volume); (3) scalar in that we can distinguish changes that are more or less empowering than others; (4) describable as durable or failing to endure; and (5) relational. To fill out the claims of the first four, Drydyk argues that while agency refers to a *state of affairs* achievable by an individual through his or her own control or power over actions, empowerment refers to a *process of change* that enables one to shape one's own (or a group's) life by one's own (or a group's) choices *for the better*. Moreover, empowerment suggests measures that are scalar and durable; one can be more or less empowered and empowerment can be said to be durable or fail to endure in and through particular sorts of processes, institutions, strategies, and policies. If agency captures the subjective elements of agency freedom, then empowerment joins this with an analysis of the objective elements of well-being freedom. By putting these together, Drydyk's account sheds a different light on the value of the 'exercise of *public* reasoning'. This must happen in relationships and collectives that assess and come to understand what will be more or less empowering or more or less durable to well-being freedom.

I take the last feature, (5) that empowerment is relational, to be the most significant in its contribution to a new literature on empowerment. Drydyk's account gives empowerment a meaning that retrieves its once close connection to power in the idea of needing to transform social relations of power by enabling individuals and communities to shape their lives for the better. One is not empowered unless one is able to *challenge* or *use* political, social, or economic power to shape their own lives in ways that change their lives and/or those in one's community *for the better*. But there is more to Drydyk's account: putting power back into empowerment draws attention to the relationships within which individuals or groups are embedded and in and through which their agency or well-being freedoms are thwarted or hindered. This relational feature of empowerment speaks to how agency and possibilities for enhancing it are shaped by one's status and position in asymmetrical relations of power. Drydyk summarizes these points in the following, 'a group is *empowered* when its asymmetrical group subjection and subjection to dominance are reduced, particularly when their asymmetric vulnerability is reduced as a result' (page this volume). Drydyk's sums up the role of the three dimensions in his account of empowerment:

> the concept of empowerment contextualizes agency in two ways: in relation to well-being freedom and in the relational context of power. Or, to put this another way, empowerment has three distinct but related dimensions: agency, well-being freedom, and power. Development that is defective in any one of these dimensions is less empowering than it might have been, or, arguably, than it ought to be. (page this volume)

As I understand it, Drydyk does not challenge Sen's account of agency, but it can be understood as clarifying, distinguishing, and expanding the role and significance of agency and well-being freedoms – away from individuals as such and to the structures and relations of power that disempower individuals and groups. I support three important aspects of Drydyk's account: that he adds to empowerment an understanding of agency as being able to expand well-being freedoms through a process of change that can endure; that he introduces the important dimension of rela- tionality that immediately points to the asymmetrical relations of power that make some people vulnerable to little or no gains in agency or well-being freedoms; and that his account, like Sen's, is contextual and deliberative.[2] Theory and policy cannot demarcate in advance how to attend to or strengthen each element in the triad of agency, well-being freedom, and power. Attending to the relational elements of power will necessarily be sensitive to the particularities of the insti- tutions, conditions, practices, norms, and traditions in specific contexts. Moreover, adding the relational dimension in empowerment casts new light on the importance of the exercise of public reasoning in that direct attention is paid to relations of power that thwart or block efforts to enhance agency, improve well-being, or sustain empowerment for some people. I would add that this will be particularly so for members of traditionally disadvantaged groups who are vulnerable to norms and institutions that shape perceptions and self-perceptions of what they are able to be and to do.

The next task will be to evaluate the implications of Drydyk's account for the specific kind of power that emerges from gender norms that assume or entrench male domination. Drydyk rightly points out that possibilities for women's empowerment depend on openings for develop- ing reciprocal relations and challenging the often asymmetrical relations in which women are dominated by men. At the end of his paper, one of the three examples he uses to apply this insight to his account is to that of gender:

> The group subjection in this case is subjection to a cultural group, including women among its members. Naturally, it remains to be seen whether women participate reciprocally either in cultural choice or in family decisions. However, this case reveals an important strength of the framework of choice relations that I have presented: it allows for understanding culture as involving relations of subjection. (page this volume)

While I entirely agree with Drydyk's move of putting power back into empowerment (a long time feminist commitment to *transforming gender relations*), we will need to unpack the role of culture in creating relations of domination and subjection in order to analyze the dimensions of agency, well-being freedom, and power for an account of empowerment as it applies to gender. The concept of 'sticky' gender norms, a description that has made its way into the some- what remarkable 2012 World Bank report, *Gender Equality and Development*, is a good way to explore how the relational feature of empowerment that Drydyk defends is also being discussed in this literature. I will argue that we need to further expand and develop the relational feature in Drydyk's account and recent World Bank reports, both of which already take us beyond Sen, to better understand empowerment as it relates to possibilities for challenging 'sticky' gender norms; understanding the force of relations of power in women's lives; enhancing agency and well-being freedoms; and creating possibilities for empowering women.

Where the action is for empowering women: norms embedded in relationships of power

The *World Development Report,* the annual flagship publication of the World Bank, devotes its 2012 report to its first time examination of the theme *Gender Equality and Development*. Let me begin the summary and analysis of this momentous report by saying that the report is explicit about borrowing Sen's notion of the centrality of freedom to an account of development: 'Fol- lowing Amartya Sen, we see development as a process of expanding freedoms equally for all people' (2011, 3). Chapter 1, 'A Wave of Progress' details the ways in which women's lives have changed for the better with large and fast gains in the second half of the twentieth century. The report admits that progress has been slow and limited for some women in some domains and then goes on to identify four areas where gender gaps are most significant 'and where growth alone cannot solve the issues': (1) Reducing excess female mortality and closing the education gaps where they remain; (2) Improving access to economic opportunities for women; (3) Increasing women's voice and agency in the household and in society; and (4) Limiting the reproduction of gender inequality across generations (abstract).

It would seem that (1) and (2) connect well with what Sen advocates for enhancing women's agency. Can we say that (3) and (4) have the report move beyond Sen in being explicit about increasing voice and agency in the household and society and about undermining gender norms so as to enhance agency and well-being freedoms? A quick answer is that Sen is certainly aware of the importance of women's voice and agency in the household – even if he is less explicitly aware of the 'reproduction of gender inequality across generations'. So the real question may be whether (3) needs to be connected with an analysis of (4)? Another question is whether endorsing Sen's goal of expanding freedoms makes the report susceptible to the criticism that it too is individualist and subjective? In other words, might attention need to be paid to women being able to *recognize and challenge* relations of power that entrench and perpetuate gender inequalities 'across generations'? Finally, does the report move in the direction that Drydyk advances – of understanding empowerment as a triad of agency, well-being freedom, and power, the deficiency of any one of which 'is less empowering than it might have been'? In the course of exploring answers to these kinds of questions, I will argue that the report supports Drydyk's move of putting power back into empowerment and of drawing out the relational aspects needed for an analysis of power. I will also argue, however, that the report goes beyond Drydyk in dealing explicitly with the 'stickiness' of gender norms, a point that is forcefully advanced in Patti Petesch's background paper for the 2013 *World Development Report*. A discussion of these contributions pushes *in the direction* of using relationships as the focal point in an analysis of empowerment, but it falls short of fully utilizing a relational framework.

While only specific sections of the 2012 report discuss empowerment explicitly, the report as a whole has implications for new insights into empowerment and its implications for gender. As captured by a section entitled 'Women's Pathways to Empowerment: Do all Roads Lead to Rome?', several aspects of the report signal a departure from previous work by the World Bank. The first is the explicit turn to qualitative analyses that emerges from interviews in which women in 19 countries around the world are asked what it means to be powerful and free. The result of the qualitative research (also published by the World Bank) is a context-specific and multifaceted analysis of various pathways to women's empowerment. This is a departure from early work by the World Bank that took itself to be providing a framework for *defining* and *measuring* empowerment (as evidenced in titles such as *Measuring Empowerment: Cross-Disciplinary Perspectives* [Narayan 2005]. The earlier work suggested more of a one-size-fits-all *pathway* to empowerment than of various *pathways* to empowerment. This change is also supported, as suggested by the section title above, by their claim that 'no single factor can explain changes in empowerment' (94) and that 'each community had its own stories to explain changes in women's power' (95). This direction in the *WDR 2012* follows both Sen and Drydyk in their defense of the need for contextual, information rich, and multifaceted analyses. Thus far, however, it seems to more clearly follow Drydyk in defending the need for an analysis of power.

In the final chapter, the report turns to recognizing the importance of acquiring knowledge of what will work in particular contexts and argues that both quantitative and qualitative research is needed:

> We adopt an empirical approach, preferring rigorous and evidence-based analysis and highlighting causality where feasible. For this, we draw on a large and growing body of quantitative gender research, complemented by new analysis, particularly on time use, domestic violence, mortality risks, and inputs into agriculture and entrepreneurship. *We also draw on new qualitative field*

> *research with more than 4000 men and women in 98 communities from 19 developing countries, exploring how gender affects their everyday lives and their aspirations, education, job choices, decision making and other aspects of well-being.* (7, my emphasis)

While the quantitative research pays attention to assessments of well-being freedoms, the qualitative research pays attention to assessments of agency freedoms. It would seem, then, that giving voice to women's own assessments of agency and well-being freedoms in the contexts of women reflecting on their lives and relationships moves away from Sen and in the direction of Drydyk. But there may also be departures from Drydyk, ones that emerge from the explicit turn to seeking women's views on what it means to be powerful and free *and* in the context of reflections on the 'reproduction of gender inequalities across generations'.

This is evident in the report's recognition of the force and influence of gender norms with respect to women's lack of power and voice and how these persist across generations (the unpacking of (4) above): 'Perhaps the "stickiest" aspect of gender outcomes is the way patterns of gender inequality are reproduced over time. Part of this persistence is rooted in slow-moving social norms and how they affect what happens in the household' (21). The report also recognizes that effective solutions very much depend on context specific factors of social and political structures, histories, traditions, and practices:

> Gender disparities persist for multiple reasons: there may be a single institutional or policy 'fix' that is difficult and easily blocked; there may be multiple reinforcing constraints in markets, formal institutions, and households that combine to block progress; or they may be deeply rooted in gender roles or social norms that evolve very slowly. Effective policy design requires a good understanding of which of these situations prevails in a particular context, and of where and what the binding constraints are. (37)

Perhaps the best way to understand how these insights play out in real world contexts is to turn to an example of the qualitative research; that done by Patti Petesch in *The Clash of Violent Conflict, Good Jobs, and Gender Norms in Four Economies*, one of the background papers for the *2013 World Development Report*. Petesch's research is contextual in limiting the analysis to contexts of violent conflict in specific countries (Afghanistan, Liberia, Sudan and West Bank and Gaza) and to exploring 'women's and men's understandings about how they gain and lose power and freedom in their lives and the normative frameworks that are shaping their agency and economic participation' (2012, 1). More specifically, Petesch examines possibilities for women's empowerment as these emerge from contexts of conflict that bring sudden challenge and change to gender norms. Petesch argues that

> post-conflict periods seem to offer a rare opportunity to accelerate local development in ways that advance gender equality because of the shock of conflict to local norms and structures, and because of women's and men's strong determination to recover peace and rebuild their lives. (2)

Importantly, Petesch also argues that whether women are empowered through changes to norms and structures needs to be analyzed in the context of relationships in specific contexts of violent conflict.

The relational dimension is present in Petesch's account of gender norms as 'products of *social interactions* between men and women – interactions where men almost always dominate women. Such mechanisms of control, however, operate mainly through routine conducts, and through hidden and subconscious psychological processes' (3, my emphasis). In contexts of violent conflict what is 'hidden and subconscious' is often revealed in ways that create surprising openings for 'a relaxation of these norms and roles, with women perceiving more voice and control and men acutely frustrated by poor security and a stifled local economy' (10). But Petesch also wants to reject the too quick conclusion that a relaxation of norms and rules calls for optimism with respect to what can empower women in these contexts. She argues that possibilities for women's empowerment are tied to possibilities for empowering men in the interactional dynamic of reasoned deliberation about the relationships that shape but also allow a reshaping of norms and rules:

> Men's and women's agency seems to be interdependent. For each to realize their potential, ideally both need to feel in control of their destinies. Gender equality and development goals that aim narrowly at transforming women's lives will likely miss their targets. (27)

Where Petesch differs from Drydyk, then, is in highlighting the *interactional and dynamic* features of the relational dimension of empowerment. This unpacking of elements in the relational dimension is needed in a framework that assesses empowerment in and through the triad of agency, well-being freedom, and power. In the section that follows, I do this unpacking by using insights from relational theory as defended by feminists and developed in my own work.

Power back in: in and through an analysis of relationships

Though not part of the mainstream literature and less well-known, feminist relational theorists argue that focusing on the network of relationships in which individuals are situated can uncover relationships of power, the values that are hidden and sustained in them, and the norms that may need to be challenged or changed in and through them. A central feature of the relational approach as it has developed over the years has been to expand the network of relationships beyond those of dependency on which some feminists, and early care ethicists in particular, tended to focus: 'relations of power, oppression, dominance, exploitation, authority, and justice form identities and self-concepts just as much as relations of dependency, benevolence, care, self-sacrifice, and friendship do' (Koggel, 1998, 163).[3] This expanded relational approach, therefore, can provide a framework for analyzing the effects of relationships at all levels of the individual, institutional, local, national, and global.

On a relational approach, liberal theory's cherished notions of agency, justice, or equality are not relinquished; instead they are reinterpreted in and through the network of complex and ever-changing relationships in which each of us is situated. A relational account of agency, for example, would explain this as a capacity to shape one's life that cannot but emerge through engagement with particular others in a network of relationships – thus the importance of the interactional and dynamic features of empowerment's relational dimension. Moreover, the relationships and possibilities for evaluating or exiting them are in turn nested in and shaped by social practices and political contexts – thus the force of norms and structures that hinder possibilities for women's empowerment. It can be said, then, that as broad as Sen's informational base for assessing inequalities is it does not cover information about inequalities that are shaped in and through relationships (and the institutional norms embedded in them) that one is powerless to exit, challenge, or change.

By putting power back into empowerment, Drydyk's account has implications for assessing and analyzing the freedoms that matter to Sen: if participation and public reasoning serve key roles in enhancing agency and well-being and in helping to shape and reshape values and policy, then attention needs to be paid to relationships of power that thwart the capacity of some to participate and engage in deliberation and debate. If Drydyk can be said to expand on Sen in developing an account of empowerment, my argument expands on Drydyk in using a relational approach to hone in on and analyze people's abilities to engage with power strategically and effectively. In other words, the approach attends to relationships of power that make women vulnerable to the disempowering effects of 'sticky' gender norms.

Attending to the broad network of relationships in which people are situated highlights several features distinctive to the feminist relational approach that I have developed elsewhere.

A relational approach (1) is contextual in that it allows us to attend to the details of the lives of those affected by various kinds of unequal and oppressive relationships, relationships that are in turn shaped by particular social practices and political contexts; (2) uncovers the governing norms and practices that sustain various inequalities for those who are powerless and disadvantaged; and (3) reveals the importance of the perspectives of those adversely affected by relationships of power as sources for learning about various kinds of inequalities and the structures that sustain them. Point (3) is captured in Petesch's research that explores women's understandings of power and freedom in their lives – and through the deliberation and reasoning that happens in relationships assessed in light of dynamic and interactional changes to those relationships. As described above, Petesch finds openings for changing relationships and norms in the unlikely contexts of violent conflict and their aftermath.

In order to further unpack the significance of the interactional and dynamic elements of relationships to an account of empowerment, I want to incorporate two features in addition to the three outlined above.[4] First, (4) human beings have needs and being able to respond in morally appropriate ways to these needs matters to accounts of what is needed to enhance agency or empower people to achieve well-being freedom. The second additional feature (5) draws attention to the fact that people's needs are increasingly shaped by factors of globalization.[5] An analysis of relationships of power at local, national, and global levels is needed to understand how needs are shaped and people are disempowered by the very structures and relationships in which they are embedded. Expanded in this way, relational theory can highlight the workings of power and its detrimental effects on relationships of all kinds and at all levels – including those in the contemporary global context. The expanded account can explain how social processes and political structures that are part of an increasingly interdependent global order determine which bodies are or become needy. It thereby presses for an account of responsibilities to respond to those needs. I think that these relational features are missing in Petesch's account that abstracts the violent conflict happening in specific countries from the global contexts in which conflict is created or perpetuated through the dynamics of relationships of power between rich and poor/developed and developing/powerful and powerful countries. We may, in other words, be even less optimistic than Petesch that openings for challenging gender norms can happen when attention is paid to policies for enhancing women's and men's agency in post-conflict contexts. An account of empowerment in terms of processes of change that can be durable for people in contexts of violent conflict will need an analysis of the dynamics of relationships of power that play out on the global stage. Moreover, contexts of violent conflict are ones in which needs and the difficulty of responding to them are often created by political and economic factors at national and global levels over which people in post-conflict countries have little to no control.

Conclusion

I will end by summarizing the implications of the turn to a relational dimension in accounts of empowerment. The accounts by Drydyk, the World Bank, and Petesch discussed thus far support several features of a feminist relational approach: they (1) attend to contexts and to the concrete details of varied aspects of people's lives; (2) pay attention to assumed and entrenched norms (the values that underlie and are implicit or taken-for-granted in theory and policy), and seem, thereby to (3) legitimize marginalized perspectives on norms and institutions. However, even in its acknowledgement of the 'stickiness' of gender norms and the relation between norms and a lack of power and voice the *WDR 2012* report and Petesch's account fail to (4) identify needs and responsibilities to others in and through networks of relationships and to analyze the ways in which (5) people's needs can be created or worsened in and through relationships of power at local, institutional, national and global levels. Attending to these factors can reveal the lack of freedom that some people have to challenge relations of power so as to enhance their agency and well-being freedoms or to generate durable empowerment.

While a relational approach can explain the power residing in dominant norms, structures, and institutions and how power shapes possibilities for enhancing agency and well-being freedoms or for challenging power, can it identify policies that will empower people in particular contexts? In other words, is a relational approach better at providing a lens or framework through which power can be described and exposed than it is at prescribing strategies or policies for challenging or changing relationships of power? My work gravitates toward the approaches by Sen, Drydyk, the *2012 World Bank report*, and Petesch precisely because they also defend a broad informational base that is sensitive to the diversity and particularity of people and contexts. On this sort of account there is no one theory or set of policy recommendations that will emerge. What is sought instead is an adequate framework for describing and assessing factors that hinder agency and well-being freedoms and disempower people in specific contexts. The relational approach I defend broadens the potential contained in the interactive and dynamic aspects of relationality in the current literature on empowerment. It does this by opening up inquiry into responsibilities to respond to people's needs as they are shaped in personal, institutional, and political relationships that exploit gender norms and disempower those affected by them.

Together the five features of the relational approach identified in this paper shape a framework that is particularly adept at revealing and analyzing gender norms that block possibilities for agency, well-being freedom, and empowerment. Care in relationships, for example, involves the vitally important activities of meeting and satisfying the needs of others, but it is also marked by gender norms and roles. The possibilities for adequate care are shaped by and dependent on the network of relationships in which caring for others is hindered or diminished by relationships at institutional, public, political, economic, and global levels. So for example, globalization's commitment to market structures as the way to maximize profits and increase wealth (and thereby enhance agency) cannot but utilize gender norms in ways that have specific and detrimental effects on opportunities to provide the kind and level of care appropriate to satisfying people's needs in a global context and created by global factors. All five features in a relational framework need to be front and center in the analysis of why it is and has been so difficult to challenge gender norms and empower women.

A focus on the networks of relationships that shape individuals and what they can do and be supports but also enriches Drydyk's account of empowerment in terms of a triad of agency, well-being freedom, and power. It also goes beyond the work now being done on the role of 'sticky' gender norms and how these hinder possibilities for empowering women by providing a critical lens through which to highlight the relational features of sticky gender norms; understand the role of norms in the shaping of possibilities for agency and well-being in particular contexts; and open up possibilities for challenge in the dynamics of relationships themselves, where reasoning and deliberation about the stickiness of gender norms can create pathways to empowerment through processes of change that are durable.

Both Drydyk and Petesch make important contributions in their attention to the relational dimension of empowerment: women's agency often depends on men's choices in asymmetrical relationships that affect possibilities for durable empowerment. We can add to the accounts by Drydyk and Petesch the relational insight that these relationships are embedded in broader networks that are in turn shaped by relationships of power. This would have us pay attention to the ways in which interventions (aid, globalization, changes to law and policy, and even interviewing, studying, and analyzing what will empower women in various contexts) are themselves relational and may set up or sustain relationships of power rather than remove them.

By focusing on the interactive aspects of the relationships themselves when public reasoning is being exercised by people in spaces where they were once absent or invisible (including the new spaces opened up by the *WDR 2012* report), we can achieve a better understanding both of the importance of democracy as public debate and of the force and influence of gender norms in perpetuating the gender inequalities that persist across generations. The engagement with concrete others as they set about to satisfy needs, struggle with barriers, advocate for others, or challenge structures and policies, holds promise for drawing out the ways in which power and relationships of power can be used in positive ways to enact and implement new policy ideas and initiatives.

Acknowledgements

Ideas for this paper emerged from the Ninth International Conference of the International Development Ethics Association (IDEA) at Bryn Mawr College, PA, USA, that I helped organize in June 2011. I would like to thank Bryn Mawr College, IDEA, and participants at the conference for providing a forum that promoted research and discussion by people from around the world on issues related to the conference theme, 'Gender Justice and Development: Local and Global'. I would also like to thank specific people at the conference and after for helping to clarify and shape the arguments in the paper: Madhavika Bajoria, Jay Drydyk, Naila Kabeer, Jennifer Llewellyn, Jan Newberry, Eric Palmer, Patti Petesch, and Joan Tronto as well as Bryn Mawr students in my courses on development ethics and feminist theory.

Notes

1. For a different account of the role of public reasoning that moves in the direction of formulating an ideal of public reasoning through an account of deliberative democracy, consult Crocker (2008).
2. Similarities between Drydyk and Sen in their approaches to formulating theory and policy can also be found in *Displacement by Development* (Penz, Drydyk, and Bose 2011).
3. Examples of theorists working on relational theory include: Brennan (1999); Campbell (2003); Code (1991); Downie and Llewellyn (2012); Koggel (1998, 2002, 2009); Minow (1990); Mackenzie and Stoljar (2000); Nedelsky (1989, 1993); Sherwin (1998).
4. I first developed an expanded feminist relational approach (for a global context) in 'Agency and Empowerment: Embodied Realities in a Globalized World' (Koggel 2009). Also consult the entire collection on similar themes in *Agency and Embodiment* (Maynell, Campbell, and Sherwin 2009).
5. Though my work is in the area of feminist relational theory and of expanding it to the global context, my approach has similarities with postcolonial feminists attending to globalization and relationships of power in the global context. On postcolonial feminism, consult, for example, Mohanty (1997) and papers in Alexander and Mohanty (1997) and Narayan and Harding (2000).

References

Alexander, M. Jaqui, and Chandra Mohanty, eds. 1997. *Feminist Genealogies, Colonial Legacies, Democratic Futures*. New York: Routledge.
Brennan, Samantha. 1999. "Recent Work in Feminist Ethics." *Ethics* 109 (July): 858–893.

Campbell, Sue. 2003. *Relational Remembering: Rethinking the Memory Wars*. Lanham, MD: Rowman & Littlefield.

Code, Lorraine. 1991. *What Can She Know: Feminist Theory and the Construction of Knowledge*. Ithaca, NY: Cornell University Press.

Crocker, David. 2008. *Ethics of Global Development: Agency, Capability, and Deliberative Democracy*. Cambridge: Cambridge University Press.

Downie, Jocelyn, and Jennifer Llewellyn, eds. 2012. *Being Relational: Reflections on Relational Theory and Health Law and Policy*. Vancouver: University of British Columbia Press.

Drydyk, Jay. 2013. "Empowerment, Agency, and Power." *Journal of Global Ethics*. http://dx.doi.org/10.1080/17449626.2013.818374

Koggel, Christine M. 1998. *Perspectives on Equality: Constructing a Relational Theory*. Lanham, MD: Rowman & Littlefield.

Koggel, Christine M. 2002. "Equality Analysis in a Global Context: a Relational Approach." In *Feminist Moral Philosophy*, edited by Samantha Brennan, *Canadian Journal of Philosophy* Supplementary Volume (28): 247–272.

Koggel, Christine M. 2009. "Agency and Empowerment: Embodied Realities in a Globalized World." In *Agency and Embodiment*, edited by L. Maynell, S. Campbell and S. Sherwin, 313–336. College Park, PA: Penn State Press.

Mackenzie, Catriona, and Natalie Stoljar, eds. 2000. *Relational Autonomy: Feminist Perspectives on Autonomy, Agency, and the Social Self*. New York: Oxford University Press.

Maynell, Letitia, Sue Campbell, and Susan Sherwin, eds. 2009. *Agency and Embodiment*. State College, PA: Penn State Press.

Minow, Martha. 1990. *Making all the Difference: Inclusion, Exclusion and American Law*. Ithaca, NY: Cornell.

Mohanty, C. 1997. "Women Workers and Capitalist Scripts: Ideologies of Domination, Common Interests, and the Politics of Solidarity." In *Feminist Genealogies, Colonial Legacies, Democratic Futures*, edited by J. Alexander and C. Mohanty, 3–29. New York: Routledge.

Narayan, D. 2005. *Measuring Empowerment: Cross-Disciplinary Perspectives*. Washington, DC: World Bank.

Narayan, Uma, and Sandra Harding, eds. 2000. *Decentering the Center: Philosophy for a Multicultural, Postcolonial, and Feminist World*. Bloomington: Indiana University Press.

Nedelsky, Jennifer. 1989. "Reconceiving Autonomy: Sources, Thoughts, and Possibilities." *Yale Journal of Law and Feminism* 1 (1): 7–36.

Nedelsky, Jennifer. 1993. "Reconceiving Rights as Relationship." *Review of Constitutional Studies/Revue d'etudes constitutionnelles* 1 (1): 1–26.

Penz, Peter, Jay Drydyk, and Pablo Bose. 2011. *Displacement by Development: Ethics, Rights and Responsibilities*. Cambridge: Cambridge University Press.

Petesch, Patti. 2012. The Clash of Violent Conflict, Good Jobs, and Gender Norms in Four Economies. Background Paper for the World Development Report 2013. Washington, DC: World Bank.

Sen, Amartya. 1999. *Development as Freedom*. New York: Anchor Books.

Sen, Amartya. 2009. *The Idea of Justice*. Cambridge, MA: Harvard University Press.

Sherwin, Susan. 1998. "A Relational Approach to Autonomy in Health Care." In *The Politics of Women's Health: Exploring Agency and Autonomy*, edited by The Feminist Health Care Ethics Research Network, 19–47. Philadelphia: Temple University Press.

World Bank. 2011. *World Development Report 2012: Gender Equality and Development*. Washington, DC: World Bank.

Women's empowerment: the insights of Wangari Maathai

Gail M. Presbey

CLAE, University of Detroit Mercy, Detroit, USA

Wangari Maathai of Kenya has written about empowerment, practiced it in many ways in her own life, and shared her reflections on it with many other women in the Green Belt Movement. Yet to date, no study has been devoted to her ideas on the topic. This paper will highlight Maathai's insights regarding empowerment, tracing several important themes in her approach, namely, empowerment's relationship to self-esteem, teamwork, and political action, its ambivalent relationship to formal education, and the role of cultural traditions in providing alternatives to colonial-era cultural impositions and current exploitative effects of neo-liberal capitalism. After reviewing Maathai's thoughts on each of these topics, I will briefly draw upon other East African thinkers and Africanists' studies of East African communities to present corroborating evidence for Maathai's views or for challenges to her position. Listening to the perspectives of Maathai and other East Africans provides several important correctives to current popular uses of the term 'empowerment'.

Women's empowerment, women's education, and women's equality: everyone agrees that these are all good things and worthy goals. But what exactly do these things mean? And what do they mean in an East African context? What forms of empowerment, education, and equality are truly liberating and what forms are deceptive, seeming to offer liberation while in reality serving to tie women down in some new and subtle way? The purpose of this paper is to explore these issues from the perspective of a remarkable East African woman, Wangari Maathai. For too long, we in the West have approached issues of empowerment, education, and equality from our own perspective only, as if we were the only ones in the world who truly knew what these words meant. But even a cursory glance at our own societies, rife as they are with problems and injustices of all kinds, should give the lie to such presumption. In our dialog with our third world neighbors, it is we who have the most to learn.

But perhaps a quick biographical note is in order before we begin. Wangari Maathai was born in Kenya in 1940. She studied biology in the USA during the 1960s and then held research and teaching positions at the University of Nairobi. In 1971 she completed her doctorate in Veterinary Anatomy, becoming the first East African woman to earn a Ph.D. Maathai began her career as an activist while still at the university, campaigning for equal benefits for the female employees. But it is as founder of the Green Belt Movement (GBM) that she has had her greatest impact. This movement has involved 100,000 women activists establishing 600 community networks, running 6000 nurseries, and planting 30 million trees to reverse environmental damage in Kenya (2007, 175). In addition, Maathai has worked for a whole host of other activist organizations and written several books about her experiences. Nixon correctly describes

Maathai as a 'writer-activist', whose writings 'give imaginative definition to the slow violence inflicted in the global South' (2011). In addition to numerous protests, Maathai also became active in traditional politics, serving as a Member of Parliament and also as Assistant Minister for the Environment, Natural Resources, and Wildlife. In 2004, she was awarded the Nobel Peace Prize and in 2006, the French Legion of Honor.

Surprisingly, though, Maathai's work and writings have received little notice from the philosophical community. A search through past issues of the *Journal of Global Ethics* finds only one mention of Maathai, a mention which basically just notes that she was the recipient of the Nobel Peace Prize for 2004. And a search in *Philosopher's Index* across all categories finds no mention of Maathai at all. Wondering how Maathai's and others' writings from the global South can so often be excluded from the lists of key course readings in environmental humanities courses, Nixon terms this 'Americanist bias' (2011).[1]

To be sure, Maathai's writing has been the subject of several good studies focusing on her rhetoric, especially her use of narrative, effective tropes, and 'suasory argumentation' (Gorsevski 2012; Kirkscey 2007), as well as gender analyses of how the media has portrayed her (Worthington 2003) and analyses of how she was able to effectively use nonviolent action to bring change to Kenya (Cesar 2010; Nixon 2006–2007, 2011). But the magnitude of her accomplishment points to the need to study her writings more seriously. We need to attend not just to her style of rhetoric, or how the media has portrayed her, or what tactics she has used, but also and most importantly to the content of her message.

Empowerment: more than just increased purchasing power or career-building

What do we mean by the term 'empowerment'? We must avoid thinking of empowerment only within a western capitalist context. For example, Lewis argues that state-engineered 'transformation' based on neo-liberal development paradigms often uses the phrases 'gender equality' and 'women's empowerment' in ways that are 'superficial and complacent' (2008, 83). In other words, they use these popular phrases in ways that do not ask for justice but only 'power within the status quo', presuming that women's only aspirations are to gain men's privileges for themselves (84). She in fact recommends simply dropping empowerment talk because of the way it has failed to promote 'situations and conditions that may lie beyond existing class and gender models of material achievement and public success' (Lewis 2008, 84).

Still, women theorists have addressed the topic of the concept of empowerment, and before turning to Maathai's contribution I would like to survey a few helpful studies. Ibrahim and Alkire have constructed a table of different connotations of the term 'empowerment' from a survey of development literature (2007, 380–381). They found great commonality among the different descriptions of empowerment, with the majority focusing on developing insight into social and structural inhibitors of flourishing, so that individuals can change their perspectives and actions, and join in community with others, to change their context so that they can more easily achieve well-being. I found this emphasis on empowerment acting as a counter to existing inhibitors to be described succinctly by Allen as 'the capacity of an agent to act in spite of, or in response to, the power wielded over her by others' (1998, 34).

I found that Koggel supplied a particularly helpful definition of empowerment as 'the expansion of freedom of choice and action to shape one's life. It implies control over resources and decisions' (2009, 250). Koggel sees empowerment as a process of change on both individual and collective levels that enhances social agency so that people can take purposeful and effective action to change their world and to combat systemic impediments to their freedom. Importantly, Koggel insists that we should not think of empowerment as an individualistic or competitive process.

Narayan points out that the equality of all persons is not simply a 'Western' philosophical notion: 'the doctrines of equality and rights, rather than being pure "products of Western imperialism" were often important products of such struggles *against Western imperialism*' (2000, 91). Narayan refers to the many political struggles of women and excluded groups – such as racial, ethnic, and religious minorities in both Western (abolitionist and suffragette movements) and non-Western (the anti-colonial struggles of India, Africa, and elsewhere) contexts – who helped to give new meaning to an anemic and minimalist conception of equality in the Western philosophical tradition.

While the US Declaration of Independence, based on Lockean philosophical principles, declared 'all men are created equal' and 'they are endowed by their creator with certain inalienable rights' (1776/2013), the US Constitution did not prevent practices of slavery and the disenfranchisement of American Indians and women. Narayan's critique would suggest, not just that there was a discrepancy between stated ideals and policies, but that the concept 'equality' was not yet fully understood and that its contemporary understanding is not the result of Euro-American male philosophers. It is with this hope of more fully understanding the concept 'empowerment' that we take into account the struggles and writings of African women like Wangari Maathai.

Empowerment: both individual and collective

One of the strengths of Maathai's work is that she emphasizes empowerment on both the individual and community levels. In *The Green Belt Movement* ([1985] 2004), Maathai explains how her organization promoted empowerment (which she termed boosting women's confidence) through civic education. She promoted empowerment on the community level so that it could lead to community mobilization (2004, 68–69). In her latest book, *Replenish the Earth* (2010), she explains that she started her work in the GBM with a focus on saving trees and the environment. Eventually, she noticed the need to increase women's self-confidence, help them to find their authentic voice, and expand democratic space so that their voices could be heard (14).

Chapter seven of *Replenish the Earth*, entitled 'Self-Empowerment', focuses on improving one's own life through self-reliance. She drives home her message: the power to change is within yourself (2010, 15, 130). Nonetheless, her goal is not to foster narrow, self-interested behavior even though responsibility rests with the individual. Her next chapter emphasizes committing oneself to selfless service for the common good. Clearly, this understanding of the term resonates with Koggel's opinion that empowerment does not need to be understood in individualistic or competitive terms.

It is important to note that we have to be careful to avoid becoming caught in a chicken–egg dilemma regarding individual and community empowerment. We cannot presume that individuals are suddenly going to gain self-confidence on their own and then join a group. Self-empowerment grows best in a context of group support. Indeed, as far as which comes first, according to her own description in the previous paragraph, Maathai worked with groups first and then came to appreciate the fact that belonging to a group is not enough: one must internalize the positive messages one hears in the group in order to have courage to act alone or with others. But then, she went back to the group experience and realized she had to build within the group learning experiences that paid particular attention to the need for growth in self-confidence of each individual person.

Not all group activities are liberatory. Maathai recognized sources of disempowerment in her community's practices. For example, she saw the Pentecostal vigil, seemingly vigorous in its use of active song and dance, as an example of 'disheartening passivity', as participants beg God to turn attention toward the people's plight and save the day, 'forsaking all belief in their own ability' (2010, 143). She bemoaned people forsaking the opportunity to empower themselves by leaving all in God's hands. By contrast, GBM seminars teach women that God wants them to do something about their situation (143, 147).

Maathai developed a personal philosophy that helped her to cope with adversity. She realized the importance of cultivating a higher consciousness within oneself to become willing to do what one believes is right, regardless of popular opinion. One of the first pamphlets that she wrote for the GBM told about searching for what she calls the 'roots' of disempowerment (2004, 165). In conversations with many Kenyans, she found that they tended to blame the government for all their problems, belittling the role that citizens could play. Maathai would instead point out to them that they themselves were part of the problem, 'by not standing up for what they strongly believed in' (173). Also, they had internalized foreign values by reducing the value of the environment to money (174).

Looking at Maathai's memoir, *Unbowed* (2007), we see a complex consideration of the influence of 'foreign' values. For while Maathai claimed that foreign capitalist values were a bad influence that replaced local traditional values, she also valued new perspectives and talents she gained while abroad. She attributes her emphasis on self-starting – finding new solutions to problems when they arise – [as] due to the influence of her education and her time in the USA (125).

That long-term, deep, and widespread change comes at a cost to the individual is something Maathai knows through personal experience. Regarding *Unbowed*, Schaeffer-Duffy (2007) comments, 'failure and obstacles define her journey', as she bears imprisonment, violent attacks, and divorce during the pursuit of her goals; but these experiences do not derail her because 'adversity can clarify and strengthen commitment'. In Maathai's own words, 'A stumble is only one step in the long path we walk and dwelling on it only postpones the completion of our journey' (2007, 162). Maathai's experience is relevant when empowerment happens in a context of resistance (Allen 1998, 34).

Women's empowerment groups emphasize that by joining together, women can change their world for the better. Participating in electoral politics is just one way, and not the only or best way, of becoming politically active. Anytime people come together for concerted action to change their world is an example of 'political action' in the broad sense.

Maathai explains that much of her life was involved in civil society and voluntary associations like the GBM, and she worked in cooperation with nongovernmental organizations (NGOs) (for example, the Norwegian Forestry Society) that funded environmental projects. Maathai formulated an easy to follow 10-step process for starting a GBM group. Recruiting others to start additional GBM groups/projects was an important step for each group. The enthusiasm was infectious. She explains that 'this was a breakthrough because it was now communities empowering one another ... the process replicated itself several thousand times' (2007, 137). They did not wait for government to fix things.

Nixon sees Maathai's movement in the larger context of civil society. He thinks that many disaffected constituencies in Kenya, including students, and others feeling marginalized, joined her group not due to environmental concerns per se but because they appreciated her emphasis on activism and they wanted to be part of her 'dramatic initiative to repossess for the polity not just plundered public land and resources but also plundered political agency' (Nixon 2006–2007, 22). Clearly, Maathai cannot be considered *merely* as an environmentalist, since she taught, through demonstration, self and group empowerment techniques that could be used to address a host of societal problems.

Taking into consideration Maathai's contributions as a role model and author, what conclusions can we draw regarding empowerment and its relationship to self-esteem, community activism, and political action? As we saw earlier, according to Lewis, 'empowerment' is one of those terms often used lately to mean, in a shallow sense, 'success' in terms accepted by the status quo. Maathai's understanding and use of 'empowerment' did not conform to the status quo in Kenya, but changed the existing framework in many ways. For example, she challenged current understandings of women's role (in leadership/politics), as well as environmental values (rather than reducing everything to cash value). She dared to criticize those who wanted God or the government to rescue them and encouraged and demonstrated women coming together to make changes in their communities and country in conformity with their values. Her challenges to the status quo did not entail simplistically jettisoning the past for an uncharted future (or for copying foreign ideas); she carefully rescued important but neglected values from the past and championed them anew, while at the same time, in other areas, creatively modeling new practices and mindsets.

Maathai's participation in electoral politics and political protest

Aili Mari Tripp explains that the 1990s brought new opportunities for women in Africa to engage in politics. She explains that women's extensive experience in associations such as churches, savings clubs, community improvement associations, and NGOs helped to prepare them for political work. Tripp also notes that once they entered politics, women were fierce opponents of the corruption, patronage, and ethnic division they found in the existing political systems. She mentions both Wangari Maathai and Charity Ngilu (a Minister of Parliament who also ran in Presidential elections in 1997) as key Kenyan examples of this larger trend in Africa (Tripp 2004, 144, 151–152).

In a majority of countries around the world, including Kenya, women struggle to be adequately represented in electoral politics. In 1982 Maathai attempted to run in a by-election for a seat in Parliament. At this time, there were only two women seated in parliament (Maathai 2007, 159–160) and the bias against women in politics was high. In fact, the courts disqualified Maathai from running due to a technicality (the government claimed she should have re-registered to vote). Then, to add insult to injury, the University of Nairobi, which had earlier insisted that she resign in order to stand for election, refused to reinstate her when she was found ineligible to run (2007, 160–163).

Many years later, she tried again to enter electoral politics. Maathai admits that she entered the November 1997 election only five weeks before the election day and that she had little funds for her campaign. She says that she chose to run for a parliamentary seat in Tetu constituency (which includes her birthplace) as well as campaigning for the Presidency, in order to have access to dialogs with other candidates so as to encourage opposition candidates to maintain a united front against Kenya African National Union (KANU), the ruling party. She became 1 of 15 presidential candidates. But she was accused of being a 'spoiler' for the campaign of the one other woman Presidential candidate, Charity Ngilu, who already held a parliamentary seat. The press printed a rumor on election day saying that she had dropped out and endorsed another candidate. She concluded in retrospect in her memoir that she had been a 'dreamer' to have thought that voters could transcend the local political culture and vote for the best qualified candidates (2007, 256–259).

The sexist views of male Kenyan politicians posed constant challenges for Maathai. Worthington (2003) notes that media coverage of politically active women tends to portray women as unnecessarily aggressive and ill-equipped to lead. Reviewing media coverage of Maathai's 1989–1990 campaign to stop the business development project proposed for Uhuru Park, Worthington notes three phases in the media coverage. In an early phase, news media acknowledged Maathai's stature as an expert, quoted her directly, and attributed authority to her words, even when she questioned a government minister (149). But this changed once President Moi spoke out against Maathai's criticisms of his development project. Moi invoked gender to explain his outrage at Maathai's opposition, saying that she 'shows no respect for men as required by African traditions' (157). The press even quoted Moi's incredulity that the GBM planted any trees (Maathai 2007, 157). Moi challenged women, saying, 'Can't you discipline one of your own?' (Cesar, 2010, 132–33). Moi's statements were repeated with great deference. In the third phase, Maathai was being called 'indomitable', then 'obstinate' and 'desperate'. When she was persecuted for her views, she was accused of having brought down the wrath of the authorities upon her. Her actions were portrayed as 'a lonely fight' despite the fact that her position had broad support (Worthington 2003, 155–57).

Such attacks did not deter Maathai from protesting. Cesar (2010) points to Maathai's dramatization of reclaiming public lands such as the Karura Forest that had been distributed to private individuals by President Moi in a system of rewards for favors rendered. Only 2% of Kenya was forested, so Maathai engaged in 'guerrilla' reforestation of public lands (128) and through this publicity worked to stop public land allocations. Ellen Gorsevski explores the importance of the choices of symbolic expression, such as women sneaking into the Karurua Forest (accompanied by the press) 'armed' with a 'watering can' to engage in their nonviolent resistance (9). Nixon (2006–2007) considers the short-sighted pillage of Kenya's natural resources as possible due to male-dominated politics in Kenya. He contrasts Maathai's slow, intergenerational focus on trees and the future with current emphases on making a quick buck. He notes that Kenya's booming economy is filled with increasing polarity between the rich and the poor (20–23, 25, 30–31).

Maathai finally won a parliamentary seat in 2002. Her campaign slogan was 'Rise up and walk!' (287), which alluded to the Bible passage in Acts 3:1–10. Maathai explains that the passage is about apostles Peter and John encountering a lame beggar 'who has all the characteristics of a disempowered person: he is poor, self-effacing, dejected, and has no sense of pride in himself' (287). But Peter encourages him to rise and walk and he can do it. According to Maathai, the moral of the story was that 'together, we could lift ourselves up and address the conditions of our poverty and disempowerment and regain our self-respect' (287). So even when campaigning for office, her message was a broader one of encouraging Kenyans to have the confidence and fortitude to change their country for the better.

Maathai's efforts finally bore fruit. In 2003, at a time when few women held ministerial positions in Kenya, Maathai was appointed Assistant Minister for Environment and Natural Resources, a post in which she served until 2005.

Maathai could be seen as a trailblazer regarding her early entry into electoral politics. Kenya has been going through rapid changes regarding women's participation in electoral politics. For most decades since Independence in 1963 up to just a few years ago, women held 10% or less of electoral and appointed positions in government. But many countries in Africa have gone through rapid change in the past decades, often with the help of affirmative action quotas for women. With the help of such quotas, neighboring countries Tanzania and Uganda rank twentieth and twenty-first internationally for rates of women's participation in national parliaments, while Kenya ranks seventy-sixth and the USA ranks seventy-eighth (Inter-Parliamentary Union 2013). Seeing and wishing to copy such gains, Article 27, point eight of the new Kenyan Constitution (2010) stipulates that no more than two-thirds of elected and appointed representatives can be of one gender. Despite this constitutional requirement, there were not enough women candidates running in the 2013 elections to be able to fulfill that mandate. The Kenyan Supreme Court ruled that the one-third gender requirement would not apply to the 2013 elections, but should be implemented progressively (Commonwealth Observer Group 2013, 15). Maria Nzomo has argued that without attention to campaign finance reform and without a change in the perceptions of Kenyan voters, women will continue to be at a disadvantage in elections

(Nzomo 2012). Women politicians considered to be outspoken still face backlash from men, as illustrated by the recent case of Governor Evans Kidero slapping Nairobi women representative Rachel Shebesh at Nairobi City Hall in September 2013 (Michira 2013). Still, milestones reached in 2013 include 6 out of 18 members of the Cabinet being women, including Amina Mohamed as the first woman Minister of Foreign Affairs and Rayechelle Omamo as the first woman Minister of Defense (Rotich 2013).

Education: what kind of education engenders empowerment?

Contemporary campaigns such as Girl Rising (2012) and Girl Up (2013) try to reach audiences in the USA by suggesting that the solution for the problems of poverty and violence against women in Africa and many parts of Asia is to focus on educating girls. By education, they mean having girls attend school. Recently, focusing on the brutal murder attempt of Malala Yousufzai, a Pakistani girl who insisted on attending school, which gained wide media attention, organizations such as UNESCO (2012) and UNICEF United States Fund (2013) are using the spotlight created by the media to reinforce the idea that girls' education is a priority. Rarely do any of the groups raise the question of the *kind* of schooling the girls will receive. It is presumed that they will learn literacy and job skills. Girl Rising (2012), drawing upon a World Bank working paper by Chabaan and Cunningham (2011), argues that a girl who receives an extra year of education will make 20% a year more income as an adult. The study, which surveys 14 countries in Asia and Africa, including the three East African countries we are focusing upon, claims that investing in girl's education will raise the country's Gross Domestic Product significantly.

No doubt schooling for girls is an important goal, but the arguments made in support of it have usually been made within the capitalist framework, promising increased income for girls and improvement of the country's economy. Each use of the word 'empowerment' in the World Bank study specifically mentions boosting girl's/women's earning power and not any other possible aspects of empowerment.

Perhaps we should pay attention to the kind of schooling we are advocating. As Jay Drydyk (this volume) explains, the presence of any particular means to empowerment, such as literacy or education, cannot in itself be directly interpreted as generating empowerment *simpliciter*. While education is no doubt a good thing, women need educational skills in a range of methods for social expression and agency, to not just fit into the status quo system, but to challenge and change it, for a fuller expression of empowerment.

The statements made above must not be construed to suggest that girls' formal education is unimportant. In Jane Osongo's study she found that in Kenya, unequal division of household chores begins during childhood for girls, when many are not able to concentrate on their education due to their workload (Osongo 2011, 27). It would indeed be an important project for Kenyan parents to learn to prioritize their daughters' school attendance or at least to ensure that they attend on par with the sons in the family.

Maathai herself had an extensive formal education, more than most Kenyan women were able to achieve, and yet in her work with GBM, she realized that she had to change her mind about what kind and methods of education women needed most. She explained that having women learn forestry from male experts was counter-productive. The men would use complicated jargon and describe procedures that depended on expensive machinery. Maathai realized that women among themselves had the environmental knowledge they needed to succeed. After all, they were farmers with loads of practical experience, all of which was being discounted by professional foresters. She concluded that women could teach each other (2007, 135–36).

Anke Wolbert (2011) argues that Maathai used critical pedagogical principles akin to what Paolo Freire called the 'conscientization process'. Women learned from each other to demystify oppressive structures and to exercise courage to challenge the social order (95–104). Her side-stepping around stultifying formal education is something that Nagel (2005) sees as an example of what Patricia Hill Collins calls 'wisdom' in the Afrocentric feminist epistemology (4). This educational maneuver was matched, according to Rob Nixon, by Maathai's rejection of masculinist ideas of saving the environment, a paradigm that removed all humans in its quest to protect nonhuman nature. Instead, Maathai defined environment as the place of women farmers with their deeply grounded knowledge of ecology and agriculture (2006–2007, 24).

In an epilogue to *Unbowed*, written after she received the Nobel Peace Prize in 2004, Maathai announced that she was going to create an empowerment center in Nairobi that would offer experiential learning opportunities as well as civic and environmental education, as she believed this to be the kind of education most important for a woman's life (2007, 305). Since her death in September 2011, the GBM continues to offer three- to four-day seminars in community empowerment (see http://www.GreenBeltmovement.org/what-we-do/community-empowerment).

Maathai did not completely discount higher formal education, but she did want the current education system to be radically changed. While academic institutions may prepare professionals to write journal articles, Maathai thought that their students often display insensitive behavior toward rural communities suffering dire problems. And an academically trained student has simply not been prepared to tackle the real-life problems of abject poverty and under-development.

The University of Nairobi now houses the Wangari Maathai Institute for Peace and Environmental Studies. The Institute's mission is to address the problem of academic institutions' failures to translate environmental knowledge into concrete help to Kenya's rural people. It follows up on Maathai's recommendation to focus on ethics and values, instilling character traits such as earnest work, respect for others, gratitude for the earth's gifts, and responsibility to work for the common good (http://wmi.uonbi.ac.ke/node/3991).

Emphasis on having young women participate in existing structures of formal education was criticized as misplaced by Elinami Veraeli Swai, a Tanzanian scholar who recently earned her Ph.D. in Education at Pennsylvania State University and now teaches Women's and Gender Studies at University of Toledo, Ohio. Swai (2010) argues that in Tanzania, the term 'empowerment' has been used in a narrow sense to describe the process of formal education and professionalization of women, which she considers to bring unexpected unhappiness to many women in rural Tanzania, as they find themselves misfits in their communities and cope with difficulties in finding a marriage partner and raising children. A main drawback to pursuing education, from her perspective, is the marginalization of women's knowledge that already exists outside of formal education. Women who provide food security for their families as well as care for family members in need or who can practice medicine, in some cases curing infection, food poisoning, and snake bite, for example, are considered less important than the formally educated (at best) or are deprecated as heathens (at worst). As a particularly vivid example of the suppression of women's knowledge, Swai recounts her interview with a woman who remembered her grandmother who, under pressure from the local missionary, had three of her fingers cut off to deter her from continuing her healing practice, which the missionary insisted was against Christianity (126–136).

What is the ideal way for educated women to work with rural women? Maathai designed the GBM to work with rural women and insisted that in her group, educated (including herself) and rural women worked side by side. But she notes that politicians have exploited the urban–rural distinction to divide women. Maathai's early work with forestry had been part of the work of the National Council for Women in Kenya (NCWK). One of the many other groups affiliated with

NCWK was Maendeleo ya Wanawake (meaning Progress for Women). According to Maathai, when the Kenyan government wanted to oppose her efforts, they used their political connections to Maendeleo, having the group's leaders charge that NCWK was run by educated, urban women who marginalized rural women. The members of Maendeleo therefore left NCWK and the government continued to financially support Maendeleo, leaving NCWK almost bankrupt (until it found foreign donors) (2007, 137–138, 155–156).

Maathai wants her readers to be able to distinguish between a real urban-rural split and one manufactured for political reasons. Researchers in Kenya have observed how politicians often try to manipulate rural women, even trying to buy their votes with bags of sugar and other staples (Abwunza 1997, 115–118). From the perspective of politicians trying to maintain status quo power, encouraging a social rift between urban and rural women may be a divide and conquer tactic that purposely disempowers women. However, Swai still has a point well taken. Urban or educated women who are not self-aware of how their attitudes may prejudice them against rural women (who do not have a formal education like themselves) could in fact be alienating rural women.

Swai judges that construing empowerment as formal education usually strengthens 'a patriarchal and capitalist agenda', since rather than create an alternative to the status quo, it rather merely encourages women to succeed in the current status quo (7).[2] Abwunza (1997) explains how women's groups, ostensibly created by drawing upon traditional sentiments of solidarity with others (*silica* in Swahili) often end up reinforcing capitalism. In her study of women's groups in Maragoli, in the Western Province in Kenya, she notes that the groups' activities are 'pervaded by a capitalistic ideology of progress and accumulation of wealth' (158). But since it 'takes money to make money' (158) and since poor women often do not have their own start-up funds, groups often stagnate unless they receive start-up loans from outside sources.

Swai has encountered many women's 'empowerment' groups in Tanzania that are led by educated middle-class African women, whom Swai thinks cannot relate to rural women as equals, since they are convinced that due to their education they are superior to other women. These attitudes alienate rural women. Swai also notes that there are sometimes monetary requirements for being able to join these mutual aid groups, and while the amounts of money involved may seem nominal to outsiders, they are prohibitive for many rural women (Swai 2010, 162–165).

Cultural traditions and their relationship to colonial history and capitalism

Maathai says that upon returning to Kenya after pursuing education abroad, she considered herself entirely Westernized, even at home with her family. It was only through her work with rural women in the GBM that she realized her need to connect to her own cultural roots. This revelation stemmed from her insight that when traditional cultures are destroyed by Westernism, Africans are left with the 'gods of commercialism, materialism, and individualism', which leave both stomachs and souls empty (2009, 164).

Many Kenyan communities had traditions that respected nature. In Brendon Nicholls' study (2005) of the so-called Mau Mau – insurgents who fought against the British during colonialism – he found that Gikuyu elders (Maathai's ethnic group) would talk to the fighters about their sacred relationship to the forest. He said:

> These elders invested the landscape with spiritual significance, in which the slightest human action (such as cutting down trees, killing animals needlessly or shooting towards mountains in which spirits dwelled) interacted with a network of taboos and portents and could invoke adverse meteorological, military or even cosmological consequences. (185)

Such a system of taboos could reinforce respect for nature.

An important aspect of cultural traditions has been story telling. Maathai herself became a storyteller, practicing this oral art in many of her public appearances. Her storytelling ability was highlighted and illustrated in animation as part of a film called 'Dirt: The Movie'. In this documentary about environmental challenges caused by contemporary agriculture techniques, Maathai tells the story of a hummingbird who, while very small, does all it can to stop a forest fire, while the other larger animals stand by, paralyzed by the sight of the big blaze (Rosow and Benenson 2009). And the fact that she tells the story in the context of an American-made documentary on the environment, with the larger world as her audience, shows that such stories not only reach Kenyans of all ages, but are indeed accessible (and memorable) to many people worldwide.

Maathai is not the only one of her generation to use oral storytelling as an educational tool based in Africa's traditions. Currently across Africa, oral literature, including proverbs and tales, is incorporated into the curriculum of schools from primary to tertiary education. Folk tales have practical advice and moral guidance. While they can be studied as literature, their value is more than mere artistry. They can serve as guides to life as well as encouragement. They are important educational tools that provide not just knowledge as in information, but also help to reinforce identity and purpose in life. In the Kenyan context, it was Kenyan faculty at the University of Nairobi who played a key role in making the curriculum (which up to this point had been based on British models) more inclusive of African literature and history. Taban lo Liyong and Ngugi wa Thiong'o, as well as Okot p'Bitek were some of the key proponents of this new African-centered approach in the 1970s (Ogot 1995, 217–220, 230). When Maathai uses storytelling, she can reach out simultaneously to young and old Kenyans. In this way her message is not limited to the audience of school attendees but can spread more easily throughout the entire society.

In workshops Maathai conducted for women, participants often referred to loss of traditional cultures as contributing to contemporary problems such as drug and alcohol abuse, theft, and school dropouts. This led Maathai to emphasize the need for self-knowledge (*kwimenya* in Kikuyu) (2010, 169–170). Some of the traditional knowledge that protected the environment has already been lost (167). Maathai admits that it is not possible or desirable to turn back the hands of time to return to an African past, but it is important to try to view the past through eyes other than the colonizer's (182–183). As well, she does not want to return to a patriarchal society, but wants instead a genuine partnership that respects gender equity and involves both parents in raising children (278).

'Cultural roots' not only involve spiritual beliefs and practices; there are also cultural traditions of family and economic organization. Some of those traditions have been destroyed during colonial times. In *The Challenge for Africa* (2009), Maathai notes that in Kenya, practices of labor migration reinforced during colonialism have separated men from their families. Fathers who are absent from rural areas leave children vulnerable. Women often find themselves raising families alone, and single heads of households are prevalent, with women even giving last names to their children (276–277). Much of the suffering of East African women has to do with poverty that has historical, political, and economic causes. So it would be erroneous to think that East African women's suffering is mostly due to their husbands (Comaroff and Comaroff 2012, 18). Maathai commented that traditionally, land in Kenya was held by a family; only during colonial times would there be a title deed for property that would only be given to men (Maathai 2009, 227). Nixon points out the ways in which colonial theft, the 'masculinizing of property', the focus on cash crops and the resulting environmental degradation have made rural African women farmers' lives harder (2006–2007, 25). Adding to the complexity of the anti-colonial narrative, a Kenyan woman researcher found that Maragoli widows thought life was easier for them under colonialism. This imperial nostalgia is due to disillusionment with politics in the context of postcolonial Kenya (Mutongi 2007).

There are African women scholars who have argued that women have not always been oppressed and that African understandings of relations between the sexes have been different than Euro-American conceptions. They have decried Northern feminist scholars' presumption that Africans have the same ideas of gender subordination found in Europe and the USA (Oyĕwùmi 2003a, 2003b; Okome 2003; Kolawole 2006). One key theme of their comments is that in the African context motherhood is more important than wifehood, and so a focus on the latter issue is Eurocentric. Also, focusing on wifehood neglects multiple identities and statuses that women hold in large extended families, narrowing concepts of their status to the relation to the husband (Nzegwu 2004). Many of the scholars who criticize Euro-American gender theorists come from West Africa, but their ideas might apply to some East African communities as well.

The almost exclusive focus on 'wifehood' decried above can be seen in the coverage of the topic 'empowerment' in the *Kenya Demographic and Health Survey 2008–09* (Kenya Bureau of Statistics, 2010). All surveys on topics in this section of the report have to do with women's decision-making power vis-à-vis her husband. While the results can be fascinating, the choice of focus shows that the concept of empowerment is too limited and too greatly influenced by Euro-American studies that focus on the nuclear family. In a study that draws upon data of the *2008–09 Kenya Demographic and Health Survey* but uses latent class analysis, sociologist John Musalia says that respondents to the questions on women's empowerment can be categorized in four ways, as holding pragmatic, traditionalist, egalitarian, or independent positions. A significant number of Kenyan women, and especially a large percentage of women who head households, hold an independent position in which they think that they do not need to consult men when they are making decisions (Musalia 2013).

One could add that among those women who do not want to consult men would be included the women who opt for traditions of woman-woman marriage, which can still be found in contemporary Kenya, including in Wangari Maathai's home area in Central Province. Gikuyu and Nandi 'muhikania' (woman-woman) marriages give women rights to land and to become the heads of their lineage, an option that was not possible in Christian patriarchal marriages (Njambi and O'Brien 2005). Recent Kenyan courts have upheld the right of women to own and pass property to their heirs, based on *muhikania* traditions (Mwobobia 2011). Interestingly enough, the *Kenya Demographic and Health Survey 2008–09* (236) shows Central Province to be the most likely to approve of women's decision-making participation. Women's gains since the 2010 Constitution have been expressed by a host of rulings upholding women's rights to inherit property that had been part of their fathers' estates. Significantly, these cases have been decided by several women Justices – Mary Kasango, Martha Koome, and Kalpana Rawal (Wambugu 2011).

Wangari Maathai has become a role model for Kenyan women who want to express themselves rather than live a life subordinate to their husbands. This ability to chart one's own course in life rather than follow the dictates of a husband is one of many senses of empowerment that Maathai discusses and models through her actions, although, unlike the demographic report, it is not the only way in which she expresses women's empowerment.

Men experience a lot of pressure to be seen by others to be in charge in the household. Maathai admits that she underestimated this problem within her own marriage: 'Nobody warned me – and it had never occurred to me – that in order for us to survive as a couple I should fake failure and deny any of my God-given talents' (2007, 140). Not only African traditions but also British colonial traditions favor men's power. Maathai wrote that she saw the early stages of the unraveling of her marriage as she was pressured by her husband to take his surname, Mathai, when African traditions would have named her for her father or her own children (2007, 140).

When Maathai's husband, a successful Minister of Parliament, decided to divorce her, the British court traditions made things difficult. At that time, Kenyan law granted divorce only for cruelty, adultery, mental torture, or insanity. Accordingly, her husband accused her of cruelty and adultery based on hearsay. Maathai (who changed the spelling of her last name after the divorce, when her then ex-husband insisted she could no longer use his name) not only lost her case, but was jailed for six months for contempt of court after 'slandering' a judge, because she opined to a reporter that the judge must have not used reasonable standards in his decision.

In her memoirs, Maathai expressed happiness that the laws regarding divorce have changed from the British model to spare couples from similar embarrassing and harmful legal procedures (Maathai 2007, 140, 148). While she was shocked to realize that she could not only be divorced by the courts but also thrown in jail (all for daring to speak her mind as a woman), she saw this, the first of her many incarcerations, to be a time that strengthened her inner resolve. Maathai, through personal example, shows women that they can have meaningful lives and feelings of connection and community with each other and with nature and the earth, without depending on men, and perhaps that is one of the reasons why so many people identify her as a feminist – at least, she was considered to be one by the many mainstream and feminist publications and websites that wrote about her after her winning the Nobel Prize and also in eulogies written at the time of her death.

Conclusion

To summarize, Maathai and other Kenyan thinkers have expanded the meaning of 'empowerment' beyond the narrow or shallow uses of the term that signify only the ability to obtain formal schooling for career and economic advancement. The reader is asked to recall the deeper meaning of the term 'empowerment' drawn from Ibrahim and Alkire's inventory of the word's use, where the term meant developing a person's insight into social and structural inhibitors of flourishing, so that the person can change their individual perspectives and actions, and join in community with others, to change their context so that they can more easily achieve well-being.

Having learned about Maathai's form of civic education for empowerment and seeing it actualized by the political actions of members of the GBM to reform their society, we see the term 'empowerment' taking on a deeper meaning. This is not education for 'success' in a narrow understanding. Rather, it involves searching for one's community traditions and cultural roots in order to ground oneself in a firm context of values that can withstand the temptations to forget the value of nature and hold a profit motive as the highest priority. It means building on the aspects of tradition that give women significant roles of responsibility as well as giving them liberty, while resisting traditions that bestow upon men the privilege of making life decisions for women. It also means joining with each other and accomplishing much, through a multiplier effect, as women's movements grow to the point, for example, of planting millions of trees. It also means changing our institutions to ensure women's greater participation. It means paying attention to courageous women role models from East Africa.

One might think that one understands a concept, but the understanding might be abstract. To test understanding, ask whether you can recognize the concept at work. Can you notice if it is absent? White male philosophers of earlier days thought they understood the concept and the value 'equality', but apparently failed to notice the aspects of their society that were unequal and unfair. We still have that narrow view. But, our view can be widened by learning from Maathai and others, who can see empowerment where once we could not see it (in some African traditions regarding women), and notice where it is being taken away or hindered (in

Kenyan politics, during colonialism, or in certain practices of religion). At the end of this learn-ing experience, we no longer have the same concept of empowerment; we have a fuller, richer understanding of it.

In closing, it seems appropriate to reiterate one final time that Wangari Maathai and other women's empowerment theorists from East Africa have much to teach on theoretical and practical levels. The authors discussed herein are accomplished writers, activists, teachers, and deep thinkers. They have access to complex customs and histories and the confidence of many who confide in them, so that they can really know what people in their respective countries think about certain topics and practices and what they want for the future of East Africa. Also, they pinpoint problems that are experienced by women in contexts beyond Africa. It would behoove us to listen closely and to read and study their works, both to learn more about them and to ask better and deeper questions about our own societies and our experiences.

Acknowledgement

The author would like to acknowledge and thank Eric Palmer and Josef Velazquez for their edi-torial help.

Notes

1. Nixon suggests that courses should cover

    figures like Wangari Maathai, Indra Sinha, Ken Saro-Wiwa, Abdul Rahman Munif, Njabulo S. Ndebele, Nadine Gordimer, Jamaica Kincaid, Arundhati Roy, and June Jordan [who] have recorded the long-term inhabited impact of corrosive transnational forces, including petro-imperialism, the megadam industry, the practice of shipping rich nations' toxins (like e-waste) to poor nations' dumping grounds, tourism that threatens indigenous peoples, conservation practices that drive people off their historic lands, environmental deregulation for commercial or military demands, and much more. (2011)

    He also suggests the following anthologies: DeLoughrey and Handley, *Postcolonial Ecologies* (2011); Hunt and Roos, *Postcolonial Green* (2010); and Caminero-Santangelo and Myers, *Environ-ment at the Margins* (2011).

2. In the South African context, Gibson critiques Thabo Mbeki's advocacy of 'black economic empower-ment' (2005, 93). In 1999, Mbeki encouraged black South Africans to overcome their inferiority com-plexes and become 'prosperous' and begin to grow a 'black bourgeoisie' (quoted in Gibson 2005, 93). Gibson considers this an example of what Frantz Fanon called 'social treason', involving a 'nauseating mimicry' of white colonial masters, in which (in contrast to African values) 'being' is reduced to 'having' (Gibson 2005, 93).

References

Abwunza, Judith M. 1997. *Women's Voices, Women's Power: Dialogues of Resistance from East Africa.* Orchard Park, NY: Broadview Press.

Allen, Amy. 1998. "Rethinking Power." *Hypatia* 13 (1): 21–40.

Caminero-Santangelo, Byron, and Garth Myers, eds. 2011. *Environment at the Margins: Literary and Environmental Studies in Africa.* Athens: Ohio University Press.

Cesar, Dana. 2010. "Jane Addams and Wangari Maathai: Nobel Laureates on Educating and Organizing Women for Local Food Security." *Vitae Scholasticae* 27 (2): 123–141.

Chabaan, Jad, and Wendy Cunningham. 2011. "Measuring the Economic Gain of Investing in Girls: The Girl Effect Dividend." Policy research working paper; no. WPS 5753. Washington DC: The World Bank. Accessed October 4, 2013. http://elibrary.worldbank.org/content/workingpaper/10.1596/1813-9450-5753

Comaroff, Jean, and John L. Comaroff. 2012. *Theory from the South: Or, How Euro-America Is Evolving toward Africa.* Boulder, CO: Paradigm Publishers.

Commonwealth Observer Group. 2013. "Kenya General Elections 4 March 2013." Commonwealth Secretariat. Accessed October 4, 2013. http://thecommonwealth.org/sites/default/files/news-items/documents/130411.pdf

Constitution of Kenya. 2010. Accessed October 4, 2013. http://www.kenyaembassy.com/pdfs/The%20Constitution%20of%20Kenya.pdf

Declaration of Independence. 1776. Accessed June 21, 2013. http://www.archives.gov/exhibits/charters/declaration_transcript.html

DeLoughrey, Elizabeth, and George B. Handley. 2011. *Postcolonial Ecologies: Literatures of the Environment.* New York: Oxford University Press.

Gibson, Nigel. 2005. "The Limits of Black Political Empowerment: Fanon, Marx, 'the Poors,' and 'the New Reality of the Nation' in South Africa." *Theoria* 52 (107): 89–118.

Girl Rising. 2012. Ten Times Ten LLC and Vulcan Productions. Accessed June 21, 2013. http://girlrising.com/

Girl Up. 2013. Accessed June 21, 2013. http://www.girlup.org/about/

Gorsevski, Ellen. 2012. "Wangari Maathai's Emplaced Rhetoric: Greening Global Peacebuilding." *Environmental Communication: A Journal of Nature and Culture* 6 (3): 1–18.

Hunt, Alex, and Bonnie Roos. 2010. *Postcolonial Green: Environmental Politics and World Narratives.* Charlottesville: University of Virginia Press.

Ibrahim, Solava, and Sabina Alkire. 2007. "Agency and Empowerment: A Proposal for Internationally Comparable Indicators." *Oxford Development Studies* 35 (4): 379–403.

Inter-Parliamentary Union. 2013. "Women in National Parliaments." Accessed June 21, 2013. http://www.ipu.org/wmn-e/classif.htm

Kenya Bureau of Statistics. (2010). *Kenya Demographic and Health Survey 2008–09.* Accessed October 4, 2013. http://www.measuredhs.com/pubs/pdf/FR229/FR229.pdf

Kirkscey, Russell. 2007. "Accommodating Traditional African Values and Globalization: Wangari Maathai's Nobel Prize Lecture." *Women and Language* 30 (2): 11–17.

Koggel, Christine. 2009. "Agency and Empowerment: Embodied Realities in a Globalized World." In *Embodiment and Agency*, edited by Sue Campbell, Letitia Maynell, and Susan Sherwin, 250–268. University Park, PA: Penn State Press.

Kolawole, Mary. 2006. "Re-conceptualizing African Gender Theory: Feminism, Womanism and the Arere Metaphor." In *Rethinking Sexualities in Africa*, edited by Signe Arnfred, 251–266. Uppsala: Nordic Africa Institute.

Lewis, Desiree. 2008. "Discursive Challenges for African Feminisms." *QUEST: An African Journal of Philosophy/Revue Africaine de Philosophie* 20: 77–96. Accessed June 21, 2013. http://www.quest-journal.net/volXX/Quest_XX_Lewis.pdf

Maathai, Wangari. 2004. *The Green Belt Movement: Sharing the Approach and the Experience.* Revised edition. New York, NY: Lantern.

Maathai, Wangari. 2007. *Unbowed: A Memoir.* New York, NY: Anchor/Random House.

Maathai, Wangari. 2009. *The Challenge for Africa.* New York, NY: Anchor/Random House.

Maathai, Wangari. 2010. *Replenishing the Earth: Spiritual Values for Healing Ourselves and the World.* New York, NY: Doubleday.

Michira, Moses. 2013. "Governor Evans Kidero Slaps Rachel Shebesh, Then Quickly Forgets." September 6. *Standard Media.* Accessed October 4, 2013. http://www.standardmedia.co.ke/?articleID=2000092952&story_title=kidero-slaps-shebesh-then-quickly-forgets

Musalia, John. 2013. "Determinants of Women's Autonomy in Kenya." Paper presented at Kenyan Scholars and Studies Association 6th annual conference, "Kenya at 50: Lessons for the Future," Bowling Green State University, September 6.

Mutongi, Kenda. 2007. *Worries of the Heart: Widows, Family, and Community in Kenya*. Chicago: University of Chicago Press.

Mwobobia, Emma Kinya. 2011. "Court Affirms the Right of Inheritance in Woman to Woman Marriage." *Kenya Law Reports*. Accessed June 21, 2013. http://www.kenyalaw.org/newsletter/20110708.html

Nagel, Mechthild. 2005. "Environmental Justice and Women's Rights: A Tribute to Wangari Maathai." *Wagadu* 2 (Summer): 1–9. http://appweb.cortland.edu/ojs/index.php/Wagadu/issue/archive

Narayan, Uma. 2000. "Essence of Culture and a Sense of History: A Feminist Critique of Cultural Essentialism." In *Decentering the Center: Philosophy for a Multicultural, Postcolonial, and Feminist World*, edited by Uma Narayan and Sandra Harding, 80–100. Bloomington: Indiana University Press.

Nicholls, Brendon. 2005. "The Landscape of Insurgency: Mau Mau, Ngugi wa Thiong'o and Gender." In *Landscape and Empire, 1770–2000*, edited by Glenn Hooper, 177–194. Burlington, VT: Ashgate.

Nixon, Rob. 2006–2007. "Slow Violence, Gender, and the Environmentalism of the Poor." *Journal of Commonwealth and Postcolonial Studies* 13(2)/14(1): 14–37.

Nixon, Rob. 2011. "Slow Violence." *Chronicle of Higher Education*. Accessed June 21, 2013. http://chronicle.com/article/Slow-Violence/127968/

Njambi, Wairimu Ngaruiya, and William E. O'Brien. 2005. "Revisiting 'Woman-Woman Marriage': Notes on Gikuyu Women." In *African Gender Studies: A Reader*, edited by Oyèrónké Oyěwùmi, 145–166. New York, NY: Palgrave MacMillan.

Nzegwu, Nkiru. 2004. "Feminism and Africa: Impact and Limits of the Metaphysics of Gender." In *A Companion to African Philosophy*, edited by Kwasi Wiredu, 560–569. Malden, MA: Blackwell Publishing.

Nzomo, Maria. 2012. Interview on "Capital Talk." K24TV, October 30. Accessed October 4, 2013. http://www.youtube.com/watch?v=u1f55MTmnq4

Ogot, Bethwell A. 1995. "The Construction of a National Culture." In *Decolonization and Independence in Kenya, 1940–1993*, edited by B. A. Ogot and W. R. Ochieng, 214–236. Athens: Ohio University Press.

Okome, Mojúubàolú Olúufúnké. 2003. "What Women, Whose Development? A Critical Analysis of Reformist Evangelism on African Women." In *African Women and Feminism: Reflecting on the Politics of Sisterhood Trenton*, edited by Oyèrónké Oyěwùmi, 67–98. Trenton, NJ: Africa World Press.

Osongo, Jane. 2011. *Promoting Gender Equity in Selected Public Universities in Kenya*. Addis Ababa: Organization for Social Science Research in Eastern and Southern Africa (OSSREA).

Oyěwùmi, Oyèrónké. 2003a. "Introduction: Feminism, Sisterhood and Other Foreign Relations." In *African Women and Feminism: Reflecting on the Politics of Sisterhood*, edited by Oyèrónké Oyěwùmi, 1–24. Trenton, NJ: Africa World Press.

Oyěwùmi, Oyèrónké. 2003b. "The White Woman's Burden: African Women in Western Feminist Discourse." In *African Women and Feminism: Reflecting on the Politics of Sisterhood*, edited by Oyěwùmi, Oyèrónké, 25–44. Trenton, NJ: Africa World Press.

Rosow, Gene, and Bill Benenson. 2009. "Dirt: The Movie." *Common Ground Media*. Accessed October 25, 2013. http://www.thedirtmovie.org/

Rotich, Jerono. 2013. "Kenya at 50: Kenyan Women Reach Some Milestones." Paper presented at Kenyan Scholars and Studies Association 6th annual conference, "Kenya at 50: Lessons for the Future," Bowling Green State University, September 6.

Schaeffer-Duffy, Claire. 2007. "She Plants Trees." *America the National Catholic Review* (Feb. 5): 32–33. Accessed June 21, 2013. http://americamagazine.org/issue/culture/she-plants-trees

Swai, Elinami Veraeli. 2010. *Beyond Women's Empowerment in Africa*. New York, NY: Palgrave MacMillan/St. Martins Press.

Tripp, Aili Mari. 2004. "The New Political Activism in Africa." *Journal of Democracy* 12 (3): 141–155.

UNICEF United States Fund. 2013. "Believe in ZERO Girls Denied Education." Accessed June 21, 2013. http://www.unicefusa.org/campaigns/stand-with-malala/

UNESCO (United Nations Education, Scientific, and Cultural Organization) 2012. "Stand up for Malala." http://www.unesco.org/new/en/education/themes/leading-the-international-agenda/gender-and-education/about-us/stand-up-for-malala-girls-education-is-a-right/

Wambugu, Benson. 2011. "Women's Right to Inherit Set to Shake Up Traditional Way of Life." *Saturday Nation* (March 4). Accessed June 21, 2013. http://www.nation.co.ke/News/-/1056/1119334/-/view/printVersion/-/ocxwgb/-/index.html

Wolbert, Anke T. 2011. "Saving the Home of the Tadpoles One Tree at a Time: A Framing and Pedagogical Analysis of Wangari Maathai's Green Belt Movement." PhD diss., Wayne State University. Proquest (3454297).

Worthington, Nancy. 2003. "Shifting Identities in the Kenyan Press: Representations of Wangari Maathai's Media Complex Protest." *Women's Studies in Communication* 26 (2): 143–164.

Agency vulnerability, participation, and the self-determination of indigenous peoples

Stacy J. Kosko

Department of Government and Politics, Center for International Development and Conflict Management, University of Maryland, College Park, MD, USA

Development, understood as a process of social and economic change, can be a source of great freedom. But when individuals and groups have little or no control over that process, it can be a source of vulnerability as well. This paper proposes the concept of 'agency vulnerability': the risk of being limited in one's ability to control the social and economic forces that propel one into change. All individuals and groups are susceptible to harm, but indigenous groups often face the gravest constellation of such threats. In particular, indigenous peoples struggle against both individual and societal vulnerabilities and often have the least control over processes of change that affect them. The language of human rights is frequently used to justify policies aimed at reducing vulnerability. For indigenous peoples, this often takes the form of a right to self-determination, a right in part intended to reduce agency vulnerability. This paper draws a distinction between the process and the substantive aspects of self-determination, and identifies participation as a key component of the process aspect, defending its importance in decision-making in any residual areas of shared rule between indigenous and non-indigenous groups or entities. Finally, it proposes a framework for evaluating the extent and quality of participation of indigenous (or any other) peoples in decisions that affect them.

Denis Goulet argues that vulnerability is a characteristic of both individuals and societies. 'An individual is vulnerable when he is exposed to injury, societies when they have no adequate defenses against the social forces which propel them into processes of change' (Goulet 1971, 38). Both are also vulnerable when they lack power to effect those changes they desire. Development, understood as a process of social and economic change, can be a source of great freedom. Crocker has something like this in mind when he describes development as 'beneficial social change' (2008). But when individuals and groups have little or no control over that process, it can be a source of vulnerability as well. I call this *agency vulnerability*: the risk of being limited in our ability to control the social and economic forces that affect us.

In this paper, I propose this concept of agency vulnerability and argue for its particular relevance for indigenous peoples. I next defend a conception of self-determination that emphasizes participation and substantive freedom. Then, suggesting a distinction between the substance and the process of self-determination, I identify participatory development as the key process aspect of self-determination. However comprehensive a group's powers of self-rule, one way to reduce the agency vulnerability of indigenous peoples, I argue, is through robust non-elite participation in residual areas of shared rule. Finally, I propose a modest framework for evaluating this participation, deploying Goulet's concept of 'entry points' into participatory processes (1989), followed by Crocker's delineation of 'thin' versus 'thick' 'modes of participation' (2008). This framework offers one possible way to determine whether a people enjoys significant self-determination. The ability to be self-determining even within governing orders that retain some element of shared rule with other groups has powerful implications for that group's particular societal vulnerability, an existential concern for many if not most indigenous peoples.

Vulnerability and self-determination

Vulnerability, or 'susceptibility to harm' (Camacho 2010, 142), has many forms. Its sources are multifaceted and intersecting. Human beings face countless threats to their physical security and well-being, including vulnerabilities to poverty, violence, and disease. Individual *identity* (whether simple or complex), intimately bound up with (often multiple) group identities, is also vulnerable, threatened by linguistic marginalization, cultural oppression, religious intolerance, and worse. These threats also have implications for individual *agency*, including that which is exercised in concert with one's peers.[1] Individual security, well-being, identity, and agency on the one hand, and group identity on the other, are connected and interdependent. A reduction in or restriction of one of these can greatly impact the other.

All individuals and groups are susceptible to harm, but minority and indigenous groups often face the gravest constellation of such threats. In particular, indigenous groups, or 'peoples', are among history's greatest losers in the processes of social and economic change – development – that have transformed the geo-political landscape in the last half-millennium. They struggle against both individual and societal vulnerabilities and often have the least control over circumstances and processes of change that affect them. The language of human rights is frequently used to justify or promote policies aimed at reducing vulnerability. Where indigenous peoples are concerned, this often takes the form of a right of self-determination. James Anaya, scholar and former UN Special Rapporteur on the Rights of Indigenous People, explains that

> [u]nderstood as a human right, the essential idea of self-determination is that human beings, individually and as groups, are equally entitled to be in control of their own destinies, and to live within a governing institutional order that is devised accordingly. (2008, 49–50)

The 'self-determination bomb' and the 'right to effective participation'

Often assumed to imply that every group that considers itself a 'people' has a right to its own state, the concept of self-determination has not always enjoyed broad acceptance in the post-Westphalian club of sovereign states. Scholars, too, remain sorely divided over its connotations and many worry about its possibly dangerous implications for minorities in newly independent territories. Although Ignatieff and others are correct in important respects when they argue that the 'painful truth is that national self-determination is not always favorable to individual human rights' (2001), the assumption of a trade-off is often predicated on a narrow conception of self-determination as secession. What Buchanan calls the 'self-determination bomb' (2004, 332) has only recently begun to be defused by legal and political scholars and indigenous leaders who have worked to decouple the principle from the idea of a universal right of secession.[2]

Anaya, for example, recognizes the 'secession' problem, but rather than scrapping what has proven to be a powerful legal and rhetorical tool for political mobilization, he seeks to explain the concept of self-determination more clearly, offering a conception that neither includes a universal right of secession nor seeks to prescribe specific institutional arrangements. He argues that 'for most peoples ... *full* self-determination, in a real sense, does not require or justify a separate state' (Anaya 2004, 7). Instead,

> self-determination means that peoples are entitled to participate equally in the constitution and development of the governing institutional order under which they live and, further, to have that governing order be one in which they may live and develop freely on a continuous basis. (Anaya 2008, 51)

Thus, according to Anaya, the emphasis today is not on statehood but on participation and freedom, twin entitlements hard won in the global indigenous movement.

If we understand societal vulnerability as Goulet does, as arising in part from a lack of control over the social processes that propel us into change (or keep us from changing), then self-determination can be understood as one way to reduce (certain aspects of) the vulnerability of indigenous societies. However, indigenous peoples have struggled to have their right of self-determination recognized as the same right that 'all peoples' enjoy, as per Common Article 1 of the 1966 UN Human Rights Covenants: 'All peoples have the right of self-determination. By virtue of that right they freely determine their political status and freely pursue their economic, social and cultural development' (United Nations 1966a, 1966b). Today, the accepted norm of self-determination requires governments to be set up in a way that, returning to Anaya's language, allows 'individuals and groups [to] live and develop freely on a continuous basis' (1993, 133). In an effort to legitimize their claim to jurisdiction over indigenous peoples and their territories, and ensure the consent of the (indigenous) governed, some governments have established specific mechanisms for the exercise of indigenous collective agency. But do these mechanisms – and the way they operate in practice – actually permit the people in question to participate fully in decisions that affect them or is 'participation' being used to cover up and legitimize governing structures that amount to an infringement on indigenous people's right to self-determination?

This question begs two others, though. First, ought not the meaning of 'participation' for indigenous peoples reflect their cultural traditions of governance, for instance the value they may or may not place on consensus or on the role of elders? This paper proceeds from the assumption that, regardless of their traditional understanding of participation for internal decision-making, indigenous peoples – or any other non-elite group that desires a role in decisions made by a powerful elite – have reason to value participatory processes that privilege thicker forms of participation, that begin earlier in the decision-making process, that seek consensus, and that include mechanisms for the exercise of real power by all involved. This assumption might be incorrect and it is worth pursuing this question – as well as others provoked by interrogations of indigenous epistemology – but for now it is the basis of the discussion that follows.

Second is not the whole point of self-determination to ensure for indigenous peoples (at least some degree of) self-rule, rather than simply the generic right to participation that minorities, and all members of society, (ought to) enjoy? This question has two answers. First, Anaya importantly, and rightly, emphasizes participation as a key *constituent element* of self-determination, not its sole defining characteristic, and it is complemented by the indispensable guarantee of a governing order that permits a people to 'live and develop freely on a continuous basis' and 'to be in control of their own destinies' (2008, 49–51) carrying at least some implication of self-rule. Moreover, this participation for self-determination takes the concept beyond the more limited right to 'effective participation' guaranteed to (non-indigenous) minorities in, for example, the Declaration on the Rights of Persons Belonging to National or Ethnic, Religious and Linguistic Minorities (United Nations 1992) and the European Framework Convention for the Protection of National Minorities (Council of Europe 1995). Unlike the 'effective participation' guaranteed to minorities, self-determination, on Anaya's interpretation, requires participation of indigenous peoples in the very establishment of the 'governing institutional order' (2008, 51), not merely in cultural, religious, social, economic, and public 'life' and the governing decisions that 'concern' them.[3]

The second answer to this question lies in the reality that self-determination, far from an all or nothing condition, is in practice a jigsaw of overlapping jurisdictions in which the degree of self-rule can vary from absolute to equally shared, provided that the areas of shared rule are consensually shared. No society – indigenous or otherwise – is absolutely autarkic, and indigenous peoples often pursue a hybrid status in which they remain citizens of the state in which they live, but enjoy substantial (sometimes verging on comprehensive) rights to self-rule, while still leaving in place some areas where shared decision-making is necessary. It is in these residual areas of shared rule where the indigenous right to participation remains important: if an indigenous people enjoys self-rule in some or most areas in which they have an interest, but remains marginalized from the decision-making process in the remaining ones, we cannot say that they are a fully self-determining people. By contrast, an indigenous people that, having consented to shared rule in certain areas, is able to exercise its collective agency through robust participatory processes remains a self-determining people, with important implications for its particular societal vulnerability.

So the question remains: do existing mechanisms for indigenous peoples to exercise collective agency permit their full participation in decisions that affect them? Put another way, do these peoples actually enjoy self-determination? Before returning to this question, I will propose the concept of agency vulnerability and locate participation within what I call the *process aspect* of self-determination.

Agency vulnerability

The word 'vulnerability' comes from the Latin for wound, or *vulnus*, and translates roughly to 'the inability to defend oneself against wounds' (Goulet 1971, 38). In the literature, the term is commonly associated with susceptibility to environmental hazards, and increasingly to poverty or ill health, but here we can retain its original, context-sensitive meaning and define it more broadly, as Luis Camacho does, as simply 'susceptibility to harm'. As Goulet points out, both individuals and societies can be susceptible to harm. Development – understood as human-induced social change intended to be beneficial – can bring great freedom and help to reduce both individual and societal vulnerabilities, but if individuals and groups have little or no control over these changes, then development can be a source of vulnerability as well. Penz, Drydyk, and Bose identify seven values of what they call 'worthwhile development'. These values are: human well-being and security, equity (which gives priority but not exclusive concern to reducing inequality), empowerment, cultural freedom (or what Will Kymlicka and the 2004 *Human Development Report* refer to as 'cultural liberty'), human rights, environmental sustainability, and integrity (in relation to corruption), with non-maleficence as a 'trump value' (Penz, Drydyk, and Bose 2011, 116–118). Those development processes and outcomes that do not in some way conform to these values, they argue, constitute 'maldevelopment' (Penz, Drydyk, and Bose 2011, 117). Development processes over which individuals and societies have little or no control are more likely to leave some behind or prevent them from getting ahead, to displace them or keep them from preserving what they value. These and other processes of 'maldevelopment' can, and almost certainly do, produce vulnerability.

The poorest members of society are often the least able to defend against the potential harms of maldevelopment. Camacho, following Goulet, makes explicit the link between poverty and vulnerability as susceptibility to harm, arguing that '[p]oor people experience underdevelopment as vulnerability' (2010, 144). But this is also true when individual (physical and economic) well-being is improving but one lacks any meaningful control over the ends and means of those improvements. Vulnerability, then, is a concept that can be applied equally to economic and physical security and to agency. What we might call *agency vulnerability* – the risk of being limited in our ability to control the social and economic forces that affect us – can remain, perhaps acutely so, even as physical or economic vulnerability is greatly reduced.[4] The importance of agency vulnerability stems in part from the greater risk that maldevelopment will occur when (even otherwise well-off) individuals lack agency but it also stems from the recognition that agency can be an end in itself, not only a means to protect oneself and one's community against maldevelopment (or other harms).

Here, following Amartya Sen and David A. Crocker, the term 'agency' refers to one's ability to reflect critically upon the options one faces, to choose deliberately between them, to act on those choices, and possibly to make a difference in the world, or at least in one's own life (Crocker 2008, 219–220). This is very different from the use of the term in economics to distinguish a principal from an agent, in which the agent is (supposed to be) an instrument of the principal and to do the principal's bidding. Also, Crocker (like Rob Reich) describes agency (in Reich's terms, 'autonomy') as a 'scalar concept': one can have more or less agency (be more or less autonomous).[5]

Agency vulnerability is concerned with the potential for limitations on what Crocker, following Adela Cortina, refers to as being the 'master of one's own life ... to be self-determining not only with respect to one's conduct but also with respect to one's moral commitments and beliefs' (Crocker 2008, 219). Clearly no person or group has total control over the future or over processes of change that affect them. The point is that neither should someone else. According to Reich, '[t]he sovereign or self-determined life is one in which *no outside person or force* controls a person's destiny' (2002, 98, emphasis mine). In this sense, then, I am referring to the control that might be reasonably expected of autonomous actors, what the *Arctic Human Development Report* calls 'fate control – guiding one's destiny' (Arctic Human Development Report 2004). One can imagine 'well-kept' slaves who enjoy outstanding health and modest material security but who are nevertheless not the authors of their own lives in this sense. They may even enjoy significant agency within limited domains (e.g. they control other slaves or make independent decisions about certain aspects of their day-to-day labor). However, they do not have control over their being bought and sold and over many aspects of how they are treated. They are not 'the masters of their own lives'.

That agency vulnerability can remain even in the face of relative physical or economic security is true of societies as well as individuals. In advancing the idea of the agency vulnerability of societies, I rely on Goulet's useful concept of 'societal vulnerability', occurring 'when [societies] have no adequate defenses against the social forces which propel them into processes of change' (1971, 38). This might occur, for example, when an indigenous group is forced by circumstance or law to give up a valued form of livelihood. However, societal vulnerability can also arise when societies are *blocked* from pursuing desired change. This would be the case, for example, when an indigenous society is constrained by well-meaning national legislation intended to 'preserve' traditions and culture, but which in fact excludes the group from important means of social or economic development. Agency is compromised by conditions that *block* change as well as by conditions that bring about change over which the agents have no or little control. This is the essence of agency vulnerability. In either case, agents are the tools of others or the victims of circumstance. I am therefore using Goulet's concept of societal vulnerability as shorthand for any situation in which a society finds itself unable to exercise reasonable control over its social and economic future, whether that future be one in which traditions are maintained, discarded, or – more likely – some combination of the two. In this way, agency vulnerability applies to groups.

The legal and political space of human rights is one place where we might seek remedies to vulnerability. Bryan S. Turner argues that vulnerability 'defines our humanity' and is 'the common basis of human rights' (Turner 2006, 1). Thus, if we agree that human rights are a response to human vulnerability then, in a legal sense, we can understand serious vulnerability as a rights deprivation. Nickel situates the concept in this way, placing vulnerability together with rights deprivation on a sliding scale.

> Let's say that the holder of a legal right is exceptionally vulnerable when that person's condition or circumstances make it unusually difficult and expensive to respect or implement his or her right ... Claims about exceptional vulnerability are comparative; they say that exceptionally vulnerable people are far more likely than average people to experience the violation, inadequate implementation, or nonimplementation of some right. (2008, 258)

The extent of one's vulnerability, then, can be evaluated according to the likelihood of experiencing a rights deprivation.

Vulnerability of minorities and indigenous peoples

Whatever their moral foundation or source of legitimacy – and reasonable people need not agree on just one – human rights laws are designed to play a protective/preventive role.[6] As Ignatieff argues, their purpose is to *protect* human agency, which in turn helps to *prevent* the cruel, inhuman, or degrading treatment or oppression of human agents because 'when individuals have agency, they can protect themselves against injustice' (2001, 57).[7] Quite often, it is minority individuals who face these threats most acutely and who experience the most severe, frequent, or multiple rights violations (or, following Nickel, inadequate implementation, or non-implementation of rights), and thus might be said to be 'exceptionally vulnerable'.[8] Ethno-cultural minorities, in addition to a host of socio-economic deprivations, often face an additional, collective vulnerability: threats to their cultures, traditions, or ways of life. In Goulet's terms, this may be understood as societal vulnerability. Will Kymlicka calls this cultural vulnerability of minorities as their 'particular disadvantage' and, along with Nickel, argues that minorities ought to (and sometimes do) have different rights than members of the majority in order to 'overcome vastly different kinds of disadvantages' (Kymlicka 1992, 141). Certain types of rights are designed to target these threats.

> [M]any countries give language rights or political autonomy to those who are members of vulnerable minority cultures, since these policies help rectify their particular disadvantage (i.e., their cultural vulnerability). We match the rights to the kinds of disadvantage being compensated for. (Kymlicka 1992, 141)

Such rights are sometimes formulated as group rights, those that aim to protect the range of opportunities and possible ways of being and doing that are bound up in some way with group affiliation. Language use and worship are two such rights (Nickel 2007). These (like all) rights, Nickel argues, respond to actual, not hypothetical, threats. A specific human right protects against the possibility that a specific harm will be done to an individual or group, but that harm has been identified and a corresponding right articulated because the violation has previously (frequently and preventably) occurred and because it continues to occur. In this sense, therefore, rights have both a preventive (or protective) and a remedial character. To say that rights are at their core remedial is not to deny their protective role, nor is it to suggest that their purpose is to right past wrongs, nor is it to say that the wrong must have been committed against the *specific* groups or individuals in questions in order for the right to apply to them. Rather, it is to highlight the *historical and present* realities presented by certain kinds of threats: the establishment and legal recognition of a right is a way of saying 'never again'. In Henry Shue's terms, in order to justify a legal 'right', a threat must be shown to be ordinary, severe, and yet remediable; in Nickel's terms the threat must be 'substantial and recurrent' and the corresponding right 'feasible [to implement] in a majority of countries' (2007, 70–79). Shue calls this 'the notion of a standard threat' (1980, 17, 29–34).[9] Both Nickel and

Kymlicka argue persuasively that many kinds of rights mentioned above address precisely such standard threats. *Group* rights are a direct response to the *particular*, ordinary, and severe, but remediable threats that minority individuals face. They are needed to protect the *agency* of minority individuals whose identity is, at least in part, bound up in some way with group affiliation.

In the case of indigenous peoples, whose 'particular disadvantage' is intimately connected to an historic loss (that continues today) of sovereignty and, often, traditional territory, the prescribed 'right' is typically self-determination. Collective in nature, it responds to the societal vulnerability of certain peoples, fitting Kymlicka's, Nickel's, and Shue's requirements. In seeking to reduce one or more particular forms of societal vulnerability (agency vulnerability, I argue, among others), the right of self-determination has a preventive character, but it is also a remedial right in the sense that it addresses a particular violation (the infringement of sovereignty at some earlier period). Moreover, it is not a *sui generis* right, different (or narrower or lesser) somehow when applied to indigenous peoples than when applied to other 'peoples'. As Anaya, Buchanan, and others argue, indigenous peoples are not a distinct category of peoples somehow possessing different rights than the rest of humanity. It is the recognition that they possess the *same* rights as all human beings, that these rights have been and continue to be violated, and that there is a real risk that they will again be violated in the future, which underpins the strong claim of indigenous peoples to a right of self-determination.

Nevertheless, the bearers of the right of self-determination are understood to be only those collections of individuals that might be deemed 'peoples'. The precise meaning of the term 'peoples' thus becomes one of 'threshold importance' for determining whether this right can be claimed by a particular group (Anaya 1993, 138). However, the international community lacks consensus on the meaning of the term. According to Anaya, some argue that a 'people' can be identified using criteria such as ethnicity and a history of some kind of sovereignty. Others consider only the aggregate population of a state to be a 'people' (2008, 49). Anaya contends, however, that if 'self-determination' is to be understood as a human right, in contrast with a 'sovereign right' of a state, then its attribution to 'peoples' must refer to something other than a statist or quasi-statist corporate entity. It must refer to a collection of human beings.

> More in keeping with the human rights character of self-determination is to see the reference to 'peoples' as designating rights that human beings hold and exercise collectively in relation to the bonds of community or solidarity that typify human existence. Because human beings develop diverse and often overlapping identities and spheres of community – especially in today's world of enhanced communications and interaction on a global scale – the term 'peoples' should be understood in a flexible manner, as encompassing all relevant spheres of community and identity. (Anaya 2008, 49)

While rejecting its *exclusive* application to a corporate entity like a state, this elucidation of the term leaves open its application not only to ethnic groups or 'nations' but also to groups of people bound by political affiliation (with or without shared citizenship). In an earlier work, Anaya highlights the possibility, but not necessity, of invoking statehood in the identification of a 'people':

> 'Peoples' is appropriately understood as simply denoting the collective character of the human impulse toward self-determination and as affirming the value of community bonds, notwithstanding traditional categories of human organization associated with statehood or sovereignty. (1993, 162)

Whatever the precise characteristics of a 'people' might be,[10] and whatever other groups might fall into this category, there is a growing international consensus that is moving toward including indigenous groups among the 'peoples' of the world. This has implications for the application of the several international human rights instruments that establish the right of all 'peoples' to self-determination.[11] Although the debate over the term 'peoples' is by no means settled, and although the question of what exactly the right of self-determination means for these peoples in practice remains the subject of much disagreement, this paper proceeds from the assumption that indigenous peoples are just that, peoples, and that they ought to enjoy the same rights as all other peoples.[12]

Until now, this discussion has loosely conflated 'minorities' and 'indigenous peoples', in so far as we understand each to possess some kind of 'particular disadvantage', to have particular kinds of vulnerabilities (including agency vulnerability), and to be justifiably the objects of certain types of group rights. However, in the international system, the two groups are categorically distinct, and with this distinction come different sets of normative assumptions which have been the foundation for different sets of legal protections. The starkest point of contrast is in the perceived legitimacy of states to govern them. While the 'minority' model – most thoroughly elaborated in Europe and embodied in the European Framework Convention (Council of Europe 1995) – assumes the legitimate authority of the state to govern its territory and the people therein, the 'indigenous' model – most clearly elaborated in the United Nations system and embodied in the Declaration on the Rights of Indigenous Peoples (United Nations 2007) – assumes that states cannot claim legitimate governing authority over indigenous peoples and their territories without their consent. The minority model does not recognize an inherent right to self-rule for minorities, and instead offers a right to effective participation as protection against injustice and domination. The indigenous model, however, does recognize such a right and claims for indigenous peoples the right to reject the authority of the state or to agree to share or cede some aspects of self-rule.

However, despite the very different legal regimes that have emerged in recent decades, the assumed stark contrast between self-governing indigenous peoples and minority members of multi-ethnic states is in fact not so stark. There is a great deal of gray area concerning which groups are 'indigenous' and which are (national or ethnic) 'minorities', and the people in question sometimes clash with their government over their status.[13] Moreover, even minority groups that do not seek indigenous status still sometimes attempt to lay claim to self-determination, a claim that in almost every case is soundly rejected by international law but still muddies the waters. To complicate matters further, few if any indigenous groups are in fact fully self-governing. Given the interdependencies of the modern world, even the most autonomous indigenous peoples are inevitably still involved in some form of shared rule with the larger society. And these systems of shared rule, both in their substantive and their procedural dimensions, still affect the vulnerability and agency of indigenous peoples and individuals, particularly in the presence of asymmetries of power.

Therefore, the model this paper will propose can be helpful both for evaluating the quality of participation that non-self-governing minorities enjoy and for evaluating the procedural dimensions of the residual areas of shared rule involving indigenous peoples. It is, in fact, particularly well-suited to the latter, for reasons I shall address below. While the effective participation of minorities gets a great deal of attention in the literature, 'effective participation' is rarely emphasized for indigenous peoples because it is perceived as undermining their stronger claim to self-determination.[14] Moreover, although the literature canvasses a wide range of substantive issues related to self-determination, it largely fails to address the process aspect of self-determination, a process that depends heavily upon quality ('effective') participation. Let us now explore this distinction.

Self-determination: substance and process

The norm of self-determination can be understood as consisting of two distinct (though inseparable) components: what I refer to as the 'substantive aspect' (the 'What?') and the 'process aspect' (the 'How?') of self-determination. Crocker identifies four key dimensions of democracy along which we might evaluate a system or a set of practices: breadth, depth, range, and control.

The 'substantive aspect' of self-determination, in my sense, is akin to Crocker's idea of 'range' in democratic decision-making or 'the *range* of questions that citizens should democratically decide' (2008, 299). The self-determination of peoples is typically summarized as covering a 'range' of questions that focus on political status and on economic, social and cultural development. These broad *substantive* categories translate in practice into a variety of policy areas in which participants must make decisions. In the case of indigenous peoples, these might include policies for cultural protection, support of traditional economic activities, natural resource management, education and schooling, and governance. In Shue's words, 'the substance of a right is whatever the right is a right to. A right is not a right to enjoy a right – it is a right to enjoy something else, like food or liberty' (1980, 15). The 'substantive aspect' of self-determination, then, covers the 'something', the 'What?'

This use of the term 'substantive' should be distinguished from a few others. Anaya understands the 'substance of the norm' of self-determination as 'the precepts that define a standard of governmental legitimacy' (1993, 144). He distinguishes these from remedial *measures*, or responses to violations of the norm, such as those that accompanied the mid-twentieth century wave of decolonization (Anaya 1993, 133–134).[15] I use the term differently. My term also differs from that which is used broadly to refer to the *normative principles* underlying or embodied in certain institutions, processes, or laws. Such is the meaning of 'substance' that Rawls (1971) and Nozick (1974), for example, have in mind when distinguishing process from substance in procedural justice. A procedure is 'substantive' when it is structured to some extent by free-standing normative principles. Like the procedural justice theorists, I refer to the *substance* of self-determination in order to distinguish it from the *process* of exercising self-determination, but my use of the term is nevertheless different than theirs. It does not refer to norms but instead to something more like the 'range' of issues over which self-determination is exercised.

If the substantive aspect is the 'What?', then the 'process aspect' covers the 'How?' What I refer to as the 'process aspect' of self-determination does not map onto a specific policy area and can be applied to a variety of political or social goals. It refers to the avenues through and processes by which collective decisions are made, avenues and procedures that might take any one of a number of forms in accordance with the traditions and needs of a given people at a given time. The processes and venues through which the North American indigenous Haudenosaunee people make collective decisions about their political future and policy aspirations might differ markedly from those through which the Scandinavian and Russian indigenous Sámi make their decisions. These decision-making systems might be modeled on the group's own traditional procedures or on Western-style parliamentary ones (or, as in the case of the Haudenosaunee, Western democracies might be modeled on theirs!). The point is not to offer a prescription for how that process ought to look, but to draw attention to the fact that there are processes at work in the exercise of self-determination and that the quality of these processes is important for the extent of self-determination a people enjoys. As in Sen's 'process aspect' of development, the processes by which self-determination unfolds 'cannot be seen as being – at best – among the *means* to development [or self-determination]..., but have to be understood as constitutive parts of the *ends* of development [or self-determination] in themselves' (1999, 291). In the language of Common Article 1 of the 1966 UN Human Rights Covenants and Article 3 of the UN Declaration on the Rights of Indigenous Peoples, this process aspect is captured simply by the terms 'freely determine' and 'freely pursue' (United Nations 1966a, 1966b, 2007).

In addition to Common Article 1 of the Covenants and its twin in the UN Indigenous Declaration (Article 3), Declaration Articles 18 and 19, on participation and consent, address the process aspect:

> Indigenous peoples have the right to participate in decision-making in matters which would affect their rights, through representatives chosen by themselves in accordance with their own procedures, as well as to maintain and develop their own indigenous decision-making institutions. (United Nations 2007, Article 18)

And

> States shall consult and cooperate in good faith with the indigenous peoples concerned through their own representative institutions in order to obtain their free, prior and informed consent before adopting and implementing legislative or administrative measures that may affect them. (United Nations 2007, Article 19)

Other articles laying out specific rights also allude to processes by which these rights must be fulfilled, using phrases like 'in conjunction with ...' and 'in consultation and cooperation with the indigenous peoples concerned'. These requirements have also found their way into the operating procedures of major multilateral development organizations. The World Bank, for example, requires borrowing countries and Bank staff to engage in 'free, prior, and informed consultation' with indigenous peoples who stand to be affected by a project (2005). Thus, it is not that international treaties – or development institutions – fail to recognize the need for indigenous participation or that the right to self-determination obviates the weaker right to 'effective participation', but rather that self-determination itself entails certain processes and participation is chief among them. To invoke the importance of indigenous participation, therefore, is not to weaken or downplay the broader, stronger right to self-determination that all peoples (ought to) enjoy, but to draw attention to one important mechanism through which it operates. While international laws and institutional operating procedures such as the World Bank's nod to the right of indigenous peoples to participate (or at least consult) in decisions that affect them, this process aspect has not been explicitly articulated as a key component of the right of self-determination itself. As a result, while the substantive aspect gets much attention in academic and policy circles, and is most often the touchstone by which national indigenous policies are judged, the process aspect is often neglected, and with it the importance of indigenous participation in policy-making. It is to this process aspect that we now turn.

Participation as the key process aspect of self-determination

Amartya Sen has called development 'a process of expanding the real freedoms that people enjoy' (Sen, Development as Freedom 1999, 3). Likewise, we might understand self-determination as the freedom of a people to do and be what they choose. In this sense, Sen's concept of development as freedom, captured by the Capability Approach, seems promising as a freedom-centered and arguably 'universalizable' (Nussbaum 2000) way of thinking about the norm of self-determination since '[f]or Sen, groups as well as individual persons can and should be the authors of their own lives' (Crocker 2008, 15). We need not elaborate on the nuances of applying the Capability Approach to indigenous peoples or groups generally[16] – as others have done in exploring the idea of 'group' or 'collective capabilities' – in order to borrow this broad understanding of 'development as freedom' as a helpful way to think about the content of self-determination. According to Anaya, 'self-determination entitles individuals and groups to meaningful participation, commensurate with their interests, in episodic procedures leading to the development of or change in the governing institutional order' (1993, 133), presumably with the aim of 'expanding the real freedoms that people enjoy' (Sen, Development as Freedom 1999, 3). Crocker's 'agency-focused [version of the] Capability Approach' (2008, 159), with its normative emphasis on agency freedom and achievement and its practical emphasis on public participation, is especially relevant in light of Anaya's words, encouraging us to concentrate not only on the substantive (policy-specific) aspect of self-determination but also on the *process* aspect as well.

Both Goulet and Crocker argue that participation is a crucial component of any development project or approach, a view echoed in the two main international instruments for the protection of indigenous peoples – ILO 169 and the UN Indigenous Declaration – and in Anaya's and others' understanding of the meaning of 'self-determination'. Crocker argues that development policies should be evaluated based on how much they promote, protect and restore human agency and not only on the concrete results they produce: sufficient food or higher income, for example. A challenge for this perspective, of course, is to give an account of *mechanisms* for collective agency (Crocker 2008). Public deliberation, Crocker argues, can meet that challenge. According to Goulet,

> [w]hen people are oppressed or reduced to the culture of silence, they do not participate in their own humanization. Conversely, when they participate, thereby becoming active subjects of knowledge and action, they begin to construct their properly human history and engage in processes of authentic development. (1989, 165)

Crocker goes a step further, making the very concept of 'authentic development' dependent on participation. 'Authentic development occurs when groups at whatever level become subjects who deliberate, decide, and act in the world rather than being either victims of circumstance or objects of someone else's decisions, the tool of someone else's designs' (2008, 339). Participation, we might say, is the very essence of the process aspect of self-determination.[17] However, to judge whether any specific participatory episode is meaningful, we need an evaluative framework.

Participation: building a framework for evaluation

Like Crocker's concept of participation and Rob Reich's concept of autonomy, self-determination is a 'scalar' concept. Just as Reich argues that an individual might be more or less autonomous, it is also possible for a people to enjoy more or less self-determination. Importantly, Reich distinguishes between the exercise of and the respect for (individual) autonomy. 'While the extent to which people *exercise* autonomy may vary, respecting autonomy is a different matter ... Governments (or people) either respect the autonomy of an individual or not' (2002, 93–94). By 'respect' he means something like 'have respect for the principle of', a general condition that is distinct from permitting the exercise of that autonomy in practice. The actual exercise of autonomy that a government is willing to countenance will vary by degree and domain and will almost certainly be constrained by other principles that the government also 'respects' (i.e. respect for human rights, freedom of religion, environmental sustainability, individual property rights, and so on). This paper seeks to illustrate this point as it applies to groups: while a government might on paper respect the autonomy (or self-determination) of a minority group, the real autonomy that that group is able to exercise in practice can vary along any number of dimensions as well as over time. Thus, it is possible to evaluate the key dimensions of self-determination on scales of their own in order to begin to arrive at a sense of *how much*, or *what degree of*, self-determination a people really enjoys. My project here is to choose one of those key dimensions, the one most closely connected with the process aspect of self-determination: participation.

We might ask: do existing mechanisms for indigenous peoples to exercise collective agency permit their full participation in decisions that affect them? To answer this question, we might examine policy areas in which self-determination is particularly important and assess not just the structural opportunity for, but the actual enjoyment of, self-determination in these areas. But evaluating the space for indigenous peoples' participation in political processes that affect them requires a framework. Goulet offers several 'axes' along which 'non-elite participation' might be classified. One of these is according to the moment at which it is introduced. 'At any point in the sequence, a nonexpert populace may "enter in" and begin to share in its dynamics' (1989, 167). In order from earliest to latest, these moments, or 'points of entry', are:

> initial diagnosis of the problem or condition; a listing of possible responses to be taken; selecting one possibility to enact; organizing, or otherwise preparing oneself, to implement the course of action chosen; the several specific steps entailed in implementing the chosen course; self-correction or evaluation in the course of implementation; and debating the merits of further mobilization or organization. (Goulet 1989, 167)

The quality of the participation, Goulet argues, depends upon the initial point of entry of non-elite, or non-expert, participants. 'Therefore, if one wishes to judge whether participation is authentic empowerment of the masses or merely a manipulation of them, it matters greatly when, in the overall sequence of steps, the participation begins' (Goulet 1989, 167). While Goulet does not go on explicitly to say 'and the earlier the better!' it seems clear that this is what he wishes to convey.

Although this insight is important for evaluating any kind of participation, it is crucial for the kind of participation that I argue is part and parcel of the right to self-determination which, at least on Anaya's influential articulation, requires participation of indigenous peoples in the *establishment* of the governing institutional order in which they live, not simply in the governing decisions which concern them. While this requirement extends to all decisions that affect indigenous peoples, demanding opportunities for indigenous entry into joint decision-making at the very start of the process, it may also be the basis for a radical reorganization of existing governing institutions in which indigenous and non-indigenous peoples have agreed to shared rule, though I will not pursue this possibility here.

Crocker adds to Goulet's insights. Although he applauds Goulet's emphasis on non-elite participation, especially that which is not compromised by manipulation or co-optation, he argues that Goulet is not entirely correct in suggesting that 'the quality of the participation depends on its initial point of entry' (1989, 167) – though to be fair Goulet says that this 'matters greatly', not exclusively – and he criticizes Goulet for not adequately emphasizing other aspects of the 'process' of participation (Crocker 2008, 344). He points out that there are various 'modes' of participation that could still exist in each, or at least the first six, of Goulet's seven categories. Whether these modes are thicker or thinner forms of participation, Crocker argues, also affects the quality of the process. He adds to Goulet's typology by distinguishing *how* a group's non-elite members participate, especially in the group's decision-making (Crocker 2008, 342). Crocker's seven modes of participation are: (i) nominal, (ii) passive, (iii) consultative, (iv) petitionary, (v) participatory, (vi) bargaining, and (vii) deliberative (2008, 343–344).[18] (See Appendix for his explanations of each.) 'The further we go down the list, the 'thicker' is the participatory mode in the sense of more fully expressing individual or collective agency' (Crocker 2008, 344). Thicker modes of participation, he argues, offer less opportunity for elite domination, a concern of many minority groups to be sure, but often an arguably greater concern for many indigenous peoples whose historical and present position has left them with so little bargaining power in their relations with states.

Below I offer a framework for evaluating non-elite participation along the dimensions that Goulet and Crocker emphasize. Because of the centrality of participation to the process aspect of self-determination, this framework is particularly helpful for analyzing this aspect of the self-determination of indigenous peoples. We begin by asking at which point or points the group (through its representatives or in some other way) enters the group decision-making process. We then assess the 'thinness' or 'thickness' of their role in decisions affecting them.[19] The later they enter the process, and the thinner their role, the less we are able to say with confidence that they exercise their agency and, thus, that they are able adequately to defend themselves

Table 1. Two accounts of participation 'quality': entry-points and modes of public participation.

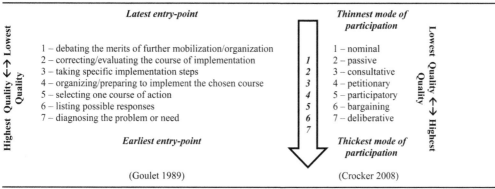

	Latest entry-point		*Thinnest mode of participation*	
Highest Quality ←→ Lowest Quality	1 – debating the merits of further mobilization/organization		1 – nominal	Lowest Quality ←→ Highest Quality
	2 – correcting/evaluating the course of implementation	*1*	2 – passive	
	3 – taking specific implementation steps	*2*	3 – consultative	
	4 – organizing/preparing to implement the chosen course	*3*	4 – petitionary	
	5 – selecting one course of action	*4*	5 – participatory	
	6 – listing possible responses	*5*	6 – bargaining	
	7 – diagnosing the problem or need	*6*	7 – deliberative	
		7		
	Earliest entry-point		*Thickest mode of participation*	
	(Goulet 1989)		(Crocker 2008)	

against forces that propel their society into change. That is, the less robust is indigenous participation in relevant policy decisions in those areas where shared rule remains, the more vulnerable is their society. Table 1 offers a visual representation of this framework. On Crocker's scale, the higher the number, the thicker is the participation. For convenience (though somewhat counterintuitively), I have also numbered Goulet's sequence of entry-points from one to seven: the higher the number, the *earlier* the non-elite entered the process. This way, on both scales, a higher number represents a higher 'quality' of participation. I thus refer to these as 'quality points'.[20]

Together, these complementary tools can offer a more complex picture of the process aspect of self-determination than what we might achieve by simply asking whether or not a central government appears to have devised mechanisms for (indigenous) self-determination, or even by using one of these two metrics alone to evaluate those mechanisms. Goulet's classification by entry-point would rate very highly, for example, a process in which a group of non-elites identified a need in their community, instigated a broad-based discussion with those powerful elites in the position to make policy changes, and succeeded in framing the discussion as one over a wide range of relevant matters from the structural sources of the problem to the details of addressing its effects. But if the way in which these non-elites actually participated once this process was underway proved thin – if they were kept at the margins of community meetings or if their views were listened to but not taken into serious consideration, for example – then this same process would earn a poor rating along Crocker's scale. Conversely, one can imagine a group of non-elites engaged with policy-makers in robust deliberation over the minutia of implementing some new policy or over how this new policy is working in practice. However, without having been involved in identifying the problem or in helping to decide on the best policies to solve it, there is no way to know whether this 'problem' is something that really mattered to them in the first place. Moreover, the policy responses might create a whole new set of problems that the elites could not have foreseen without the benefit of deliberating (or at least consulting) with the non-elites at an early stage. This process, then, while ranking very highly on Crocker's scale would do poorly on Goulet's.

It is also important to note the possibility that a multi-stage policy-making process could have a single non-elite entry-point (and thus a single ranking on Goulet's scale), but comprise numerous modes of participations at different stages (thus having several different rankings on Crocker's scale). In this case, the non-elite group imagined above might enter into the process at the very beginning, and might even be robustly engaged in helping to diagnose the problem and list the possible responses to be taken, but it may then be largely marginalized at the implementation and evaluation stages. In this case, a single process might be broken down into its component parts and analyzed separately. The key is that any process that does not score well on both scales is flawed in some important way and its quality as a whole is substantially compromised. This framework can be applied to indigenous participation in policy-making as well as to any number of political processes in which we are interested in evaluating the degree of agency enjoyed by a non-elite population in decisions that affect them.

Conclusion

The 'spirit' of the norm of self-determination, whatever a group's political aims, emphasizes freedom, participation, and reasonable control over one's life and destiny. 'All peoples have the right of self-determination' (United Nations 1966a, 1966b). In practice, however, this norm often remains thinly applied. If we understand self-determination to mean 'that human beings, individually and as groups, are equally entitled to be in control of their own destinies, and to live within a governing institutional order that is devised accordingly' (Anaya 2008, 49–50), then our assessment of its application in practice needs to be fleshed out. I argue that the norm of self-determination would benefit from an elaboration of its core content, not only in a *substantive* sense, which already receives a fair amount of attention in the literature and in policy circles, but also in a *process* sense.

Indigenous peoples are particularly vulnerable in ways both numerous and complex; minorities also confront many complicated forms of vulnerability. As individuals, both indigenous persons and minorities are especially susceptible to harm, and their societies face a 'particular disadvantage' both in protecting themselves against unwanted change and in effecting change that they desire. If human rights offer a way to reduce human vulnerability, then in the case of indigenous peoples the right of self-determination is a protection against a certain type of human vulnerability, what I call 'agency vulnerability'. The value in a *process*-focused analysis of self-determination is in its ability to help better reveal the real opportunity that an indigenous people – or any other – have to be and do as they choose, independently to define and pursue a life they value and have reason to value, to reduce their agency vulnerability.

The framework suggested here offers one way in which to evaluate this process aspect of self-determination: by identifying the points at which indigenous peoples enter into the decision-making process with the governments of their respective states or other indigenous or non-indigenous populations and the modes of participation through which they engage. To the extent to which all indigenous peoples, no matter how extensive their rights of self-rule, must continue to engage in various forms of 'shared rule' with the larger society, evaluating participation in this way remains important.

While this framework does not differ conceptually from one that might be used to evaluate the effective participation of minorities (or any group in their dealings with a more powerful elite), it is especially relevant for indigenous participation for two reasons. First, the equal weight it gives to entry-points speaks directly to the requirement that indigenous people be involved in the very establishment of the governing order under which they live, a requirement not typically associated with the European minority right to 'effective participation'. And if (any level of) state jurisdiction over indigenous peoples is to be legitimate, then the people must consent to these areas of shared rule, which therefore requires early participation in the identification of those areas. Participation in schemes of shared rule over areas that the people in question had no part in identifying seriously erodes any claim that that people truly enjoys self-determination.

Second, the weight that this framework puts on the mode of participation can help us to evaluate whether indigenous peoples participate in a way that ensures that their 'consent' to those areas of shared rule, and the execution of that rule from there forward, is not the product of manipulation or domination but rather is a full expression of their free and informed agency. Again, this dimension is important for many minority groups as well, but it may be more important for indigenous groups whose relative bargaining power vis-à-vis the state is often even lower than that of other non-dominant groups.

In those areas where shared decision-making remains between indigenous peoples and states (or certain state apparatuses), with such a framework in hand, we can more easily put the onus on governments to demonstrate that a thick concept of 'quality' participation is at work in their protection and promotion of the wider 'right of self-determination'. With attention to both the entry-point and the mode of participation, governments will better live up to their normative and legal obligations toward indigenous peoples, and those peoples might better hope to reduce both their societal and individual agency vulnerabilities.

Acknowledgements

The author would like to thank Alexandru Cojocaru, David A. Crocker, Will Kymlicka, and Eric Palmer, as well as participants at the 2011 Human Development and Capability Association annual conference, for very helpful comments on this paper.

Notes

1. See Section 1: Vulnerability and Self-Determination for a discussion of the concept of 'agency' at work here.
2. See Allan Buchanan on self-determination, secession, intra-state autonomy, and reform in Buchanan (2004, especially Chapters 8–10).
3. In the next section, I will briefly return to and clarify the oft-assumed categorical distinction between indigenous and minority peoples, and the distinct models of protection that have arisen in response, in particular with regard to the right to effective participation. Whether the distinction is valid and the laws justifiable – and thus whether minorities do not also have a claim to self-determination – is a matter that I will not address here.
4. This dynamic concept is distinct from Amartya Sen's idea of 'agency freedom', 'one's freedom to bring about the achievements one values and which one attempts to produce' (Sen 1995, 57), as it explicitly highlights the risk of harm that arises from a lack of agency at any given time. By naming this important form of vulnerability we make it visible.
5. For a useful discussion of the concept in Sen's work, see Part II of the Crocker and Robeyns chapter 'Capability and Agency' in *Amartya Sen*, Christopher Morris, ed. (Crocker and Robeyns 2009). For a discussion of the role of one's 'highest values or moral principles' in the exercise of agency, as well as its relationship to Adela Cortina's, Flavio Comim's, and Rob Reich's concepts of autonomy, see Crocker 2008, Chapter 7, especially footnote 12, 249–250. See also Reich (2002), Chapter 4, on 'minimalist autonomy.'
6. Here and throughout this discussion the term 'human rights' refers specifically to 'human rights laws.'

7. By 'agency,' Ignatieff means 'more or less what Isaiah Berlin meant by "negative liberty," the capacity of each individual to achieve rational intentions without let or hindrance' (Ignatieff 2001, 57). Ignatieff says that 'to emphasize agency is to empower individuals.' See Drydyk's and Keleher's essays in this volume for interrogations of the concepts of agency and empowerment and their relationship to one another.

8. Here I use the term 'minority' as shorthand for any non-dominant group, including both non-indigenous persons such as national minorities and members of indigenous groups. I return below to the more unique and specific case of indigenous peoples. For a discussion of Western democratic trends in the recognition of different 'types' of minorities and the different protections and accommodations that each claims, see Kymlicka 2007, especially 67–77.

9. Shue says that identifying such threats is a 'largely empirical question' (Shue 1980, 33). For a thorough discussion of, and framework for, justifying certain rights to protect against those threats, see Nickel 2007, Chapter 5 (and references therein).

10. John Rawls, for example, in *The Law of Peoples*, offers a similar conception to Anaya's but makes explicit the requirement of shared political institutions. To this he adds 'common sympathies' in John Stewart Mill's sense and a shared 'moral nature,' a feature understood as 'a firm attachment to a political (moral) conception of right and justice' (Rawls 1999, 23–30).

11. The first to establish a right of all peoples to self-determination are the two 1966 UN Human Rights Covenants: the International Covenant on Economic, Social and Cultural Rights (ICESCR) and the International Covenant on Civil and Political Rights (ICCPR) (United Nations 1966a, 1966b). Common Article 1 of the two Covenants establishes this right.

12. A robust defense of the application of the term 'peoples' to indigenous groups, and of the justifications for their right to self-determination, is beyond the scope of this paper, but see Anaya's *Indigenous Peoples in International Law* (2004) for a thorough discussion of the 'developments over time' and analysis of current debates. The work itself, and its many references and primary texts available in the appendix, offer a rich account.

13. Despite the grey areas, insofar as the arguments in this paper rest upon accepted human rights norms, and their expression in international law, I will respect this distinction with the caveat that it can be difficult to apply in practice.

14. See Will Kymlicka's 'The evolving basis of European norms of minority rights' (in McGarry and Keating, Routledge, 2006) for an introduction and critique of the norm of 'effective participation' for minorities in the European context.

15. For Anaya, the organization and continuation of the governing institutional order – what he calls the 'constitutive' and 'on-going' elements – together make up the substance of the norm of self-determination.

16. See for example Gigler 2005 on the former and Stewart 2005 on the latter.

17. The role of 'participation' in development has been the subject of much debate, with critics rightly arguing that its implementation can easily reproduce inter- and intra-group inequalities and structures of domination and can thus be detrimental to or at least unhelpful for the interests of women, minorities, children, and others. Crocker (2008) attempts to answer a number of these challenges in his discussion on the value of public deliberation for democracy and development. See Chapter 10, particularly his responses to the 'indeterminacy' and 'autonomy' criticisms. Jay Drydyk recognizing the important role of participation in democracy, cautions against valuing participation for its own sake, and argues for the importance of consequences in assessing the social worth of democratic processes. 'Greater access to political activity makes political life more democratic, but it is yet more democratic if that activity *influences* decision-making, and more democratic still if the decision-making affected has a real *impact* on the capabilities that people value as building-blocks of a good life' (Drydyk 2005, 256, emphasis mine).

18. 'Negotiation' is not a category Crocker uses, given its ambiguity: there may be thinner and thicker forms of negotiations, with the thickest forms merging with deliberation.

19. There are, of course, other dimensions we might consider, such as the inclusiveness of the participatory arrangement with respect to the breadth of group membership (see Crocker 2008, 342), or the degree of control over resources necessary for implementation of decisions (see Gaventa and Valderrama 1999), or even the actual impact those decisions ultimately have on the capabilities that people value (Drydyk 2005). Crocker also highlights the importance of several other of Goulet's dimensions of participation, including the 'originating agent' (does non-elite participation originate from below, from above, or from the outside?) and the normative role and scale of participatory processes. Furthermore, both Crocker's and Goulet's scales might be challenged for having omissions (or requiring subtractions),

but I am not going to challenge them here except to show that, used together, they provide a helpful lens for evaluating public participation. In future research I may offer a more comprehensive evaluation tool.

20. Of course, neither of the two 'scales' was ever meant to be used empirically to 'measure' the quality of participation. I use the numbers as an easy way to conceptualize where on each scale the various processes fall. These judgments, while assigned numerical values for conceptual convenience, are qualitative, not quantitative.

References

AHDR. 2004. *Arctic Human Development Report*. Akureyri: Stefansson Arctic Institute.

Anaya, S. J. 1993. "A Contemporary Definition of the International Norm of Self-Determination." *Transnational Law and Contemporary Problems* 3 (1): 131–163.

Anaya, S. J. 2004. *Indigenous Peoples in International Law*. New York: Oxford University Press.

Anaya, S. J. 2008. "The Right of Indigenous Peoples to Self-Determination in the Post Declaration Era." *Gáldu Čála – Journal of Indigenous People's Rights*, no. 2/2008: 47–57.

Buchanan, Allen. 2004. *Justice, Legitimacy, and Self-Determination*. Oxford: Oxford University Press.

Camacho, Luis. 2010. "Goulet on Vulnerability as a Key Concept in Development Ethics." In *New Directions in Development Ethics: Essays in Honor of Denis Goulet*, edited by Charles K. Wilber and Amitava Krishna Dutt, 142–154. Notre Dame, IN: University of Notre Dame.

Council of Europe. 1995. *Framework Convention for the Protection of National Minorities*. Strasbourg: Council of Europe, February 1.

Crocker, David A. 2008. *Ethics of Global Development*. Cambridge: Cambridge University Press.

Crocker, David A., and Ingrid Robeyns. 2009. "Capability and Agency." In *Amartya Sen*, edited by Christopher Morris, 60–90. Cambridge: Cambridge University Press.

Drydyk, J. 2005. "When is Development More Democratic?" *Journal of Human Development* 6 (2): 247–267.

Gaventa, John, and Camilo Valderrama. 1999. "Participation, Citizenship and Local Governance." Paper presented at the Institute of Development Studies workshop: Strengthening Participation in Local Governance, Brighton, June 21–24. http://www.uv.es/~fernandm/Gaventa,%20Valderrama.pdf

Gigler, Björn-Sören. 2005. "Indigenous Peoples, Human Development and the Capability Approach." Paper presented at the 5th international conference of the Human Development and Capability Association, Paris, September 11–14.

Goulet, D. 1989. "Participation in Development: New Avenues." *World Development* 17 (2): 165–178.

Goulet, D. 1971. *The Cruel Choice: A New Concept in the Theory of Development*. New York: Atheneum Press.

Ignatieff, Michael. 2001. *Human Rights as Politics and Idolatry*. Princeton, NJ: Princeton University Press.

Kymlicka, Will. 1992. "The Rights of Minority Cultures: Reply to Kukathas." *Political Theory* 20 (1): 140–146.

Kymlicka, Will. 2006. "The Evolving Basis of European Norms of Minority Rights: Rights to Culture, Participation and Autonomy." In *European Integration and the Nationalities Question*, edited by John McGarry and Michael Keating, 35–63. New York: Routledge.

Kymlicka, Will. 2007. *Multicultural Odysseys: Navigating the New International Politics of Diversity*. New York: Oxford University Press.

Nickel, James W. 2007. *Making Sense of Human Rights*. 2nd ed. Malden, MA: Blackwell.

Nickel, James W. 2008. "Rights and the Exceptionally Vulnerable." In *Genomics and Environmental Regulation: Science, Ethics, and Law*, edited by Richard Roy Sharp, Gary Elvin Marchant and Jamie A. Grodsky, 258–266. Baltimore, MD: John's Hopkins University Press.

Nozick, Robert. 1974. *Anarchy, State, and Utopia*. New York, NY: Basic Books, Inc.

Nussbaum, Martha. 2000. *Women and Human Development: The Capabilities Approach*. New York: Cambridge University Press.

Penz, Peter, Jay Drydyk, and Pablo S. Bose. 2011. *Displacement by Development: Ethics, Rights, and Responsibilities*. Cambridge: Cambridge University Press.

Rawls, John. 1971. *A Theory of Justice*. Cambridge, MA: Harvard University Press.

Rawls, John. 1999. *The Law of Peoples*. Cambridge, MA: Harvard University Press.

Reich, Rob. 2002. *Bridging Liberalism and Multiculturalism in American Education*. Chicago, IL: Chicago University Press.

Sen, Amartya. 1995. *Inequality Reexamined*. Cambridge, MA: Harvard University Press.

Sen, Amartya. 1999. *Development as Freedom*. New York: Anchor Books.

Shue, Henry. 1980. *Basic Rights: Subsistence, Affluence, and U.S. Foreign Policy.* 2nd ed. Princeton, NJ: Princeton University Press.

Stewart, Frances. 2005. "Groups and Capabilities." *Journal of Human Development* 6 (2): 185–204.

Turner, Bryan S. 2006. *Vulnerability and Human Rights.* University Park, PA: The Pennsylvania State University Press.

United Nations. 1966a. *International Covenant on Civil and Political Rights.* New York, December 16.

United Nations. 1966b. *International Covenant on Economic, Social, and Cultural Rights.* New York, December 16.

United Nations. 1992. *Declaration on the Rights of Persons Belonging to National or Ethnic, Religious and Linguistic Minorities.* New York, December 18.

United Nations. 2007. Declaration on the Rights of Indigenous Peoples. New York, September 13.

World Bank. 2005. *OP 4.10 – Indigenous Peoples.* The World Bank Group. http://go.worldbank.org/TE769PDWN0.

Appendix. Crocker's 'modes of participation'

(Excerpted from Crocker 2008, 342–344, footnotes omitted)

"Here, drawing on and supplementing the classificatory work of Bina Agarwal, J. N. Pretty, John Gaventa, and Jay Drydyk, I distinguish – from thinner to thicker – a spectrum of modes of participation in group decision-making:

(1) *Nominal participation:* The weakest way in which someone participates in group decision-making is when someone is a member of a group but does not attend its meetings. Some people, of course, are not even members. Some are members but are unable to attend because of other responsibilities, or are unwilling to attend, for instance because they are harassed or unwelcome.

(2) *Passive participation:* In passive participation, people are group members and attend the group's or officials' decision-making meetings, but passively listen to reports about the decisions that others already have made. The elite tells the non-elite what the elite is going to do or has done, and non-elite persons participate, like the White House press corps, by listening and, at best, asking questions or making comments.

(3) *Consultative participation:* Non-elites participate by giving information and their opinions ('input', 'preferences' and even 'proposals') to the elite. The non-elite neither deliberate among themselves nor make decisions. It is the elite who are the 'deciders', and while they may deign to listen to the nonelite, they have no obligation to do so.

(4) *Petitionary participation:* Nonelites petition authorities to make certain decisions and do certain things, usually to remedy grievances. Although it is the prerogative of the elite to decide, the non-elite have a right to be heard and the elite have the duty receive, listen, and consider if not to heed. This participatory model, like that of consultative participation, is often used in traditional decision-making.

(5) *Participatory implementation:* Elites determine the goals and main means, and non-elites implement the goals and decide, if at all, only tactics. In this mode non-elites do more than listen, comment, and express. Like soccer players, they also make and enact decisions, but the overall plan and marching orders belong to the coach.

(6) *Bargaining:* On the basis of whatever individual or collective power they have, non-elites bargain with elites. Those bargaining are more adversaries than partners. Self-interest largely if not exclusively motivates each side, and non-elite influence on the final 'deal' depends on what non-elites are willing to give up and what concessions they are able to extract. The greater the power imbalances between an elite and non-elite, the less influence the non-elite has on the final outcome. An elite may settle for some loss now in order to make likely a larger future gain. Alliances with and support from actors outside and above tend to enhance non-elite bargaining power.

(7) *Deliberative participation:* Non-elites (sometimes among themselves and sometimes with elites) deliberate together, sifting proposals and reasons to forge agreements on policies that at least a majority can accept."

Identifying adaptive preferences in practice: lessons from postcolonial feminisms

Serene J. Khader

Department of Philosophy, Brooklyn College, CUNY, Brooklyn, NY, USA

I argue that postcolonial feminist critiques draw our attention to four phenomena that are easily confused with what I call 'paradigmatic adaptive preference' – and that the ability to distinguish these phenomena can improve the quality of development interventions. An individual has paradigmatic adaptive preferences (APs) if she perpetuates injustice against herself because her normative worldview is nearly completely distorted. The four look-alike phenomena postcolonial feminist critics help us identify are (a) APs caused by selective value distortion (SAPs), (b) APs caused by forced tradeoffs (TAPs), (c) APs caused by misperceptions of the facts (MAPs), and (d) wellbeing-compatible preferences that are misunderstood because of a lack of cultural or contextual knowledge. The first three, I argue, are non-paradigmatic forms of AP that have gone previously unrecognized and that we need to expand our conceptual vocabulary to describe; the last is not a form of AP at all. Development practitioners can grapple more seriously with the real-world complexities of moral psychology and cross-cultural moral judgments if they are capable of distinguishing paradigmatic AP from the look-alike phenomena.

Postcolonial feminist critics argue that theorists of adaptive preference (AP) depict women in the global South in ways that are inaccurate and morally objectionable. According to the critics, AP theorists represent women from the global South as 'dupes of patriarchy' (Narayan 2002) or suggest that 'the West is best for women' (Jaggar 2005, 61). These criticisms offer insights about development practice, and not only about the politics of representation – or so I will attempt to show here. The critics' allege that AP theorists default to colonial stereotypes when they attempt to explain what appears to be deprivation-perpetuating behavior by women from the global South. On the stereotypical account, Southern women perpetuate their deprivation because they have internalized the extremely distorted normative worldviews promoted by their cultures. This account fails to challenge widespread depictions of Southern women as ultra-oppressed, as unthinking victims of especially patriarchal cultures. Development practitioners who employ these stereotypes may misperceive the lives they are trying to trans-form – and thus recommend objectionable and/or ineffective interventions.

I argue in this article that postcolonial feminist critiques draw our attention to four phenom-ena that are easily confused with what I call 'paradigmatic adaptive preference' – and that the ability to distinguish these phenomena can improve the quality of development interventions. An individual has paradigmatic APs if she perpetuates injustice against herself because of a near-completely distorted normative worldview. The four look-alike phenomena AP critics help us identify are (a) APs caused by selective value distortion (SAPs), (b) APs caused by forced tradeoffs (TAPs), (c) APs caused by misperceptions of the facts (MAPs), and (d) wellbeing-compatible preferences that are misunderstood because of cultural unfamiliarity. The first three, I argue, are non-paradigmatic forms of AP that have gone previously unrecognized and undertheorized; the last is not a form of AP at all. Development practitioners can grapple more seriously with the real-world complexities of moral psychology and cross-cultural moral judgments if they are capable of distinguishing paradigmatic AP from the look-alike phenomena.

In the first section of the article, I describe the key postcolonialism-influenced criticisms of AP and the role of the concept of AP in development ethics. I show that, though they fail to show that paradigmatic APs do not exist, the postcolonial criticisms suggest that paradigmatic AP should not be our explanation of first-resort for apparent deprivation-perpetuating behavior by women in the global South. In the second section, I argue that the postcolonialism-influenced critiques offer examples of four phenomena that are easy to confuse in practice with paradigmatic AP. I discuss what the existence of these phenomena implies about the concept of AP. One phenomenon (unfamiliar wellbeing-compatible preferences) demonstrates that the range of applicability of the concept of AP is smaller than typically thought. The presence of the other three phenomena reveals the existence of non-paradigmatic forms of AP that we need a richer conceptual vocabulary to describe. I also argue in this second section that distinguishing among these phenomena can yield more ethical and effective development interventions. Finally, I recommend steps development practitioners can take to tailor interventions and to avoid seeing paradigmatic AP where it does not exist.

Is the concept of AP colonial?[1]

The two most prominent theorists of AP, Martha Nussbaum and Susan Moller Okin, are white women who spent, or have spent, the bulk of their lives in the North. Many (but perhaps not as many as the critics believe)[2] of their examples of real-world AP involve women from the global South. These facts are not in and of themselves significant. According to the critics, however, Nussbaum and Okin's positionality causes their work on APs to express and perpetuate a variety of colonial epistemic prejudices. Let us say that I have an epistemic prejudice toward another if I attempt to explain her behavior using concepts that distort it – and do so because of that person's belonging to some marginalized social group. I have a *colonial* epistemic prejudice if the distorting concepts I choose have justified imperialist oppression.

Postcolonial feminist theorists have documented two colonial epistemic prejudices relevant to our discussion here – the tendency to see all third-world women as 'victims' (Mohanty 1988) or 'unconscious reactors' (Mohanty 1995) and the tendency to treat their oppressions as caused by their 'backward cultures' (Narayan 1997). Critics, such as Ackerly (2000), Jaggar (2005), and Narayan (2002), argue that Nussbaum and Okin perpetuate the tendency to see women in poor countries as unthinking victims of patriarchal cultures. The problem with perpetuating colonial stereotypes is epistemic as well as ethical; the critics believe that Nussbaum and Okin propagate *false* beliefs about Southern cultures and how women in them navigate their options. It is clear enough that these epistemic prejudices have adverse effects on knowledge production about the global South. What is less clear is whether – and to what extent – the postcolonial critiques are relevant to development practice. My contention is that the critiques draw our attention to the epistemic complexities involved in understanding why real people appear to perpetuate their deprivation – rather than undermining the practical usefulness of the concept of AP.

The role of the concept of AP

I am about to argue that the postcolonial criticisms do not undermine the explanatory usefulness of the concept of AP. To show this, I need to clarify what concept of AP is supposed to explain.

I believe that development ethicists want the concept of AP to provide grounds for disputing two common (and related) claims about welfare. One claim is that a person's subjective attitudes (in the form of happiness, perception of want-satisfaction, etc.) are reliable welfare indicators. The other (which is a certain way of interpreting the implications of the first) is that a person's deprivation-perpetuating beliefs and behaviors somehow legitimate her deprivation. That the idea of AP evolved to undermine subjective welfarism will probably strike most readers of this journal as uncontroversial.

To justify my assertion that the idea of AP evolved to provide grounds for questioning the claim that perpetuating one's deprivation reveals underlying endorsement, we can consider the fact that most feminist invocations of AP respond to allegations that feminism is paternalistic. Feminist theorists often mention AP to dispute the claim that giving a woman opportunities she did not ask for is a way of disrespecting her – a way of assaulting her deeply held conception of the good.[3] Consider this quotation of Nussbaum's, typical of feminist discussions of AP: 'If one has never learned to read and is told that education is not for women, it is very easy to internalize one's second-class status and not strive for what is out of reach...We have good reasons...to support public investment in female literacy, even in the absence of young girls' demand for such programs' (Nussbaum 1999, 151). The idea here, and in many discussions like it, is that a person's complicity in her own deprivation neither nullifies the deprivation nor reveals deep endorsement of it.

Nussbaum and Okin's desire to give force to the point that complicity does not equal consent causes them to have a specific type of deprivation-perpetuating preference in mind. This is the type of AP I call 'paradigmatic AP'. Nussbaum and Okin claim that some deprived people's values are so distorted that they have difficulty recognizing their deprivation as such. Okin, for instance, writes that, oppressed people 'have often internalized their oppression so well that they have no sense of what they are justly entitled to as human beings' (2008, 249). Nussbaum writes in one instance that a woman does not resist domestic violence because she does not know she is a human being with rights (2001, 112–113). A person with this type of paradigmatic AP struggles to see harm to herself as harm because she, fairly consistently, sees behaviors that harm her as acceptable or helpful to her. She thus can neither value herself appropriately nor consent to her deprivation.[4]

My understanding of the reasons for which the concept of AP developed leads me to an understanding of the term that encompasses more than paradigmatic AP. We need not identify AP with near-total value distortion to argue that there is some class of preferences that should be treated as suspect indicators of either what would benefit their bearers or what their bearers actually value. Admittedly, my broad use of the term 'AP' is somewhat idiosyncratic, and those who would like a fuller defense should consult my book (Khader 2011). To summarize, I believe an AP is a behavior or belief whereby an individual perpetuates her deprivation that is also causally related to her deprivation. By 'causally related to deprivation', I mean 'would disappear upon exposure to superior conditions and/or information'. It follows from my definition that a variety of beliefs and behaviors count as APs. These range from behaviors where a person experiences no normative distortion but is simply making the best of a bad situation (a phenomenon I will later refer to as making 'forced tradeoffs') to behaviors motivated by relatively thoroughgoing value distortion (or paradigmatic AP). It also follows from my definition that behaviors that do not perpetuate deprivation cannot count as APs. My understanding of the role of the concept of AP will become important in the second section when I argue that there exist non-paradigmatic forms of AP. Now, I turn to examining three postcolonialism-influenced criticisms of AP and asking what they imply about whether we should retain the concept of AP in development practice.

The 'dupes of patriarchy' criticism

Uma Narayan argues that deprived people may perpetuate their deprivation and retain critical attitudes toward it. She responds to a rhetorical question from Okin about the behavior of Ultra-Orthodox Jewish women who accept subservience. Specifically the ultra-Orthodox women believe that their bodies are 'dangerous sexual objects' and their role in life is to facilitate men's torah scholarship. Okin asks whether their 'acquiescence in cultural practices stems from lack of power, or socialization to inferior roles, resulting in a lack of self-esteem or sense of entitlement' (Okin 1998, 675). Narayan replies that Okin sees 'other' women as 'dupes of patriarchy'. She proceeds to describe a group of 'other' women who comply with oppressive norms without being 'dupes'. These are the Pirzada women of Old Delhi who practice body veiling and female seclusion. According to Narayan, the women have a variety of motivations, including a realistic assessment of what is possible for them, a desire to move around anonymously and without being regarded as sexual objects (Narayan 2002, 420), the belief that unveiled women are sexually licentious (421), and a desire for class status (421). Despite their compliance with (and partial endorsement of) these sexist norms, the women retain a critical perspective – lamenting restrictions on their mobility and education, and joking about how they look like a 'water buffalo' (Narayan 2002, 420).

Narayan makes two distinct theoretical points in her discussion of the Pirzada women. The point about the objective benefits associated with veiling and seclusion is a version of the 'limited options criticism' I discuss in the next section. The point I am interested in now involves the Pirzada women's maintenance of a critical perspective on their own oppression. If the (empirical) claim that the Pirzada women do not wholly endorse their oppression is true, it follows that it is theoretically and actually possible to comply with patriarchal practices despite experiencing some dissatisfaction with them. But there are two significant things the example of the Pirzada women does not demonstrate: (a) that Okin is wrong about the ultra-Orthodox Jewish women and (b) that all women who comply with patriarchal norms evince critical attitudes toward them. Showing that *some* women who comply with oppressive norms retain a discernible critical perspective toward them is not the same thing as showing that *all* of them do. Narayan fails to demonstrate that there are *no* paradigmatic APs.

It may seem that we should conclude from Narayan's analysis that paradigmatic APs, though theoretically possible, are rare. I agree that cases of thoroughgoing and uniform value distortion are probably uncommon – given the simple fact that all of us have inconsistent moral beliefs. But those of us who have done gender and development practice and/or taught introductory Women's Studies courses know that women in the same group endorse patriarchal norms to varying degrees; some believe in the justice of inferior roles for women, others do not see the inferiority as unjust, and many others see the injustice in only a smattering of sexist practices. Some women's endorsement of patriarchal practices does appear to be near-total. Indeed, as Hannah Papanek argues, some oppressive practices may need near-total endorsement in order to be successfully perpetuated. According to Papanek, adult women go through a process of 'secondary socialization' to justify inflicting painful practices like female genital cutting and foot-binding on their daughters. As mothers, they remember the pain they suffered but must justify turning themselves into perpetrators, rather than mere victims, of the pain. According to Papanek, this transformation requires an especially conscious and thoroughgoing endorsement of beliefs about women's inferiority (1990, 178). We need to be aware that value distortion comes in degrees and be wary of discounting the possibility of very significant value distortion a priori.

The limited options criticism

Another critical response to Nussbaum's and Okin's claims about AP is that women may comply with oppressive norms because of limited options rather than value distortion. As part of an argument that that women may accept unjust treatment because they have 'internalized the ideas behind the traditional system of discrimination' (1995, 91), Nussbaum discusses women's low participation in a literacy program in Bangladesh. She conjectures that the reason behind it is the women's failure to 'even know what it means to have the advantages of an education' (1995, 91). Brooke Ackerly disputes this claim by describing her own interactions with over 800 women from rural Bangladesh. These personal interactions have persuaded Ackerly that the literacy program did not fail because of women's failure to value education (2001, 107). Rather, Ackerly claims, these women live under conditions where it is a welfare-maximizing move for them to educate their children – particularly their male children, rather than themselves.

Ackerly's criticism, put in more abstract terms, is that a person may engage in self-depriving behavior without having distorted values. Restrictions on her options may simply prevent her from pursuing her welfare in a comprehensive fashion. As I have argued elsewhere (2011, 2012), bad conditions often constrain an agent such that she cannot achieve basic welfare across all domains of life – so she must sacrifice it in some in order to achieve it in others. Therefore, the Bangladeshi women (correctly) value literacy; their options are just limited such that they cannot pursue it without sacrificing something else of objective value. Assuming Ackerly is right about the Bangladeshi women's reasons for failing to pursue literacy, and assuming that the norm dictating that women should not be sources of their own income is sexist, she demonstrates that a person can comply with oppressive norms without experiencing any value distortion.[5]

Ackerly's criticism may even make an additional stronger point – that there is reason to believe paradigmatic AP is uncommon in the global South. Conditions where one cannot resist one's deprivation without making extreme sacrifices in some domain of life are probably particularly common in poor countries – both because poverty involves option restriction and because neoliberal policies have, in many cases, retrenched restrictive gender roles by increasing labor demands on women (Naples 2002) and helping cultural/religious fundamentalists gain power (Brenner 2003). Despite this, however, Ackerly falls short of showing that *no one* has paradigmatic APs. She does not show that no one rejects a literacy program because of the belief that women's projects are of little value.

The logical reason for this is identical to the reason Narayan's dupes criticism fails to demonstrate the non-existence of paradigmatic AP. Arguments by counterexample can only show so much. Narayan and Ackerly's arguments show that paradigmatic AP does not explain certain cases of oppression-perpetuating behavior. Paradigmatic AP can be misapplied to cases of deprivation-perpetuating behavior that is caused by partial value distortion and limited options. But we also have empirical reason, in examples like the one from Papanek above, to believe that there are some actual cases of people failing to pursue their wellbeing because of relatively thoroughgoing value distortion.

The 'West is best' criticism

Jaggar's criticism differs in structure from those made by Ackerly and Narayan. Jaggar argues that Nussbaum and Okin only attribute APs to third-world women who endorse their own cultural practices (Jaggar 2005, 69). Jaggar argues that this pattern encourages the view that only Westerners are capable of 'naming and challenging patriarchal atrocities committed against third-world women' (Jaggar 2005, 69). Jaggar goes on to point out that some Southern women believe their cultural practices to be beneficial (2005, 68). Though Jaggar is noteworthy in directing this criticism at AP theorists specifically, it is a version of a more general criticism. A variety of non-Western feminists point out that Westerners may mistake culturally unfamiliar preferences for preferences adapted to deprivation. For instance, Vandana Shiva argues that Westerners incorrectly see the lives of those engaged in subsistence agriculture as essentially deprived (1989, 5). Leila Ahmed argues that Westerners ignore the ways in which sex segregation in some Arab cultures functions to protect women from internalizing sexist views about themselves (Ahmed 1982, 528–529). Translating concerns like these into philosophical discussions of AP, Jaggar worries about the reliability of Nussbaum's and Okin's judgments that certain culturally unfamiliar preferences are adaptive. Nussbaum and Okin may object to certain morally acceptable preferences because they reflect the values of non-Western cultures – not because they are objectively harmful to the people who participate in them. Jaggar's worry about this seems warranted, given that Nussbaum and Okin rely on their intuitions[6] to determine which preferences are adaptive – and given that they offer no method for distinguishing unfamiliar preferences from harmful ones.

Jaggar's 'West is best' criticism, like the others, does not demonstrate that there is a problem with the concept of AP. As I argued earlier, the core idea behind the concept of AP is the idea that some deprived people's behaviors and beliefs are poor guides to what their welfare requires. The problem Jaggar identifies is not conceptually related to this belief. That is, Jaggar does not seem to take issue with the idea that deprived people's existing preferences *can be* poor wellbeing indicators. Jaggar seems instead concerned about how we determine *which* behaviors are problematic wellbeing indicators. Because Nussbaum and Okin lack a clear definition of deprivation, they are susceptible to confusing unfamiliar preferences with harmful ones.

We may be tempted to construe Jaggar as making a stronger criticism – one that undermines the very concept of AP. Perhaps Jaggar points out that many Southern women do not believe their preferences to be adaptive to demonstrate that whatever a person believes is good for her is actually good for her. Jaggar clearly does not mean this; she writes that her experience with the British class system leads her to believe that injustice can cause people's preferences to become distorted (2005, 69). But even if Jaggar herself does not mean to argue that no preferences are adaptive, we can imagine someone making the argument that there are no APs because whatever a person believes is good for her is actually good for her. This claim would undoubtedly strike the conceptual core of AP, but it is implausible. Though I believe that people – even deprived people – often know what is good for them, I see no reason to accept that *anyone's* judgments about their own good are *infallible*.

Identifying the look-alike phenomena

What are the implications of the dupes criticism, the limited options criticism, and the 'West is best' criticism for development practice? On one hand, I have argued that they fail to demonstrate that there are no paradigmatic APs. The view that there exist paradigmatic APs is fully consistent with the view that the concept of AP serves an ideological function in Western feminist theorizing. If our background context presents women from poor countries as unthinking pawns of their backward cultures, and if Northern feminists treat women from poor countries as disproportionately wrong about their own needs, we should not be surprised if readers of Nussbaum and Okin walk away feeling that their colonial stereotypes have been philosophically confirmed. On the other hand, I have argued that the criticisms show real-world descriptive limitations in the concept of paradigmatic AP. The three criticisms we have looked at help us name other phenomena to which the concept of paradigmatic AP may be easily misapplied.

The implications of postcolonial theory for development are often diluted into the vague prescription that practitioners should be conscious of their privileged positionality vis-à-vis beneficiary populations. A structural similarity among Ackerly, Jaggar, and Narayan's criticisms allows a more nuanced prescription than the simplistic: 'interrogate your positionality'. All three criticisms are directed at the way Nussbaum and Okin *apply* the concept of paradigmatic AP to real-world women. Nussbaum and Okin, like development practitioners, want to explain why actual women are complicit in their deprivation. Nussbaum and Okin act as though conclusion that women have paradigmatic AP follows seamlessly from the observation that women seem to entrench their own deprivation. Ackerly, Jaggar, and Narayan demonstrate that *there are other patterned explanations for the same observed phenomenon.*

Distinguishing paradigmatic AP from other phenomena that are easily confused with it is important for practice in a way it is not for theory. Nussbaum's and Okin's points about subjective welfarism can remain intact even if they are wrong about why the individual women in their examples perpetuate their deprivation. But similar practitioner misunderstandings can lead to ineffective or woefully inefficient development interventions. Solava Ibrahim and Sabina Alkire illustrate the importance of practitioner knowledge about why women comply with unjust norms:

> [First-person data about why women seem contented with their roles as housewives] may guide policy-makers in local government to increase women's autonomy, either by investing in their 'conscientization', or by direct interventions to assist in change, such as providing training for advocacy for childcare facilities and maternity leave on jobs. However, choosing between these options requires an understanding of the women's own 'positionally objective' views. (Ibrahim and Alkire 2007, 394)

It matters to intervention design is whether the deprived are being held back by structural obstacles, their psychologies, or some combination of the two. As Ibrahim and Alkire point out, women may accept their roles as housewives because they believe they are inferior or because they lack childcare – and knowing which is the case is terribly important for effectiveness. I turn now to naming the phenomena identified by Ackerly, Narayan, and Jaggar that may masquerade as paradigmatic AP. I also explain why distinguishing these phenomena from paradigmatic AP is useful in development practice.

Look-alike 1: APs caused by selective value distortion (SAPs)

Narayan's Pirzada women perpetuate their oppression without paradigmatic AP. They have internalized some sexist values – about women's lesser entitlements to mobility, sexual agency and education. However, unlike women with paradigmatic AP, who fail to value themselves in a relatively thoroughgoing fashion, the Pirzada women express selective but nonetheless positive self-regard. We know the Pirzada women have some sense of entitlement to education and mobility, because they envy women subject to fewer purdah restrictions and with educational access (Narayan 2002, 420). Narayan draws our attention to the fact that normative distortion (or internalized oppression, to use the more popular term) comes in degrees.

Recognizing the possibility of *selective* value distortion helps development practitioners see that improving women's self-regard is not always a matter of foisting unfamiliar views about the good on them. AP is frequently discussed as enervating oppressed people's capacities to see injustice in their situations. But, if Narayan is correct, many oppressed people who endorse aspects of their oppression retain discernible critical perspectives on it. Narayan goes so far as to speculate that women in ultrapatriarchal contexts[7] are particularly likely to be aware of a system that causes their suffering. According to Narayan, such women are more aware of patriarchal restrictions, because the restrictions are not obscured by a discourse that emphasizes women's freedom and power (2002, 424).

Look-alike 2: APs caused by forced tradeoffs (TAPs)

Women may also comply with oppressive norms despite retaining appropriate values. We can distinguish two types of cases in which an individual perpetuates her oppression but expresses thoroughgoing regard for her wellbeing. One, typified by Ackerly's Bangladeshi women, involves what I call 'forced tradeoffs'. In it, an individual cannot access some threshold level of welfare in all domains of life, so she trades it away in some domains of life to achieve it in others.[8] Ackerly's Bangladeshi women cannot simultaneously pursue their own education and have income security in old age. Pursuing welfare in the cognitive domain[9] comes at the cost of pursuing it in the income domain. Under these circumstances, pursuing one element of welfare reveals no absolute failure to value the other.[10] In other words, the women value both education and income; their conditions simply prevent them from expressing sufficient value for one.

Look-alike 3: deprivation-perpetuation caused by factual misperception (MAPs)

In a second type of deprivation-perpetuating behavior without value distortion, an individual lacks non-normative information that would motivate her to more effectively pursue her welfare. The women in Ackerly's Bangladesh example are motivated by a (presumably) correct assessment of what is possible for them. This reminds us that a person's capacity to pursue her own wellbeing depends partly on her capacity to correctly identify options and predict their welfare outcomes.[11] But people may *incorrectly* assess their options – and choose not to pursue welfare-enhancing alternatives because of this. For instance, I may comply with an oppressive norm because I overestimate the penalties of non-compliance – or because I am simply unaware that non-compliance is an option. A woman from a community that treats female seclusion as a marker of class status may lose respect if she works outside the home. But she may overestimate the loss of respect she will incur; she may assume that everyone will reject her as a 'loose' woman if she goes out to work – only to discover that her leaving the house only elicits a few whispers. People may also comply with oppressive norms because they are simply unaware of the benefits of doing otherwise. For instance, there is evidence that some communities persist in severe female genital cutting because they are unaware that the practice is the cause of their health problems; in a community where all women are cut, it is easy to assume that the health problems it causes are simply a part of all women's lives (Mackie 2000). In such cases, women perpetuate their deprivation for reasons that have to do with mistaken facts – not mistaken values.

We cannot tell whether a woman experiences value distortion just by noticing that she perpetuates her deprivation. These latter two non-paradigmatic forms of AP (TAPs and MAPs) involve an agent's simultaneous possession of AP and appropriate values. But whether she experiences normative distortion is significant for development intervention design. The woman who simply *cannot* achieve welfare across a variety of domains of life will respond only to an intervention that changes the *structural* conditions of her life. Development practitioners who psychologize the structural will focus on changing beliefs where they should focus on changing external constraints. Ackerly's Bangladeshi women do not need to be convinced of the value of literacy. They need an intervention that reduces the opportunity cost (income, in this case) of pursuing it. The woman who does not know that changing her behavior would improve her life also needs a non-normative intervention – but one that provides information rather than transforms social structures.

We might wonder whether there is a practical difference between an intervention that provides non-normative information and one that engages in overtly normative consciousness-raising. An intervention that connects an existing notion of harm and benefit to a concrete practice looks quite different from one that attempts to change women's conceptions of harm and benefit. Differences between the exercises development practitioners use to elicit value discussion and those that present evidence to help people understand the effects of their practices illustrate this. Contrast two types of intervention to end severe female genital cutting in Africa. In one, undertaken in the Somali community in Kenya, practitioners worked with religious leaders and scholars to discuss whether Islam could be construed as not requiring severe female genital cutting (Abdi, Jaldesa, and Askew 2008, 6). In another, 30 Wolof women in Senegal asked women to share their health experiences after female genital cutting with one another, and this caused the women to identify a causal relationship between genital cutting and poor health (Mackie 2000, 260).[12] In the latter, exposure to facts was sufficient to change people's investment in female genital cutting.[13] The former intervention would be more appropriately targeted at women who valued women's sexual purity over their bodily health.

Look-alike 4: unfamiliar preferences that are compatible with wellbeing

Naming the last three look-alike phenomena helps us differentiate *reasons why* people perpetuate their deprivation. But the only relevant question for practical AP intervention is not *why* people perpetuate their deprivation – it also matters *whether* what they are doing actually perpetuates deprivation. Jaggar's examples help us see this. Jaggar discusses Leila Ahmed's claim that Islamic veiling and seclusion practices benefit women by creating a separate women's culture where 'women may interact freely with one another and where they resist men's efforts to impose on them an ideology of inferiority and subservience' (Jaggar 2005, 68). Let us suppose for the sake of argument that Ahmed is correct and that seclusion gives women a normative perspective from which to critique masculine culture (the truth of this claim is overall difficult to assess given the wide contextual variation in actual Muslim practices of seclusion). Let us also assume (more controversially, perhaps) that this benefit to women's self-esteem, autonomy competencies, etc. does not carry harms with it.[14] A practitioner who saw women's desires to maintain a women's culture as reinforcing an ideology of female subservience would be mistaken.

I believe there are two non-relativist (and non-exclusive) reasons development practitioners are particularly likely to reach false judgments about whether targets of development are deprived. One is that a cultural outsider may be wrong about what the good is because she wrongly believes that what are held to be goods in her culture are the only objective goods. For instance, there might be some distinct objective good called 'belonging to a women's culture' that Western feminists have difficulty recognizing. The second is that cultural outsiders may have difficulty assessing the welfare effects of unfamiliar practices. In the first case, the practitioner is wrong about what welfare *is*; in the second, she lacks the contextual knowledge to know what the *welfare effects of some practice* are. Ackerly accuses Nussbaum of this second type of error at one point in her discussion of the Bangladeshi women (2000, 108). According to Ackerly, Nussbaum mistakenly believes that women in Bangladesh need literacy classes to gain stable income, autonomy, and self-respect. Nussbaum makes the mistake, because literacy is necessary for autonomy and income in her home (American) cultural context. Nussbaum misses the fact that there are alternative routes to income and self-respect in rural Bangladesh – through credit (one can be illiterate and start a business) and consciousness-raising.[15] Ackerly does not deny that autonomy, self-respect, and access to income are valuable.[16] Her point is that Nussbaum lacks the contextual knowledge to recognize unfamiliar routes to achieving these objectively valuable functionings.

The 'West is best' criticism reveals another phenomenon that is easily mistaken for paradigmatic AP – the unfamiliar preference with positive or neutral wellbeing effects. Therefore (if Ahmed happens to be correct about the welfare effects of seclusion), a development practitioner who thinks that a preference for seclusion is adaptive sees harms that simply do not exist. The practitioner may see harm because (a) she is wrong about what the good is because of cultural biases or (b) she lacks the contextual knowledge to assess the well-being impacts of practices. Development practitioners should want to avoid confusing harmful preferences with neutral/beneficial ones for both moral and pragmatic reasons. Practitioners who intervene to change preferences that are morally unproblematic, will not improve, and are likely to worsen, the lives of the women they intend to help. Additionally, such practitioners will promote unjustified cultural homogenization.

Are the look-alike phenomena APs?

I have argued that the existence of the look-alike phenomena does not drain the explanatory power from the concept of paradigmatic AP. Instead, the existence of these phenomena implies two things: that there are non-paradigmatic forms of AP and that some phenomena that seem to be APs may not really be APs at all. Let us begin with the idea that there are non-paradigmatic forms of AP. I pause to defend the idea that the look-alike phenomena that involve actual deprivation-perpetuation – caused by factual misperception (MAPs), forced tradeoffs (TAPs), and selective value distortion (SAPs) – should be called 'APs'. Recall the role of the concept of AP: the concept allows us to refuse to take first-person data as exhaustive welfare indicators, and it allows us to deny that a person's participation in her oppression amounts to consent. Deprivation-perpetuating preferences that are caused by selective value distortion (which I have called 'SAPs'), factual misperception (MAPs) and imposed tradeoffs (TAPs) are all instances of preferences from which we cannot easily read people's 'true' or 'deep' desires. A person with SAPs may fail to express adequate self-regard in some domains of life because of a failure to integrate her values. Think here of the Pirzada woman, who, despite dissatisfaction with lack of education, fails to recognize the inconsistency between her belief that she has an inferior education and her belief that God created men and women as equals. A person may perpetuate her oppression because MAPs may simply not know she could hope for more than what she has. Think here of the woman who does not recognize that her health problems come from genital cutting and thus believes that needing 15 minutes each time she urinates is 'normal'.[17] A woman with what I have called 'TAPs' may make welfare-maximizing choices about what to do, but we should be careful not to read her preference for the lesser of two evils as expressive of deep value for the option she chooses. Think here of the error that would be involved in assuming that Ackerly's Bangladeshi women did not value education.

In sum, in each of three look-alike phenomena involving deprivation-perpetuating preferences, a person's participation in injustice against herself does not reveal deep endorsement of it. The Pirzada women are dissatisfied with some of the effects of oppressive norms on them, the Senegalese women cannot be said to have consented to a practice whose effects they did not understand, and the Bangladeshi women would clearly prefer a situation in which they did not have to choose between literacy and income. I thus argue that the look-alike phenomena whereby a person continues her own deprivation demonstrate a need for a richer conceptual repertoire for discussing APs – one that recognizes APs besides the paradigmatic type.

The existence of the fourth look-alike phenomenon – the unfamiliar but welfare-compatible preference – reminds us to be cautious about assuming that every preference that appears deprivation-perpetuating actually is. The fourth look-alike phenomenon is clearly not a form of AP, since APs must be somehow inconsistent with the welfare of their bearers. The existence of unfamiliar but welfare-compatible preferences also suggests something about the prevalence of AP in the real world. If it is easy to mistake welfare-compatible preferences for APs, actual APs may be rarer than they initially seem. We need to avoid treating AP as the only possible explanation of what appears to be deprivation-perpetuating behavior by women from the global South.

Distinguishing the look-alike phenomena from paradigmatic APs in practice

Postcolonial critics draw our attention to four phenomena that are easily confused in practice with paradigmatic AP – unfamiliar wellbeing-compatible preferences, APs caused by factual misperception (MAPs), APs caused by forced tradeoffs (TAPs), and APs caused by selective normative distortion (SAPs). How can development practitioners avoid confusing these phenomena on the ground? The most basic practical lesson we can take from the critics is that people's beliefs and values cannot simply be 'read off' their expressed preferences. We need to discern (a) whether people's behavior is genuinely inconsistent with their basic welfare and (b) if so, what is causing this welfare-incompatible behavior. Discerning this requires intimate contextual knowledge, especially the kind derived from the first-person perspectives of people who seem to have APs.

Distinguishing types of AP in practice

Let us start with distinguishing among the cases where a person's behavior is indeed inconsistent with her basic welfare. Nussbaum and Okin suggest that the correlation between oppression-perpetuating behavior and paradigmatic AP is very strong; Nussbaum in particular sometimes suggests that choices to comply with oppressive norms reflect a complete lack of self-worth.[18] It is important for practitioners to acknowledge that deprivation-perpetuating behavior happens for a variety of reasons – ranging from lack of information to lack of options to partial value distortion. Ethical and effective development practice requires more than abstractly acknowledging this fact, however. Development practitioners need to know which *type* of AP they are dealing with – and not just that non-paradigmatic APs exist.

This is where first-person accounts of people with APs can be useful. Instead of making solitary conjectures about why intended beneficiaries do what they do, practitioners can ask them about their reasons for their behavior. Social scientists are already creating assessment tools to this end. For instance, Sabina Alkire has developed a questionnaire for measuring agency with women in Kerala. Alkire's questionnaire asks women about the extent to which each of the following motivates their behavior in various valuable domains of life: (a) feeling coerced into acting by another person, (b) feelings of guilt and shame, (c) the belief that the activity in question is valuable, and (d) the belief that the activity is valuable in the context of her other judgments about value (Alkire 2007, 174). One might object to attempts to gather first-person data on the grounds that people with APs make suspect judgments. I believe this objection overstates the effects that most APs have on people's abilities to understand their own situations. If I am correct that people can perpetuate their oppression without paradigmatic AP, many deprived people have at least some undistorted values. More importantly, many of the subjective data social scientists like Alkire want to collect are unlikely to be corrupted by value distortion. We are asking people to report why they do what they do, and such judgments, though they are reports about values, are not themselves normative judgments. A person can accurately report her motivations even if some of her values are problematic. For instance, a woman who believes that women should submit to domestic violence should still be capable of making the judgment that her reason for submitting has to do with her values about fate, God, appropriate femininity, or whatever the case may be.

Of course, all of us act on motivations that are not completely transparent to us, and practitioners should not presuppose that people's descriptions of their motivations are completely accurate. But practitioners can use subjective data combined with other indicators to form considered judgments about why people contribute to their deprivation. Further – depending on the extent to which we are concerned about practitioner misunderstanding – we can recommend that practitioners ask beneficiaries for feedback about their findings. There is certainly precedent for this within participatory development practice. Knowing why people engage in deprivation-perpetuating behavior – whether they are experiencing TAPs, MAPs, SAPs, or paradigmatic APs – can help practitioners understand whether their task is to effect total value transformation, to help women achieve harmony among their welfare-promoting values and their other values, to expose them to new information, to change their option scts, or something else entirely.

Practitioners who recognize the existence of non-paradigmatic APs will know that deprived people often retain elements of the capacity to criticize injustice and be more inclined to recommend interventions that build on this capacity. Practitioners dealing with women with SAPs will be most effective when they draw out women's existing negative attitudes toward patriarchal practices. A strategy that develops women's existing dissatisfaction is more likely to articulate the problems with the status quo in terms women can recognize and identify with. Consider two different ways of intervening in the lives of secluded women who support norms of female modesty but also are frustrated at their lack of education. In one, the practitioner attempts to bring out their frustration at their lack of education and ask them to think about the relationship between this deprivation and female modesty norms. In another, a practitioner works to convince women of the wrongness of seclusion. We can conjecture that the latter strategy would face more immediate opposition than the former – even from women who do, to some extent, support oppressive norms about modesty. The case for refusing to ignore existing critical capacities is even clearer in the case of MAPs and TAPs. Where women perpetuate their deprivation without value distortion, it is, at best, a waste of resources – and at worst condescending and ineffective – to focus resources on conscientization.

Development practitioners who recognize the extent to which people with APs can retain critical capacities will also design interventions that produce the added value of cultivating agency in the deprived. As most empowerment theorists argue, there is inherent value in the capacity to recognize social problems and strategize to solve them (Ibrahim and Alkire 2007, 384–385). Attempts to use subjective data to better understand people's reasons for perpetuating their deprivation will not only lead to more effective interventions. It may also have the additional benefit of cultivating agency in the deprived – which typically contributes to their wellbeing.

Determining whether AP is present at all

Inability to distinguish the look-alike phenomena from paradigmatic AP can lead development practitioners to two types of mistakes: misunderstanding the causes of deprivation-perpetuating behavior and seeing deprivation-perpetuating behavior where there is none. Specific strategies can offset this second type. One reason practitioners are likely to see APs where none exist is that they lack the contextual knowledge required to correctly ascertain the links between observed behaviors and their welfare effects. The popular solution to this problem, preferred in the early postdevelopment/participatory development literature, is to have practitioners be cultural insiders.[19] Familiarity with a cultural context is indeed likely to help practitioners understand the welfare impacts of practices and behaviors. However, without rehashing the literature on insiders and outsiders here, I note that cultural insiders also face particular barriers to understanding the welfare effects of practices in their own communities. Insiders may belong to classes or genders that make them poor interpreters of the behaviors of intended beneficiaries (imagine an insider male practitioner who attempt to understand women's reasons for submission to their husbands); they may fail to make causal linkages between welfare losses and practices that are relatively ubiquitous (think of the women who fail to isolate female genital cutting as a cause of many of their health problems); or they may be habituated to local injustices and thus fail to see harm where harm actually exists (think of the insider who believes husbands who do not beat their wives do not love them enough).

Cultural insider status does not neatly track the ability to discern the welfare impacts of behaviors. We should want practitioners who have and/or can gain contextual knowledge – which may include class, ethnicity, culture, and/or gender-specific knowledge. However, ideally, we should not trade this contextual knowledge for the capacity for moral scrutiny. We need practitioners who understand that cultural practices and beliefs are not beyond scrutiny simply because they are familiar or endorsed. They should also understand the theoretical point that there are a variety of ways to achieve any functioning required for a good human life as well as have a sense of the variety of concrete ways of achieving any single human functioning. We can take a practical example from Naila Kabeer's work on household decision-making. In some societies, training women to leave or ignore their husbands seems to be an effective way of helping them claim power, but in communities where familial ties are important to retaining other goods, this is a non-starter (Kabeer 1999, 460). In those communities, women may still exercise household decision-making power by deceiving their husbands[20] or by negotiating with them. We want practitioners who are aware that leaving or aggressively confronting one's husband are not the only ways women can exercise household decision-making power. We want them to refuse to assume that the desire not to aggressively confront one's husband bespeaks AP and we want them to see that, in some cultural contexts, household decision-making power will be most effectively increased through means that do not sever communal ties.

There is a second reason practitioners may see APs where none exist – the belief that a good human life is simply identical with the dominant conception of a good human life in her culture. Therefore, for instance, an American practitioner may believe that owning a large number of possessions is necessary for a good human life. She may thus see AP in any person who wants a simpler life.[21] Supposing that having a lot of stuff is not necessary for a good life, the American practitioner treats the preference as harmful just because it is foreign. It seems to me that the way out of this is to begin AP identification with an explicit idea about what functionings are required for a good human life. This way, it is neither the practitioner's unquestioned intuitions nor complete practitioner skepticism that guides the process of discerning deprivation. A process guided by unquestioned practitioner intuitions would allow importing a culturally specific conception of the good. On the other hand, a process focused primarily on asking practitioners to question their own judgments is likely to produce wide-ranging acceptance of injustice.

Still, as I have argued elsewhere (see Khader 2011), not just any conception of the good will work to offset the type of error we are discussing here. We need one that is substantively minimal and cross-culturally acceptable. By substantively minimal, I mean 'confined to basic levels of well-being'. Substantive minimality allows practitioners to recognize that individuals, once they possess a threshold level of certain important goods, can lead good human lives – despite combining those goods differently. Therefore, for instance, development practitioners need a conception of the good that allows us to say something like the following: a person needs to be able to make important decisions in her life without fear of domination, and a person who accepts domination has an AP. But a person need not have maximal independence to have acceptable preferences; she may live a good life and value duty to her family as long as her sense of duty is not maintained by violence or domination. Practitioners also need a definition of welfare that refuses to equate the practices of some particular culture with a good life. Arriving at such a conception is certainly difficult work, but we can imagine a list of goods such as Nussbaum's capabilities list, Ackerly's list of things people should be able to choose, or the list of basic human rights[22] playing this role. The postcolonial critics of AP draw our attention to the danger of concluding people are deprived because their way of life is unfamiliar. An explicit and appropriately formulated conception of welfare, coupled with intimate contextual knowledge, can help practitioners avoid confusing unfamiliar but welfare-compatible preferences with APs.

Conclusion

Reasoning about why and whether real-world people perpetuate their deprivation is not simple. Development practitioners should try to avoid Nussbaum's and Okin's mistake. This is the mistake of treating fairly thoroughgoing value distortion as the default explanation of why women in the global South appear to perpetuate their deprivation. Postcolonial feminist critics of AP draw our attention to three reasons people perpetuate their oppression that are distinct from paradigmatic AP – SAPs, MAPs, and TAPs. The critics also remind us that practices that are compatible with people's welfare may appear deprivation-perpetuating just because they are unfamiliar. Development practitioners need to consciously ask about both the extent to which people endorse their deprivation and whether they are actually deprived. Doing so will lead to more effective and ethical interventions – interventions that deny neither the complexity of cross-cultural moral judgments nor the complexity of people's reasons for colluding with injustice against themselves. Simplistic colonial descriptions of the psychologies of women in the global South are no replacement for the rich contextual attention required for interventions that can actually change women's lives. Postcolonial critiques can enhance our repertoire of possible explanations of behavior that appears deprivation-perpetuating. My hope is that this richer conceptual repertoire can help practitioners avoid colonial stereotypes and move toward more genuine moral encounters with the people whose lives they are trying to change.

Notes

1. The idea that the concept of AP derives from and perpetuates colonial stereotypes should be distinguished from the idea that development practice is irreducibly colonial. This latter claim targets the entire development enterprise rather than the concept of AP. It is out of the scope of this paper to consider whether development as a whole is colonial – though I concede that my practical recommendations would become indefensible if it turned out that all development interventions were immoral.
2. Though I share the view that some Western feminists evince colonial attitudes in their writing on APs, I disagree with Jaggar's (2005) claim, that Nussbaum and Okin *only* raise issues of AP in relation to third-world women. For instance, Nussbaum refers to the APs of women in the USA in a few places (see Nussbaum 1999), and Okin (1991) discusses how American cultural traditions socialize female children to accept inferiority in the household.
3. The argument that it is paternalistic to offer unsolicited opportunities to another person trades on the assumption that whether a person is deprived depends, to some extent at least, on whether she believes herself to be.

4. The implicit feminist argument about consent in cases of paradigmatic AP is that women cannot have consented to views about women's inferiority if they were never presented with alternatives to those views.

5. Baber (2007) makes a criticism of Nussbaum that is similar to Ackerly's. She argues that Afghan women practice child marriage because it is the best way to ensure income and safety for their daughters.

6. Strictly speaking, Nussbaum uses the capabilities list and not her own intuitions to judge that the women in her examples have APs. However, both Ackerly (2000) and Jaggar (2006) criticize the method by which Nussbaum arrives at the list on the grounds that it allows her to present her intuitions as the result of cross-cultural dialogue.

7. Narayan does not use the word 'ultrapatriarchal'. I use the word 'ultrapatriarchal', despite its problematic nature, to avoid implying that all non-Western cultures are 'more patriarchal' than Western ones.

8. The idea of a forced wellbeing tradeoff presupposes that achieving wellbeing means exercising a *variety* of functionings to some threshold level. Otherwise, trading one valued functioning for another would not necessarily constitute a wellbeing loss.

9. There are, of course, other benefits to literacy – such as the ability to interact as an equal with merchants and government officials – but I focus on the cognitive benefits for the simplicity of the example.

10. On the other hand, the choice to pursue income over education may reveal the individual's perception of the *relative* values of the goods (i.e. how she ranks them compared to one another).

11. Narayan mentions people may perpetuate their deprivation because of a realistic assessment of their (limited) options (2002, 425).

12. It may seem that the women in the Senegal case actually experience some value distortion. Perhaps it seems that they initially value the cultural significance of genital cutting enough to offset the health losses. But this objection misses the fact that the women were initially unable to factor the health losses into their assessments of the costs and benefits of circumcision; it is more apt to say that they initially perceived circumcision as without costs. They have always valued health but only understood the link between circumcision and poor health at the time of the intervention.

13. I do not deny that both of the interventions described in the above paragraph have normative goals. However, they differ in that one type of intervention involves only exposing people to non-normative facts.

14. I am personally skeptical of the idea that female seclusion is often compatible with basic well-being, but I am not skeptical either of the idea that seclusion can produce female solidarity or the idea that there are non-Western cultural practices that appear to decrease welfare but are actually welfare-enhancing.

15. Ackerly's argument in this particular example depends on the belief that the value of literacy is largely instrumental, but her theoretical point does not depend on the example.

16. My point here is not that autonomy is valuable (it may or may not be); it is rather about the form of Ackerly's argument. The argument form is 'practice x promotes good y,' rather than 'good y is not a good.' We might make the same point with a different, less controversial good in mind. I may, for instance, think someone eats food that is not nourishing because I am mistaken about the nutritional content of her food. I can be wrong about whether her food is nourishing while being correct that nourishment is a good.

17. This is a belief held by an actual woman interviewed by researchers in Sudan (cited in Chambers 2008).

18. For example, see Nussbaum's description of Jayamma (2001, 113), whose acceptance of domestic violence is read to show she does not know she is a human being with rights.

19. For an overview of what is at stake the insider/outsider practitioner debate, see Crocker (1991).

20. Kabeer draws examples of women exercising household decision-making power covertly from Margrethe Silberschmidt's ethnographic work in Kenya. She discusses women who refuse to plant crops where their husbands tell them to and then claim that it is because the seeds did not germinate in the husbands' desired spots (448). Silberschmidt also mentions that women sell the crops to middlemen behind their husband's backs in order to gain cash (1992, 49).

21. The idea that one can lead a good human life without large numbers of possessions, if true, has important implications for AP theory. AP theorists sometimes argue that being contented with what one has is a sign of AP. If we believe that one can have a good life without 'always wanting more', AP is a threshold concept. That is, we believe a person has APs if she does not desire some threshold level of important goods rather than if she does not desire *more* important goods.

22. The human rights regime has frequently been criticized for reflecting a distinctly Western conception of the good. However, most of these criticisms are of the idea that human rights are rights – not of the constituents of a good human life that are on the list of human rights. Rights language would not need to be a part of AP interventions founded on the human rights regime.

References

Abdi, Maryam Shiek, Guyo Jaldesa, and Ian Askew. 2008. *Managing and Preventing Female Genital Cutting (FGM/C) among the Somali Community in Kenya*. The Population Council. http://www. popcouncil.org/pdfs/frontiers/FR_FinalReports/Kenya_FGMSomali.pdf.

Ackerly, Brooke. 2000. *Political Theory and Feminist Social Criticism*. Cambridge: Cambridge University Press.

Ackerly, Brooke. 2001. *Political Theory and Third World Social Criticism*. New York: Cambridge University Press.

Ahmed, Leila. 1982. "Western Ethnocentrism and Perceptions of the Harem." *Feminist Studies* 8 (3): 530–534.

Alkire, Sabina. 2007. "Measuring Agency: Issues and Possibilities." *Indian Journal of Human Development* 1 (1): 169–175.

Baber, H. E. 2007. "Adaptive Preference." *Social Theory and Practice* 33 (1): 105–126.

Brenner, Johanna. 2003. "Transnational Feminism and the Struggle for Global Justice." *New Politics* 9 (3): 1–20.

Chambers, Clare. 2009. *Sex, Culture, and Justice: The Limits of Choice*. State College: Pennsylvania State University Press.

Crocker, David A. 1991. "Insiders and Outsiders in International Development." *Ethics & International Affairs* 5 (1): 149–173.

Ibrahim, Solava, and Sabina Alkire. 2007. "Agency and Empowerment: A Proposal for Internationally Comparable Indicators." *Oxford Development Studies* 35 (4): 379–403.

Jaggar, Alison. 2005. "Saving Amina: Global Justice for Women and Intercultural Dialogue." *Ethics and International Affairs* 19 (Fall): 55–75.

Jaggar, Alison. 2006. "Reasoning about Well-Being: Nussbaum's Methods of Justifying the Capabilities Approach." *The Journal of Political Philosophy* 14 (3): 301–322.

Kabeer, Naila. 1999. "Resources, Agency, Achievements: Reflections on the Measurement of Women's Empowerment." *Development and Change* 30 (3): 435–464.

Khader, Serene J. 2011. *Adaptive Preferences and Women's Empowerment*. New York: Oxford.

Khader, Serene J. 2012. "Must Theorizing About Adaptive Preferences Deny Women's Agency?" *Journal of Applied Philosophy* 29 (4): 302–317.

Mackie, Gerry. 2000. "Female Genital Cutting: The Beginning of the End." In *Female 'Circumcision' in Africa: Culture, Controversy, and Change*, edited by Bettina Shell-Duncan and Ylva Hernlund, 253–282. Boulder, CO: Lynne Rienner Publishers.

Mohanty, Chandra Talpade. 1995. "Feminist Encounters: Locating the Politics of Experience." In *Social Postmodernism: Beyond Identity Politics*, edited by Linda Nicholson and Steven Seidman, 68–86. Cambridge: Cambridge University Press.

Mohanty, Chandra Talpade. 1988. "Under Western eyes: Feminist Scholarship and Colonial Discourses." *Feminist Review* 30 (Autumn): 61–88.

Naples, Nancy. 2002. "Transnational Solidarity, Women's Agency, Structural Adjustment, and Globalization." In *Women's Activism and Globalization: Linking Local Struggles and Transnational Politics*, edited by Nancy Naples and Manisha Desai, 15–33. New York: Routledge.

Narayan, Uma. 1997. *Dislocating Cultures*. New York: Routledge.

Narayan, Uma. 2002. "Minds of Their Own: Choices, Autonomy, Cultural Practices, and Other Women." In *A Mind of One's Own: Feminist Essays on Reason and Objectivity*, edited by Louise M. Antony and Charlotte E. Witt, 418–432. Boulder, CO: Westview Press.

Nussbaum, Martha. 1995. "Human Capabilities: Female Human Beings." In *Women, Culture, and Development*, edited by Martha Nussbaum and Jonathan Glover, 61–105. Oxford: Clarendon.

Nussbaum, Martha. 1999. *Sex and Social Justice*. Oxford: Oxford University Press.

Nussbaum, Martha. 2001. *Women and Human Development: The Capabilities Approach*. Cambridge: Cambridge University Press.

Okin, Susan. 2008. "Gender Inequality and Cultural Differences." In *Global Ethics*, edited by Thomas Pogge and Keith Horton, 233–257. St. Paul: Paragon.

Okin, Susan Moller. 1991. *Gender, Justice and the Family*. New York: Basic Books.

Okin, Susan Moller. 1998. "Feminism and Multiculturalism: Some Tensions." *Ethics* 108 (4): 661–684.

Papanek, Hannah. 1990. "To Each Less Than She Needs, From Each More than She Can Do: Allocations, Entitlement, and Value." In *Persistent Inequalities: Women and World Development*, edited by I. Tinker, 162–184. Oxford: Oxford University Press.

Shiva, Vandana. 1989. *Staying Alive: Women, Ecology, and Development*. London: Zed Books.

Silberschmidt, Margarethe. 1992. "Have Men Become the Weaker Sex? Changing Life Situations in Kisii District, Kenya." *The Journal of Modern African Studies* 30 (2): 237–253.

Global surrogacy: exploitation to empowerment

Vida Panitch

Department of Philosophy, Carleton University, Paterson Hall, Ottawa, ON, Canada

Commercial surrogacy has gone global in the last decade, and India has become the international centre for reproductive tourism, boasting numerous high-quality and low-fee clinics. The growth of the surrogacy industry in India raises serious concerns of global gender justice, in particular whether the option is inordinately enticing for women who lack other remunerable options and whether the conditions are adequate and the compensation fair. In this paper I argue that the moral harm of global commercial surrogacy lies in the exploitative nature of transactions involving unequally vulnerable parties. More specifically, I argue that the practice exploits Indian surrogates on the basis of an inter-contractual failure of both justice and consent. I go on to consider an important objection to my use of exploitation as the relevant conceptual tool of analysis. The ethnographic challenge holds that the exploitation lens Occidentalizes surrogacy by conceptualizing the practice in universalizing terms, thereby eclipsing the particularities of the global surrogate's lived experience. I respond by showing that in fact the exploitation and the ethnographic models are not so at odds as they might seem. Provided we are careful in our use of the former to nuance our analysis by appeal to narrative evidence supplied by the latter, we are thereby best situated to identify and address the moral difficulties generated by commercial surrogacy under conditions of global injustice.

Introduction

Commercial surrogacy, either a criminal offense or prohibitively expensive for many first-world citizens, has gone global in the last decade. India has become the international centre for reproductive tourism, boasting numerous high-quality and low-fee clinics. The growth of the surrogacy industry in India raises serious concerns of gender justice, in particular whether the option is inordinately enticing for women who lack other remunerable options and whether the conditions are adequate and the compensation fair. The growing trend of global commercial surrogacy has thus compelled many feminists to reopen the moral debate that surrounded the domestic practice some 30 years ago in the wake of the infamous Baby M trial. But what is clear this time is that the practice must now be assessed alongside the additional moral dimension of global injustice.

In this paper I argue that the moral harm of global commercial surrogacy lies in the exploitative nature of transactions involving unequally vulnerable parties. More specifically, I argue that the practice is exploitative of Indian surrogates due to a failure of consent within the contract and of justice across contracts. The upshot of my argument is that this type of exploitation is made possible by an act of omission on the part of the Indian state, specifically that of failing to protect the negative reproductive rights of its female citizens. This is a failure the state need not rectify not by criminalizing the practice, I suggest, but by investing the profits of commercial surrogacy in female empowerment goals geared to the promotion of women's agency.

I go on to consider an important objection to my use of exploitation as the relevant conceptual tool of analysis. The ethnographic challenge holds that the exploitation lens Occidentalizes surrogacy by conceptualizing the practice in universalizing terms, thereby eclipsing the particularities of the global surrogate's lived experience. I respond by showing that in fact the exploitation lens and the ethnographic model are not so at odds as they might seem, provided we are careful in our use of the former to nuance our analysis by appeal to narrative evidence supplied by the latter. This is precisely the approach I attempt to take in this paper, as this approach best enables us to identify and challenge the moral difficulties generated by commercial surrogacy arrangements carried out against the backdrop of global injustice.

Global surrogacy

Recent statistics show that 1 in 10 (first world) couples are experiencing trouble conceiving a child naturally and are turning to various forms of assisted reproductive technology (ART), surrogacy prominent among them (Twine 2011). Commercial surrogacy is, however, a criminal act in many countries, including but not limited to Canada, the UK, France, Norway, and Italy. Although it is perfectly acceptable that a surrogate be reimbursed for costs associated with her diet, clothing or medical needs, it is illegal that she receive payment for her reproductive services specifically. This is a serious deterrent for many potential surrogates given that the process is, pun intended, quite labour intensive. And in the USA, where commercial surrogacy is legal (except in a few jurisdictions), it remains a luxury of the wealthy, ranging in cost anywhere from $50,000 to $120,000 (Busby and Vun 2010, 34).[1]

Women for whom other forms of ART have proven ineffective, who cannot find a friend or relative willing to act as an altruistic surrogate, and/or who cannot afford the rates charged by American clinics, are turning in growing numbers to the global surrogacy market. India in particular has become a transnational hub for reproductive tourism, with the city of Anand in the Western state of Gujarat as its nerve centre. Although California remains the destination of choice for wealthy reproductive tourists seeking gestational surrogates, clinics such as the Akanksha Clinic in Anand provide equivalent services for a fraction of the price. Dr Nayna Patel, who founded the clinic in 2003, has alone employed 167 surrogates who have given birth to 216 healthy babies (Twine 2011, 45). Wider estimates suggest that 100–150 babies are born to surrogate mothers in India each year (Gupta 2012, 32). The total cost to prospective parents is around $10,000, and reproductive tourism is estimated to be a $445 million business in India, with the potential to grow in the near future to anywhere from $2.3 to $6 billion (Gupta 2012, 43; Nolen 2009; Subramanian 2007).

The question is whether global commercial surrogacy is morally defensible. It might be regarded as such by appeal to the liberal freedom of contract, which protects the rights of adults of sound mind and full information to contract for the performance of services they desire at a price they are willing to pay, or to offer services for a fee they find compensatory. It might also be defended on the grounds that it provides a source of independent income to developing world women whose economic options are otherwise quite limited. And finally, it might be defended on the grounds that it satisfies the reproductive rights of first-world women who have chosen to delay child-rearing to pursue a career or other projects of interest to them and who would otherwise be biologically, legally, and economically prevented from exercising that right. But there is a decidedly more pressing reason to be concerned with the practice, namely that it exploits the reproductive labour of developing world women.

Exploitation, justice, and agency

In what manner might global commercial surrogacy be viewed as exploitative? Typically exploitation is thought to occur when one party to an exchange takes advantage of the other's vulnerability to deny her a share of the cooperative surplus. But this account does not seem to capture the reality of global commercial surrogacy. The contracting parents bear a financial cost, but gain a child; the surrogate endures insemination, pregnancy, and labour, yet can earn a significantly higher wage than her other opportunities afford. This is obviously not a case where benefits only accrue to the non-vulnerable party. Rather it seems that if we want to identify global commercial surrogacy arrangements as exploitative, we must be prepared to do so as cases of what Wertheimer (1996) calls mutually advantageous exploitation.

Mutually advantageous exploitative transactions need not necessarily be prevented, according to Wertheimer (1996, 207). What is relevant to assessing their wrongfulness, on his view, is how much each party benefits relative to where each began, as compared to the other. If both parties benefit relative to where they respectively began but Party A gains enormously while Party B only gains marginally, we might well think that B has been wrongfully exploited by A. What is equally relevant on his account is whether B fully consented to the transaction. If Party B was vulnerable in some sense such that her rationality or agency was impaired, we must deny that her consent was properly authoritative. We should therefore assess the permissibility of mutually advantageous exploitative transactions on the basis of whether they meet two conditions: (1) The Justice Condition: that the distribution of benefits and harms between Party A and B is not unfair in A's favour. And (2) The Consent Condition: that B's consent is valid (Wilkinson 2003, 173).

Let us take a closer look at the Justice Condition first. With respect to global surrogacy arrangements, we must presumably assess the satisfaction of this condition on the basis of whether the surrogate is under compensated relative to the gains enjoyed by the contracting parents. But it is immensely difficult to compare the value of a wage to a surrogate with few other financial options and the value of a child to an infertile couple. This difficulty might be due to the fact that we seem to be comparing vastly different kinds of goods. But even if we hold that the real value of the surrogate's wage lies in the fact that it enables her to provide for her own children, and thus take the value of children as the point of comparison, both parties seem to do decidedly better by it as compared to where they began, so injustice does not appear to be done by the exchange.

However, while comparing gains enjoyed by the specific parties to an exchange is definitely an important way of evaluating fairness, it is not the only way. Consider the example most often given in colloquial discussions of transnational exploitation, namely that of the multinational corporation that 'exploits' its developing world workers. The intuition we encounter when this example is voiced as paradigmatic is that developing world workers are exploited by multinationals who deny them the minimum wage guarantees, pensions, health benefits, work week standards, work place safety regulations, and union bargaining rights they afford their first-world employees. What this intuition points to, and what those who raise this example are in fact decrying as unjust, is not simply that the multinational walks away with a greater benefit share than its developing world workers, but that its *developing world workers enjoy so many less benefits than their first-world counterparts, despite taking on all the same burdens.*

This example is, of course, not totally analogous to global surrogacy arrangements (assuming we deny the claim that corporations are persons). But I offer it here not so much as an analogy as to tap into the widely shared intuition that when assessing transnational exploitation our considered judgments instruct us to look not only within contracts but also across them. In order to properly evaluate whether a transaction satisfies the Justice Condition it strikes us as intuitively necessary to make comparisons not just between parties to a specific contract but also between parties across contracts of a relevantly similar sort. What we are looking to see is whether the vulnerability of one party to an exchange is being used as grounds for denying her what a less vulnerable party, performing the same contractual service in a different geographical region, receives in exchange for her services. We feel we must compare the fairness of B's benefit share *inter*-contractually and not just *intra*-contractually. Let us attempt this type of comparison with global surrogacy.

In the USA, surrogates are typically high-school graduates, often college graduates, between the ages of 22 and 38, who earn anywhere from $25,000 to $40,000 (Twine 2011, 45). According to a series of empirical studies, they opt to become surrogates not due to an absence of other equally remunerable options but because this type of work allows them to help others, and provides them the time to pursue other interests (such as furthering their education or caring for their own children). They come from working class or middle-class families, and have never except in a few rare cases been on social assistance. Indeed they are screened out by surrogacy clinics if they articulate primarily financial motives. On the whole, American surrogates report having chosen the role willingly, against the backdrop of other reasonable options. They enjoy a post-birth grace period, a pre-birth opt out clause, compensation for expenses, quality medical care, legal representation, and the opportunity for an ongoing relationship with the child and its adoptive family (Busby and Vun 2010, 40–45).

In India, surrogates are typically between the ages of 18 and 45, with limited education and often illiterate, have two or more children, and can expect to earn between $1500 and $5000. In lieu of expenses, surrogates in Anand are housed in clinical compounds where all of their meals and activities are monitored, and from which they are not permitted to leave (nor indeed go downstairs) without clinical permission. Indian surrogates are poorer both relatively and absolutely than surrogates in the USA, almost all are living below the poverty line as defined by the Indian government, and the payment they receive is often unavailable to them via other forms of work in their communities (Pande 2009, 2010; Twine 2011). They have no legal representation and no rights under the contract: they do not have a grace period following birth within which they can change their mind, and they are guaranteed no compensation should they fail to produce a child (Busby and Vun 2010; Pande 2010). The Indian surrogate's motivation is almost exclusively financial, and her decision is, as Gupta (2012, 46) puts it 'generally made in a context of limited possibilities for self-expression or development, rising unemployment, lack of financial resources … low education levels, poverty, marginalization in labour and job markets, and patriarchal social and family structures'.

This comparison confirms that there is indeed a further dimension to consider when assessing the Justice Condition of an exploitation claim as it pertains to global surrogacy arrangements. Underpayment, or unfairness of benefit sharing, must be assessed not just relative to what the other party to the contract gains but relative to what other people performing the same type of work in other parts of the world receive as compensation. This is consistent with the widely shared intuition that people should not, for arbitrary reasons (including their geographic location) be denied parity of benefit for party of burden – or equal pay for equal work. When we evaluate fairness not simply within contracts but across them, or *inter*-contractually (Party B to another Party B) as opposed to just *intra*-contractually (Party B to Party A), it seems warranted to say that the Indian surrogate's benefit share does not satisfy the Justice Condition.

One challenge to this is, of course, that while the wages of Indian and American surrogates may be asymmetric, the purchasing power of their wages may not be; $3000 in Gujarat might make available similar kinds of opportunities as $30,000 does in California. But supposing we grant this (despite how unlikely it seems, and without a proper digression on purchasing power parity), we have not necessarily established satisfaction of the Justice Condition. Along with a wage, the benefits to an American surrogate include the freedom to pursue other interests while under contract, health care, travel and dietary expenses, legal representation, a post-birth opt-out clause, and the potential for a rewarding relationship with the adoptive family (Busby and Vun 2010). If we view these additional considerations alongside income as matters of benefit, I think we can safely reassert our conclusion that the Justice Condition currently goes unfulfilled in Indian commercial surrogacy arrangements.

A second challenge is whether my view implies that American surrogates cannot be exploited. On my account, how can we make such an assessment if there is no better-situated Party B against which to evaluate their benefit shares? To effectively answer this challenge, we must appeal to the distinction between ideal and non-ideal justice. To determine whether American surrogacy arrangements fail the Justice Condition, we would have to look to an ideal form of this type of arrangement, which might be established either by an enumeration of the kinds of goods morally appropriate for exchange with the kind of good a surrogate provides, or by appeal to the share of benefits ideally placed transactors would agree to under perfectly just conditions. Ultimately, I think the latter would be the right and possibly the necessary move to determining the genuine justice of surrogacy arrangements. But I do not think we need to make this move in order to claim that *global* surrogacy arrangements are unjust. As a claim of non-ideal theory it is enough to say that they are quite obviously *less fair* than first-world arrangements, and that first-world surrogates enjoy a share of benefits closer to the ideal, whatever it may be.

I have tried to show so far that we can only properly evaluate the Justice Condition of global surrogacy arrangements if we engage in inter-contractual as opposed to simply intra-contractual benefit comparisons. I now want to show with respect to the Consent Condition that, once again, we must look beyond the arrangement itself to appreciate its coercive nature. To do so, let me again take Wertheimer as my point of departure. On his view, surrogacy arrangements are con-sensual because the contracting parents do not threaten to make the surrogate worse off than she would otherwise have been if she refuses their offer. His view is that so long as they do not threa-ten her if she refuses, they do not coerce her. That their offer is extended to someone who is likely to accept it given her circumstances does not in and of itself entail coercion, he claims; their offer would only be coercive if they had a pre-existing obligation to improve her circum-stances without demanding anything in return.

Wertheimer gives the example of a passerby who offers to save a drowning swimmer in exchange for $10,000. This scenario is coercive, he claims, because the passerby has a duty to perform easy rescues without demanding payment (1996, 111). But, he continues, this type of example is of no use in evaluating surrogacy arrangements, because prospective parents have no such duty, and so do not coerce the surrogate by offering to improve her circumstances only if she provides them with a child. Wertheimer is of course right that where no duty is owed, no duty can go unfulfilled, and no coercive offer can be made to fulfil the duty only in exchange for some good. But to properly assess the satisfaction of the Consent Condition in global surro-gacy, we must again look beyond the contract itself.

Consider for a moment the very reason that American and Indian surrogates command such differential benefits. The prospective parents who contract the services of an Indian surrogate do so precisely because they can get away with offering her less. And they can get away with offer-ing her less because the Indian surrogate is not in a position to demand better terms. The genuine acceptance of an offer, I propose, depends on the ability to negotiate its terms. Authoritative consent is possible only where one is able to consent to the terms of the offer, and consenting to the terms of an offer depends on the ability to bargain for preferable terms. If the prospective Indian surrogate attempts to bargain for better terms, the offer will just be made to someone who will not. She cannot really be said to be in a position to bargain if any attempt to do so will result in the offer's disappearance. An inability to demand better terms, I am suggesting, is thus morally equivalent to an inability to refuse.

If a prospective surrogate wants to participate she must accept whatever terms are offered to her, no matter how meagre, how much more she might want, or how much more she might be entitled to. This is precisely the point we must be concerned with when assessing coercion: not whether the offer threatens to make her worse off, but whether she is able to negotiate for a fair share of benefits. The extent to which an Indian surrogate is forced to accept the terms as presented to her depends on the quality of her bargaining power. For Kabeer (1999, 436) this 'amounts not only to the ability to define one's goals, but to negotiate for what one wants', and where this ability is lacking, she avows, agency is thereby impaired. A surrogate's bargaining power can be assessed on the basis of her fungibility, her lack of alternative options, and the urgency of her own and her family's needs. I will provide evidence in the next section that Indian surrogates are indeed unable to negotiate for these reasons. For now suffice it to say with normative purposes in mind that insofar as an Indian surrogate cannot negotiate her arrangement's terms, the satisfaction of the Consent Condition is in doubt.

Wertheimer would respond that although the Indian surrogate may not be able to bargain for better terms, this is not the fault of the contracting parents. I am in agreement with him on this point. But this does not settle the matter. Reconsider his drowning example, and let us call it 'Drowning 1' or (D1). In (D1) the passerby who offers to save a drowning swimmer for $10,000 is flouting a duty to perform easy rescues without demanding anything in return, while parents who contract a global surrogate's services are not. But this conclusion is not so straightforward. On the one hand, prospective parents may indeed have obligations of rescue, or rather, of restitution to members of the third world for returns they have already enjoyed as members of the first world (Pogge 2001). And on the other hand, passersby may not have duties of easy rescue at all (and even if they do, rescuing someone from drowning is rarely very easy).

Let us therefore change the case to (D2): in which the person making the offer is a lifeguard. In this case the offer is coercive because lifeguards have an undeniable duty to rescue swimmers (on their beach during their shift) without demanding anything in return. But this version of events is not all that analogous to surrogacy either, because prospective parents clearly do not have the same duties of rescue as lifeguards. So let us change the scenario one more time to (D3): in which the lifeguard falls asleep, whereupon a passerby offers to save the drowning swimmer for $10,000. It is this last scenario that is most analogous to global surrogacy arrangements according to Wilkinson (2003, 174). And he is correct that the scenario is clearly coercive.

The parents in (D3) are not represented by the lifeguard but by the passerby. And in this case the moral blame lies, as it does in (D2), with the lifeguard. Here the passerby makes an exploitative offer, but is only able to do so because the lifeguard is flouting his duty of rescue; had he performed his duty no such offer could have been extended. This constitutes a case of what Wilkinson calls third-party omissive coercion (2003, 177). The right of rescue owed to the drowning man in (D3) is going unmet by the relevant duty-bearer, who is thus an omissive third party to the exploitative arrangement that is struck between the passerby and the swimmer. By analogy, the parents are able to demand whatever they want from the surrogate in return for the benefit they provide her precisely because the person (or institution) that bears a duty to provide her such benefits without demanding anything in return is failing to do so. Since what matters from the point of view of the Consent Condition is whether something to which the surrogate has a right is going unfulfilled, such that her ability to negotiate the terms of the offer is impaired, we can conclude that the arrangement fails to satisfy the Consent Condition as a result of third-party omissive coercion.

From exploitation to empowerment

Where both the Consent Condition and the Justice Condition are unmet, wrongful albeit mutually advantageous exploitation occurs. Both of these conditions, I have endeavoured to show, currently go unmet in global commercial surrogacy contracts. Both analyses, however, depend on looking beyond the arrangements themselves. With the Justice Condition, we must make inter-contractual distributive comparisons. With the Consent Condition, we must take account of a third-party coercive omission. The correct solution, I will now propose, depends on holding this third party to account. It is only in ensuring that this third party satisfies its obligation to improve the conditions of the surrogate's bargaining power that we will thereby be able to promote satisfaction of both the Consent and the Justice Conditions. The task now is to identify the relevant third party and the nature of its omission.

Insofar as the Indian surrogate is not able to negotiate, her right to make reproductive decisions free of coercion is going unmet. The United Nations and the World Health Organization recognize this when they assert

> the basic right of all couples and individuals to decide freely and responsibly the number, spacing and timing of their children, and to have the information and means to have a family if and how they so desire . . . this includes the right of all to make decisions concerning reproduction free of discrimination, coercion and violence. (UN 1994; WHO 2010)

On this account, negative reproductive rights carve out a sphere of autonomy within which the individual must be free to make, exercise and authorize genuine procreative choice.

The right not to be coerced is a central component of reproductive freedom, and it is insofar as a surrogate lacks adequate bargaining power that she is coerced, and insofar as she is coerced that she is exploited. Her exploitation thus depends on a violation of her negative reproductive rights. The point, to be clear, is not that her exploitation *constitutes* a rights violation, but that her exploitation is *made possible* by a rights violation. The surrogate's lack of bargaining power is attributable to some third-party omission, and the omission we must be concerned with, I suggest, is a failure to ensure the content of her negative right not to be reproductively coerced, an omission which itself amounts to a violation of that right. Negative rights are not rights we hold against other persons but against the state. They insulate a sphere of protection against interference by the state, its laws and its agents, and assure us state protection against those who seek to transgress our rights. Insofar as the surrogate's negative reproductive right is going unfulfilled, the Indian state is thus the relevant third party whose omission creates the coercion that enables her exploitation.

The Indian state could address the surrogate's right by criminalizing the commercial practice. Criminalization is not the only option available, however, nor necessarily the most effective, insofar as it would treat the symptom not the cause. Gupta (2012, 47) concurs with my assessment that

> the problem lies . . . with the lack of a powerful welfare state that fails to ensure the basic needs of its citizens and protect them from exploitation . . . Empowerment of vulnerable people to meet their basic needs and strengthen the capabilities and rights of vulnerable women . . . [is a thing for which] the state is accountable and must take action.

She concludes from this that the Indian state must ban commercial surrogacy. But if the true problem lies in the state's failure to secure the material and social conditions of Indian women's empowerment, the solution would seem to lie with a concerted effort on its part to satisfy their reproductive rights by securing the social and material conditions of their empowerment.

I propose that Indian women therefore have a right against their state that it employ a share of the profits of surrogate tourism to address the conditions of vulnerability that affect their bargaining power and make them open to exploitation at the hands of surrogate tourists.[2] A significant portion of the state revenue from commercial surrogacy in India ought to be invested in female empowerment goals, as measured by resource, agency, and achievement gains. These gains depend crucially on investment in women's education, literacy, health, employment options, and general resource shares (Kabeer 1999, 437). Foreign nations (especially those whose citizens take part in the surrogate tourism market), and aid agencies both domestic and global committed to empowering women and girls in the developing world, should exert what pressure they can on the Indian state to invest in these areas. And the Indian state must come to see this investment as necessitated by the reproductive rights of its female citizens.

It may be asked at this point whether the prospective parents themselves have no duty to the surrogate. Surely a passerby who sees a lifeguard asleep in his chair ought to jump into the water and save the drowning swimmer without demanding payment. But why should he do this if he can instead simply wake the lifeguard? Would the passerby then be morally culpable if, once the swimmer had been brought to shore safely by the party charged with this task, he asks to rent the swimmer's goggles for less than the going rate at the surf shop? Presumably not, so long as the swimmer is able to make a counter offer which the passerby is free to accept or decline. I do not want to take this analogy too far, but the point, I hope, is clear. It may well be wrong for the contracting parents to make an exploitative offer to the surrogate, knowing they can get away with doing so because the state is failing to satisfy her rights. But were the state performing its duty this offer would not be wrong to the extent that it could be turned down.

A further challenge, however, is that even if measures are taken by the relevant third party to improve the bargaining power of global surrogates, achievements in this regard will be years away. What should surrogate tourists do in the mean time? Should they offer more, or desist altogether? If they offer more, they might make the deal not only unreasonable but actually impossible to refuse. If they desist, they would deny an economic option to women with few others, and deny the state resources I am now proposing it use to fund empowerment goals. I suggest, again, that the correct response is an institutional one. As a short-term measure the state might consider drafting and enforcing a standard contract, with terms which could include legal representation, an opt-out clause, and standards pertaining to housing and leave. The terms might also include minimum wage guarantees, although these could continue to be considerably lower than in the USA as a means of maintaining foreign interest and preventing the problem of increased coercion. This contract would be mooted once Indian surrogates are in a position to demand better terms for themselves, but in the mean time it would accord them some protection, and demonstrate to them a commitment on the part of the state to secure their interests and on the part of the adoptive parents to fair dealings.

A standard contract of this sort could be included in the ART (Regulation) Bill and Rules, currently under consideration by the Indian Government. The current bill proposes regulations, for example, on the age of surrogates, the number of children they can bear, the conditions in which they are housed, on the installation of payments, etc. The standard contract I propose – along with a tax on surrogacy revenue to fund female empowerment goals – would address some of the key concerns that Indian women's groups have voiced with respect to the inadequacies of current bill which, in their view, constitutes a move in the right direction yet pays insufficient attention to improving the bargaining power of surrogates and to protecting women's reproductive rights in an ongoing way (SAMA Women's Health 2010).

I have tried to show in this section that the omissive third party in global surrogacy arrangements is the state, who is neglecting a duty to satisfy the rights of its female citizens, and who ought to rectify this failure by investing in female empowerment goals. This solution has the virtue of addressing not only the Consent Condition by calling to account the negligent third party, but of promoting satisfaction of the Justice Condition by empowering surrogates to demand terms more proximal to those enjoyed by their first-world counterparts. I have tried to address various challenges to my version of the exploitation argument as I have proceeded, but before concluding I want to consider the challenge that exploitation itself is a problematic conceptual tool for analysing global surrogacy.

The ethnographic challenge

The exploitation model I have employed for assessing and critiquing the practice of global commercial surrogacy is not without challenges. Indeed, a number of contemporary feminists working in the area of global and reproductive justice have argued that insofar as this lens is borrowed from earlier discussions of domestic commercial surrogacy it reflects the inherently Western nature of these discussions, thereby Occidentalizing in theory something that is increasingly non-Occidental in practice. This challenge has been voiced in diverse ways, but can be summed up with the claim that the Western ethical paradigm offers only two possible analyses of surrogacy. On the one hand, there is the standard interpretation of reproductive liberalism, of the sort represented by Wertheimer. On this view, surrogacy is a contract entered into freely by two parties who believe it will promote their well-being; it is thus an expression of reproductive autonomy and as such a morally defensible practice. On the other hand, there is the exploitation critique of the sort I have offered. On this view, the Indian surrogacy contract is rife with power imbalances and coercion; it is thus exploitative of women's reproductive labour, and as such a morally harmful and condemnable practice.

According to Banerjee (2010) both views are equally flawed and for the same reason. Reproductive liberalism holds that 'insofar as women have the right to decide whether and how to procreate, they have the right to do so by contract and against payment' (Fabre 2006, 192; quoted in Banerjee 2010, 109). The exploitation critique counters that 'Legal surrogacy contracts . . . coerce women into making a choice they do not prefer, yet cannot refuse because the price of refusal is too high' (Damelio and Sorenson 2008, 274). Banerjee argues that these two positions are essentially flip sides of the same coin, as the language of choice that both employ is itself the problem. The liberal lens ignores the power imbalances and socio-political conditions that can mar or impede the exercise of reproductive autonomy. But while the exploitation lens addresses these issues, it does so by treating the surrogate as a passive victim, at the mercy of superior forces external to her and in need of rescue by Western saviours. Claims Banerjee (2010, 111): 'Each of the perspectives . . . confines its attention to the active or the passive dimension of human existence. However, agency and passivity often do not constitute a dichotomy within our lived experience. We realize this further as we begin to listen to the voices of the transnational surrogates.'

This critique underlies the 'ethnographic turn' that surrogacy scholarship has taken in recent years, in response to increasing trans-nationalism. The ethnographic model focuses on narrative evidence supplied by global surrogates themselves, with the view to highlighting not the universal vice or virtue of the practice, but lived, complex, and concrete realities. As Bailey (2011, 723) puts it, the ethnographic model

> highlights the dangers of assuming *a priori* that Western moral considerations can be exported to account for the lived experience of surrogates in third-world settings . . . [It shifts attention] from questions about the moral status of new reproductive technologies . . . to an examination of their culturally specific meanings as part of lived, contested and negotiated relations.

According to Bailey, ethnographies steer clear of normative master narratives that reduce surrogacy into the two binary logics wherein contract pregnancy is either characterized as a free choice with a win–win outcome or an exploitative practice from which Indian women must be rescued (2011, 724).

The ethnographic turn owes much to Amrita Pande's scholarship, which centres on interviews she conducted in 2006 and 2007 with surrogates working in the Akanksha clinic in Gujarat. For her, conceptualizing the practice in terms of right or wrong is simply not consonant with the fact that surrogacy has become a reality for many Indian women, one that Western moral categories cannot help them negotiate or navigate. Pande (2009, 145) argues that

> Eurocentric portrayals of surrogacy cannot incorporate the reality of a developing country setting – where commercial surrogacy has become a survival strategy and temporary occupation for some

poor rural women ... in such a setting, surrogacy cannot be seen through the lenses of ethics or morality but as a structural reality, with real actors and real consequences ... If we are able to understand how surrogates experience and define their act ... it will be possible to move beyond a universalistic, moralizing position and to develop some knowledge of the complex realities of women's experience of commercial surrogacy.

While Bailey embraces the ethnographic critique of Occidental master narratives, she nonetheless cautions that we should be wary of the 'weak moral absenteeism' of ethnography, arising from the fact that it asks moral questions only when interviewees do so themselves (2011, 724).[3] She argues that to avoid a kind of paralysis in both theory and action we must employ ethnography in our moral work, but not take it as a replacement for our moral work. Banerjee concurs, and holds that Pande's observations should not be seen as obstacles to future moral thinking, but as central points to consider in future normative discussions (2010, 117). We need not, according to both Banerjee and Bailey, respectively, set aside normative responses to Indian surrogacy, but simply proceed cautiously by listening carefully to Indian women's voices and being mindful of the ways that Western normative tools can have harmful effects when exported (Bailey 2011, 726; Banerjee 2010, 111).

Let us therefore consider some of the findings of Pande's ethnographic research, and see whether the account I have offered here has indeed proceeded 'cautiously' enough – or rather, whether it has been consonant with the surrogate's own narrative experience. Consider the following sample of statements from Pande's interviews, and whether the narrative themes that emerge support my earlier assessments of both the Justice Condition and the Consent Condition:

Salma:	Who would do this? This is not work. This is *majboori* (a compulsion). Where we are now, it can't possibly get any worse. In our village we don't have a hut to live in or crops in our farm. This work is not ethical – it's just something we *have* to do to survive. When we heard of this surrogacy business, we didn't have any clothes to wear after the rains – just one pair that used to get wet – and our house had fallen down. What were we to do? (2009, 160)
Anjali:	I am doing this basically for my daughters. Both will be old enough to be sent to school next year ... I don't want them to grow up like me – illiterate and desperate. I don't think there is anything wrong with surrogacy. But of course people talk. They don't understand that we are doing this because we are compelled to do so. People who get enough to eat interpret everything in the wrong way. (2009, 161)
Pushpa:	They said they don't care how long they have to wait – I can rest for 1–2 years, as much as I want but they only want me to carry their baby ... Almost everyone who comes here for a surrogate wants me. Doctor Madam says to me, 'Why can't you get me 10–15 more Pushpas?' (2009, 163)
Salma:	Will (the adoptive father) said: 'You will make us happy and we'll make you happy.' His wife has become like an elder sister to me so I do just want to see them happy. They said they would build a house for us wherever we want to build it and however big we want it to be. I am having twins so perhaps they will build us two rooms instead of one. But I don't want to ask. (2009, 165–66)
Raveena (former surrogate, current surrogate counsellor and hostel matron):	My task is to make sure the clients don't get fooled – they get the best deal possible. After all they are investing all this money in my surrogates ... I teach my surrogates: don't treat it like a business. Instead treat it like God's gift to you. *Don't be greedy.* (2010, 979)

Let us consider these statements first from the perspective of the Consent Condition. The first two statements point to the narrative theme of *majboori*, or compulsion – a theme that reappears consistently throughout Pande's interviews (2009, 160–63). She observes that the surrogates have a sense of moral non-responsibility for their work, insofar as they do not feel free to refuse it given their and their family's more immediate needs. The mere existence of the offer exerts such a force given their circumstances that they do not feel as though they have either the luxury of assessing its morality or of turning it down even if they do find it to be morally lacking. The second two statements highlight the narrative theme of non-disposability, according to Pande (2010, 976–78). The surrogates emphasize their unique bond with the adoptive parents as a means of coming to terms with their actual fungibility. This narrative theme is evidence that the surrogates are themselves aware of their own disposability, but deny it in order to bolster their sense of self-worth.

Pande affirms the correlation between fungibility and a lack of bargaining power when she observes that since the surrogates cannot negotiate due to their disposability, they simply deny its relevance by seeing the arrangement as a gift relationship. Thus, in attempting to bolster their sense of self-worth, the surrogates downplay their own role as 'workers' entitled to a wage and fair contractual terms (Pande 2009, 163–66). The final statement reveals that the surrogates are discouraged from seeing themselves as workers. Whilst on the one hand being told that they are gift givers, they are on the other hand reminded of their disposability by the contract, the clinic rules, and their counsellors, who reaffirm repeatedly that they are just wombs that can easily be replaced. But the underlying instruction in both cases, according to Pande, is 'not to negotiate the wages' (2010, 977). Both the themes of *majoboori* and disposability are consistent with, and indeed lend considerable support to my earlier assessment of the Consent Condition; they are in fact the very reasons I gave for being concerned about the Condition's (non) fulfilment in Indian surrogacy arrangements.

And what do ethnographies tell us with respect to the Justice Condition? Most of the information we have about Indian surrogates comes from Pande's studies. This information substantiated my earlier discussion of the motivations, conditions, and benefits enjoyed by Indian surrogates as compared to their American counterparts. That Indian surrogates are for the most part illiterate, living below the poverty line, and ineligible for other work that might pay a comparable wage is made plain by Pande's research, as are the restrictive conditions under which their work is performed and the few protections they are afforded as workers. That I was able to engage in the type of inter-transactional comparative analysis necessary, on my view, to a proper assessment of the Justice Condition, was only made possible by paying close attention to the results of her ethnographic research.

I hope to have at least suggested from this that my analysis has endeavoured to be sensitive to the lived and concrete realities of surrogacy work in India. In this regard my analytic lens, albeit one of exploitation, satisfies Bailey's instruction that we ought to only engage in normative discussions of the practice in a global context so long as these discussions are centrally informed by ethnographic research. Of course, having tried to suggest here that my argument is properly sensitive to, and indeed depends on, the output of Pande's studies, I may not have yet satisfied the concern(s) Banerjee articulates. My focus is, of course, still very much on choice, and thus, in her view, as equally culpable as reproductive liberalism of endorsing a Western master narrative that denies autonomy by casting surrogates as helpless victims incapable of making sound judgments about their own identities (Banerjee 2010, 110).[4]

There are two responses I would like to offer here. On the one hand, I want to deny that my account depicts Indian surrogates as victims, at least in the sense that I think Banerjee understands the term. What I have argued is that, in being unable to bargain, Indian surrogates do not enjoy the kind of control over their work that would enable them to demand their just share. But in identifying the problem as one of third-party omissive coercion, I have not cast them as victims of anything other than an institutional failure on the part of the state to satisfy their rights. And insofar as anyone suffers a rights deprivation that leaves them open to exploitation, they are not so much helpless victims as citizens who bear entitlements that have gone unfulfilled. Our task is thus not one of rescue (despite the possibly misleading drowning example borrowed from Wertheimer) but of demanding that the relevant institutions ensure the satisfaction of their rights.

The other response I would like to offer is that I think the exploitation lens is not in fact the appropriate target of the ethnographic challenge. Banerjee claims it is the flip side of the liberal coin, and thereby equally insensitive to ethnography. But Pande herself employs the exploitation lens. She argues that we, and the surrogates themselves, must come to appreciate that they are not providing a gift but performing a type of 'gendered, exploitative, stigmatized labour' (2009, 169). Pande also claims (2010, 972) that it is only by

> identifying commercial surrogacy as labour, susceptible to exploitation like other forms of labour, and by simultaneously recognizing the women as critical agents, [that] we can deconstruct the image of the victim that is inevitably invoked whenever bodies of third world women are in focus.

Since Pande is adamant that surrogacy is a type of exploitable labour, what does she have in mind when she chastises 'Eurocentric' master narratives that depict the practice in black or white terms as universally right or wrong?

I think that what she actually has in mind, and so too Banerjee and Bailey, is in fact the *commodification* critique of surrogacy, which is unfortunately all too often misread as indistinguishable from the exploitation critique. Banerjee herself highlights the extent to which these two critiques are blurred when she says (2010, 109) that:

> one of the dominant western ethical arguments against surrogacy is the exploitation argument that is frequently linked to the commodification argument. It is argued by this camp of ethicists that surrogacy ... ends up reducing women to their wombs and defining them in terms of their reproductive capacities. Based on this aspect of commodification the surrogate is exploited because her labour and her body are judged on the basis of their use value.

Banerjee does not differentiate the two views, but it would be helpful to do so here.

The commodification argument is central to the views of many Western feminists who wrote on the ethics of surrogacy in the wake of Baby M (Anderson 1993; Overall 1987; Pateman 1998; Warnock 1985). The argument basically runs that commercial surrogacy is wrong because it involves the assignment of a market value to a good of inherent worth, and thereby reduces a human agent to the dollar value of her body parts. The deepest articulation of the view is offered, to my mind, by Elizabeth Anderson, who contends that when a woman contracts away control over her own body (as in a surrogacy or prostitution contract) she thereby also sells her agency, because in selling her body she sells the thing she requires to be agential with respect to. In selling control of her body, the surrogate sells her agency because she becomes something that can only be moved at, or by, the will of whomever has her under contract. If she cannot move except at the direction this other, she is inert, inanimate, objectified. In this respect what she sells is too valuable to be sold: she sells her *self* (Anderson 1993, 168).

The commodification critique is often assumed to entail an exploitation claim in the sense that since one cannot possibly be fairly compensated for the sale of one's *self* no terms of exchange could ever possibly be just. What I want to insist here is that *we can deny the commodification view and still make an exploitation claim*. That is, an appeal to exploitation does not have to depend on, nor presume the conceptual or moral veracity of the commodification argument. We can and indeed should deny, with Pande, that what is being sold is a good (physical or conceptual) as opposed to a type of labour. And we can deny, with Banerjee, that agency is inevitably and irrevocably undermined by the very act of sale. We can then go on to deny that surrogacy is universally wrong in every case based on the nature of the good being sold, but is instead morally problematic (and in some cases more so than others) based on the degree to which the choice is coerced and/or the labour unjustly compensated.

I suggest that when Banerjee singles out the exploitation view as the thorny Western counterpoint to reproductive liberalism, and when Pande rejects Eurocentric views that depict surrogacy arrangements as universally right or wrong, they in fact have the commodification view in mind. This view is the true flip side of the liberal coin, insofar as it asserts that agency is universally lost in the act, just as the liberal asserts that it is universally exercised in the act. Moreover, ethnography is essentially irrelevant to the commodification view's purely conceptual, and indeed conceptually Western, analysis of agency, value, and self. Because the view sees all surrogacy arrangements as equally morally problematic for the same conceptual reason, it denies that the concrete realities of women's lives and labours in developing parts of the world can or should affect our assessment of the harms they face as surrogates (Panitch 2013).

Thus, insofar as proponents of ethnography are concerned with Occidentalizing master narratives that ignore surrogates' lived experiences, focus exclusively on yet deny the very possibility of their agency, and deem all such arrangements equally morally impermissible for the same reason, it is the commodification view that is their best and presumably their intended target. But this type of view must not be mistaken for the one I have endeavoured to offer here. While the commodification view denies the very possibility of surrogate autonomy and thereby of just contractual terms, mine seeks to understand the realities of choice making under conditions of inequality, and to promote Indian women's autonomy as a means of enhancing the justice of transnational contracts. I conclude that the exploitation argument I have offered, properly distinct from the commodification view, is indeed part of the ethnographic turn, as it addresses the concrete realities of Indian surrogacy and focuses on women's empowerment.

Conclusion

In this paper I have argued that the moral harm of global commercial surrogacy lies in the exploitative nature of transactions exhibiting a failure of both justice and consent, made possible by a failure on the part of the Indian state to protect the negative reproductive rights of its female citizens. This is a failure, I argued, that it ought to rectify by investing the profits of surrogacy in female empowerment goals geared to the promotion of women's agency and bargaining power. I went on to show that my account is properly sensitive to, and indeed depends on, information about the concrete, lived realities of Indian surrogacy, and in this regard differs from the commodification critique which should be understood as the true Occidental opponent of ethnography.

Notes

1. This fee includes wages along with brokerage and legal fees. Only three US states impose criminal sanctions on payment: Michigan, New York, and District of Columbia.

2. The idea here is a tax levied on the profits of surrogacy to generate revenue for addressing empowerment goals. The tax should not be paid directly by the consumer, and would thus not be a luxury or sales tax, as surrogacy arrangements must not be viewed as involving the purchase of a commodity (see Panitch 2013). The tax would be levied, rather, on those whose income derives from surrogacy transactions, such as physicians, clinicians, brokers, and matrons (and possibly the surrogates, but an infinitesimal rate). It might thus be a form of graduated income tax (or possibly a value-added tax). The cost would be transferred to the consumer, but would not come close to paralleling first-world surrogacy rates nor thereby undercut the state revenue earmarked for empowerment.
3. A perhaps more troubling concern is the seeming impossibility of genuine impassivity on the part of the ethnographer herself. While she may resist ethical judgments in her scholarship, is she truly capable of complete benignity in her choice of questions (which can have a leading quality), or in her reactions during the interviews themselves (which may in turn influence what interviewees to further choose to confide)?
4. This is only a partial response to Banerjee, whose concern is also that the exploitation lens shares in the same dualistic (mis)conception of relational power as the liberal, wherein a surrogate either has it or does not. Banerjee proposes a turn to ethnography precisely so as to enrich our understanding of what it might mean to 'empower' (2010, 110 and 117–119), but her nuanced discussion of the distinction between 'power-over' and 'power-with' is unfortunately beyond the purview of my project to consider in depth here.

References

Anderson, Elizabeth. 1993. *Value in Ethics and Economics*. Cambridge: Harvard University Press.
Bailey, Alison. 2011. "Reconceiving Surrogacy: Toward a Reproductive Justice Account of Indian Surrogacy." *Hypatia* 26 (4): 715–741.
Banerjee, Amrita. 2010. "Reorienting the Ethics of Transnational Surrogacy as a Feminist Pragmatist." *The Pluralist* 5 (3): 107–127.
Busby, Karen, and Delaney Vun. 2010. "Revisiting the Handmaid's Tale: Feminist Theory Meets Empirical Research on Surrogate Mothers." *Canadian Journal of Family Law* 26 (1): 13–93.
Damelio, Jennifer, and Kelly Sorensen. 2008. "Enhancing Autonomy in Paid Surrogacy." *Bioethics* 22 (5): 269–277.
Fabre, Cecile. 2006. *Whose Body is it Anyway? Justice and the Integrity of the Person*. Oxford: Clarendon.
Gupta, Jyotsna Agnihotri. 2012. "Reproductive Biocrossings: Indian Egg Donors and Surrogates in the Globalized Fertility Market." *International Journal of Feminist Approaches to Bioethics* 5 (1): 25–51.
Kabeer, Naila. 1999. "Resources, Agency, Achievements: Reflections on the Measurement of Women's Empowerment." *Development and Change* 30 (3): 435–464.
Nolen, Stephanie. 2009. "Desperate Mothers Fuel India's Baby Factories." *Globe and Mail*. February 13. Accessed February 10, 2013. http://www.theglobeandmail.com/news/world/desperate-mothers-fuel-indias-baby-factories/article1153508/?page=all.
Overall, Christine. 1987. *Ethics and Human Reproduction*. Boston: Allen & Unwin.
Pande, Amrita. 2009. "Not an 'Angel', Not a 'Whore': Surrogates as 'Dirty' Workers in India." *Indian Journal of Gender Studies* 16 (2): 141–173.
Pande, Amrita. 2010. "Commercial Surrogacy in India: Manufacturing a Perfect Mother-Worker." *Signs: Journal of Women in Culture and Society* 35 (4): 969–992.
Panitch, Vida. 2013. "Surrogate Tourism and Reproductive Rights." *Hypatia* 28 (2): 274–289.
Pateman, Carole. 1998. *The Sexual Contract*. Stanford: Stanford University Press.
Pogge, Thomas. 2001. "Eradicating Systemic Poverty: Brief for a Global Resources Dividend." *Journal of Human Development* 2 (1): 59–77.
SAMA Women's Health. 2010. "The Regulation of Surrogacy in India: Questions and Complexities." Accessed February 10, 2013. http://samawomenshealth.wordpress.com/2011/04/23/the-regulation-of-surrogacy-in-india-questions-and-complexities/.
Subramanian, Sarmishta. 2007. "Wombs for Rent." *Macleans*. Accessed February 10, 2013. http://www.macleans.ca/article.jsp?content=20070702_107062_107062.
Twine, Frances Winddance. 2011. *Outsourcing the Womb: Race, Class and Gestational Surrogacy in a Global Market*. New York: Routledge.
UN (United Nations). 1994. "Report of the International Conference on Population and Development (Cairo)." Accessed February 10, 2013. http://www.un.org/ecosocdev/geninfo/populatin/icpd.htm.

Warnock, Mary. 1985. *A Question of Life: The Warnock Report on Human Fertilization and Embryology.* Oxford: Basil Blackwell.

Wertheimer, Alan. 1996. *Exploitation*. Princeton: Princeton University Press.

WHO (World Health Organization). 2010. "Reproductive Rights and Reproductive Health." *Progress Report: Reproductive Health Strategy.* Accessed February 10, 2013. http://www.who.int/reproductivehealth/publications/general/rhr_10_14/en/index.html.

Wilkinson, Stephen. 2003. "The Exploitation Argument against Commercial Surrogacy." *Bioethics* 17 (2): 169–197.

Globalization and ecofeminism in the South: keeping the 'Third World' alive

Anupam Pandey

International Development Studies Program, St. Mary's University, Halifax, Canada

The aim of the article is to discern, highlight and thus, give due cognizance to a pattern of women's environmental activism in the South that is getting increasingly pronounced with the exacerbation of injustice and inequality due to globalization. It provides a theoretical critique and highlights a practical resistance offered by a materialist ecofeminism in combating the devastating impact of multi-national corporations in the South in the fields of food and nutritional security, deforestation and the protection of biodiversity. Furthermore, it develops a philosophical and moral critique of globalization by elucidating an ecofeminist ethic which highlights an alternate model of development, based on care and responsibility. The research combines a literature survey of the most recent and classic ecofeminist theoretical literature and practical case-study based on the author's own field research on ecofeminist activism prevalent in the Garhwal Himalayan region of India.

Introduction

While there are many different facets to globalization, this article focuses on economic globalization, i.e. the imposition of neo-liberal economic reforms and structural adjustment programs (SAPs) on the 'Third World' and the entry of multi-national corporations (MNCs) into hitherto unopened markets. Recent studies suggest a decrease in the overall income disparity in the world in the previous decade, attributable to economic globalization (Firebaugh and Goesling 2004; Conference Board of Canada document 2013). However, it needs to be clarified that this is due to an increase in the economic growth rate, engineered largely by the middle classes of India and China. But Africa, Latin America, former Communist countries as well as the rural poor of India and China, who comprise the majority of their population, have been largely untouched by the visible benefits of globalization (Milanovic 2012). Not only have the promised 'trickle-down' benefits of redistribution in the Third World not materialized, but free trade has meant greater material disparity between the rural and the urban sectors and greater polarization of classes within countries cutting across the North and the South (Wade 2004). The fact remains that the single most important factor determining the income of an individual, even in this globalized world, is still 'location' or citizenship. What it means literally is that the income of a citizen of the bottom-most rung of the developed world is still more than the income of even a middle-class citizen of most developing countries (Milanovic 2012).

Under such iniquitous circumstances, this capitalism-led globalization is the focus of attack by activists and masses and critique from the academic community. It is in this context that ecofeminism makes an especially relevant contribution. In fact, it would not be an exaggeration to suggest that ecofeminist activism guided by ecofeminist ethics has developed a thorough analysis of the global capitalist economy. It has brought ecofeminism to the center-stage of environmental, feminist, developmental and social movements and concerns. It offers a moral critique as well as a practical guide for resistance to the globalization of poverty and exploitation by international capital.

The aim of this article is to highlight the critical role of ecofeminist activism against this highly iniquitous globalized economic regime that has been imposed on the South. This article elucidates a Southern materialist ecofeminism and its underlying ethic and uses it to examine vital questions pertaining to economic globalization such as its impact on the environment, women, livelihoods and poverty, food and nutritional security, deforestation, protection of biodiversity, indigenous knowledges and cultures. It develops a critique of globalization from the perspectives of the most vulnerable and worst-affected victims of economic globalization – Southern women and nature. However, the article goes beyond critique and resistance to highlight an alternate way of life, world-view and world which is non-exploitative and harmonious with respect to nature as well as fellow human beings. The article is divided into three sections: the first section highlights just what is ecofeminism and extrapolates on a materialist ecofeminism which is the analytical perspective of this article as well as the means of resistance that is employed by ecofeminist struggles in the South. The second section is again divided into two parts: the first part develops a theoretical analysis of how economic globalization erodes the Third World's very basic means of survival, and the second part bases itself in the author's field research to enumerate examples of a Southern materialist ecofeminist resistance to the same. The final section details the philosophical and ethical bases of ecofeminism and just how it is a vital tool for analyzing, critiquing and resisting the injustices of capitalist globalization. Moreover, it shows how relationships can be based on care, ethics and responsibility in a world where capitalism is fast eroding such values.

The article relies on the more recent as well as classic ecofeminist theoretical literature and the author's own field research in 2004 on the ecofeminist activism in the Garhwal Himalayan region of India. The theoretical approach or ecofeminist lens is that of a Southern materialist ecofeminism which analyses women's environmental activism at the cusp of class as well as gender but cannot be reduced to either. It is an activism borne out of the triple discrimination of being a woman, colored, possibly indigenous and deeply materially deprived. The aim of the article is to discern, highlight and thus, give due cognizance to a pattern of women's environmental activism in the South that is getting more prominent with the excesses of globalization.

A southern materialist ecofeminism

Ecofeminism has come to the fore to resist the injustices of globalization as a social movement, a philosophy and a value-system, a practice and a way of life and in the context of this article, an analytical perspective for political analysis. A basic definition of ecofeminism is that androcentric ideologies are responsible for environmental degradation as well as the oppression of women and that, under specific circumstances, it is possible to posit an alliance between nature and women. One of the central postulates of ecofeminism is that male domination and modern civilization are built on the colonization of women, nature and nations (Mies 1986). While there is no dearth of the feminist critique of the capitalism–patriarchy nexus, ecofeminism's distinctiveness lies in its specific inclusion of nature in the category of the exploited. However, the importance of nature can best be appreciated if we *attempt to see nature as an attribute of all that man believes is inferior to himself and undeserving of being granted agency.* Here, by man, we refer (most often, though not exclusively so), to the white, male, Western elite in its treatment of women, colored peoples, colonies and the socially and materially underprivileged. The list is by no means exhaustive and leaves room to include all those who are less powerful and are deemed as being without any intrinsic, independent worth in themselves. The reason as to why all of these categories are considered part of nature is to be found in their embodied status, i.e. they are directly involved in production at the most primary level, as raw material or labor. Thus, nature itself, should be seen as a deeply exploited category, but it is simultaneously a metaphor for all subordinated groups that are subjugated and abused by the powerful.

This article makes the same argument as ecofeminist Plumwood (1993, 2002) noted that nature has been a very broad and shifting category and has encompassed many different sorts of colonialisms. She emphasizes the need to develop an integrated framework for the critique of both human domination and the domination of nature. Thus, the most significant contribution of ecofeminism lies in its ability to plumb to the very depths the entire process of 'othering' and explore the reasons for its very origins. Second, it shows the interconnections between all kinds of oppressions.

Within ecofeminism, there exist a variety of schools of thought. However, for furthering the aims of this paper, what I support and espouse as a tool for analysis of globalization is a Southern materialist ecofeminism. The concept of a materialist ecofeminism has been theorized in considerable depth and detail by both, Western (Warren 1990, 1993; Plumwood 1993; Mellor 1996, 1997; Cuomo 1998; Mies and Bernholdt-Thomsen 2000; Salleh 2004, 2009) as well as Southern ecofeminists (Shiva 1989, 1993; Nanda 1991; Mies and Shiva 1993; Pandey 2010). The core argument for both counterparts is indeed the same. They argue that the affinity that exists between women and nature is a result of the situation and the specific context women find themselves in, vis-à-vis nature. It is in the course of carrying out their materially and socially constructed duties and responsibilities, i.e. their daily household chores and work outside, in conjunction with nature, that women develop a special relationship with nature. A materialist ecofeminism serves as the antidote to all criticisms of 'essentialism' leveled against ecofeminism (Agarwal 1992, 2007; Jackson 1993, 1996) since it is based on the given material circumstances of women agents and their labor as the crucial factors in determining their emotional, physical and practical world and world-view. It does not lay any claim to any universality or essentialism based on biology or culture. It argues that both women and men are essentially materially constructed agents and it is this very aspect that shapes their relationship with nature. Wrapped around this kernel of the material existence of human beings is the performance of their socially constructed role and responsibility, i.e. their gendered division of labor.

However, the materialist ecofeminist perspective is popularized by, but not restricted to, Southern ecofeminists. It is based on a bonding between nature and women based on the labor of women, particularly in the Third World, where women are in a practical as well as emotional/spiritual interaction with nature on a daily basis. Nature is not just a source of survival for them but also shapes their identity. The vast majority of such practicing ecofeminists live in the South by sheer dint of their colonial past and neo-colonial present of exploitation and poverty. Thus, materialist ecofeminists focus on capitalist patriarchy, highlighting the devastating impact of capitalist structures on nature and, as it follows, the lives and livelihoods of poor women across the planet. The fundamental contribution of materialist ecofeminism is that it shows that feminist social justice cannot be achieved without addressing environmental issues in the South.

It is based on the simple yet entirely practical idea of the 'environmentalism of the poor', a term popularized by Martinez-Allier (2002) which is obviously the case here considering that women and girls constitute 70% of the world's poor (*WILPF, Women and Human Rights Seminar* 2008). In response to all 'essentialist' allegations where women are connected with nature, Ariel Salleh is worth quoting when she states that:

... the global majority of women do labor hands-on with nature and cope with the matter/energy transformations of their own gestational bodies. In this respect, academic attempts to silence woma-nist voices sound rather like class denial on the part of the serviced, time free and often childfree, middle class feminists. (2009, 13)

A Southern materialist ecofeminism is often traced back to the Chipko (which means 'to stick to' in Hindi) movement in the 1970s when women clung to trees in the early 1970s in the Garhwal Himalayas in India, in defiance of axe-wielding contractors. This unprecedented Gandhian tactic employed by illiterate, poor peasant Garhwali women was a strategic move to protect not just their forests but also their own survival and subsistence.

However, detractors (Guha 1989; Guha and Gadgil 1992) have characterized Chipko as a peasant movement, rather than an ecofeminist one. Determining the veracity of this criticism was the key factor in the selection of the Central Himalayan region of Tehri Garhwal as the region for a suitable case-study by the author. The entire province of Uttaranchal in India and the Garhwal region in particular is characterized by female-headed households. Due to lack of employment opportunities and underdevelopment within the region, outmigration of men is rampant, which in turn, puts the burden of running the household as well as providing for it largely on the women agents. The aim of my case-study was to garner what kind of ecofeminist activism (post-Chipko) existed, if at all, in the region. It was also a splendid representation of the aspirations and point of view of one of the most marginalized and overlooked sections of society – illiterate, peasant women of the Third World. In the course of my research, I discovered that the region is rife with examples of single-handed and collective ecofeminist courage, initiatives and activism (even if the women may not use the exact terminology to describe their ideology or its concomitant actions). In this context, it is my contention that ecofeminism continues to be a rather under-valued concept.

In the context of off-setting the ills of globalization, the Kenyan Green Belt movement is a key example of a materialist ecofeminist intervention. In the 1970s, Nobel prize winner, Dr Wangari Mathaai witnessed a shocking proliferation of commercial plantations of coffee and tea which had replaced the sacred fig tree, which is the cornerstone of the Kenyan subsistence economy, and the streams fostering the biodiversity had all but dried up. While the men embraced the export-oriented model, the women were left outside the pale of this 'development', and struggled to keep their families alive.

Maathai was roused into starting the Kenyan Green Belt Movement, which went on to plant an unprecedented 30 million trees. While the Kenyan Green Belt Movement is considered a key aspect of the food sovereignty as well as afforestation movement, one of the most significant effects it has had is the resistance to the global problem of climate change and altered patterns of rainfall in East Africa. Large tracts of African land have been sold for mining for petroleum, lumber, diamonds, bauxite, etc., and the production of export crops of cocoa, tea and coffee (Brownhill 2007, 36) to MNCs denying the African people the right to use their own forests and grow food. In the words of Dr Wangari Mathaai:

Working with women to teach them how to plant and care for trees was a natural choice. Throughout Africa, women are the primary caretakers, tilling the land and feeding their families. As a result, they are often the first to feel the effects of environmental damage as vital resources become scarce and even unusable. Environmental dégradation forces them to walk farther to attain wood for cooking and heating, to search for clean water, and to find new sources of food as old ones disappear. When the environment is destroyed, plundered, or mismanaged, it is their quality of life, and that of their children and families, that is ultimately undermined. (2008, 25)

Similarly, she states, 'Protecting the environment is often seen as a matter of luxury, when it is a matter of life and death' (Mathaai 2008, 26).

While it is important to highlight that a materialist ecofeminism is based on actual material circumstances as well as labor of the agent, it is equally important to state that this does not negate the role of identity or consciousness. In fact, one is able to better understand ecofeminist activism in the South by taking it into account, where sometimes it becomes impossible to distinguish between the spiritual and material aspects of people's lives and ecofeminist struggles and resistances. The land on which people are born is more than 'resources' to them; it is regarded as their mother and people's identity is intrinsically linked to it since generations have been reared on it.[1]

Similarly, in the course of the author's research in the Garhwal Himalayas, a constant theme that emerged was the stance of the Garhwali women who practice an alternate perspective where profit is not the guiding motive (detailed instances of the same will be discussed in the paper ahead). Instead, what is in evidence is a nurturing, caring attitude toward humans and nature. It is based on a recognition of mutual dependence and intrinsic worth of each living being. While such a relationship might find its origins in material reasons, it goes well beyond them to establish deep bonds and relationships (where the forest is regarded as the mother's home) that far surpass the understanding of the market economy. In the words of Escobar, 'The house economy is fueled not by acquisition but by material activities the central principle of which is to care for the base' (1995, 168). Nature is regarded as not just a resource, but a source of life, strength and courage and a great emotional and spiritual anchor.

The ecofeminist critique of global economic restructuring: in theory

Ecofeminist authors have developed nuanced critiques of the impact of globalization on the issues of environmental and social justice, livelihoods and employment, gender division of labor, feminization of poverty, biopiracy and intellectual property rights, toxic dumping, inequality on environmental issues between the North and the South, etc. Ecofeminist struggles as a response to these issues are numerous and increasing in number and taking place wherever people have a stake in protecting their lives, livelihoods, resources and identities from being usurped by capitalism and MNCs.

Much of ecofeminist thought that critiques globalization overlaps with critical feminist international political economy literature. The neo-liberal market economy is premised on the 'rational' economic man where rationality is equated with profit-maximizing. However, much of the work that women do lies outside the formal, productive sector of the market economy. Most women in the Third World are involved in subsistence providing roles and much of their maternal and reproductive role does not conform to the instrumental rationality of the neo-liberal economy. A materialist ecofeminism further elaborates on this by showing exactly *how* women fulfill this subsistence providing role through their direct interaction with nature, which is the very means of their survival and that of their dependents.

Ecofeminism also suggests the need for critical re-evaluation of women's domestic work. It means redefining reproductive and regenerative labor as empowering, creative work which needs special skills and intelligence and recognizes the woman as an agent and subject in her own right. While feminists have made significant critiques of the global political economy in terms of highlighting women's exploitation by showing how they are being impacted by economic liberalization, a materialist ecofeminist perspective deepens the critique to create a more nuanced understanding by showing just *how* the lives and livelihoods of poor women in the Third World are dependent upon nature and exactly how globalization impacts them through environmental degradation and usurping resources that are rightfully theirs. In both cases, it extends the critique to include questions of planetary survival and that of the well-being of other species, which are often overlooked by the anthropocentric nature of social sciences.

In this manner, an ecofeminist critique of globalization is imperative because first, it provides us with a practical critique that is premised on the real lives and actual experiences of women in the Third World. It is based on two simple practical facts: (1) that female-headed households, dependent on nature for subsistence and survival, outside the pale of the formal economy, are increasingly the norm, in the Third World and are, therefore, the most vulnerable victims of globalization and (2) it cautions us against the severe ecological consequences of this mindless consumerism and pursuit of growth rates in the West as well as countries with burgeoning middle classes such as China and India; Second, it serves us with a philosophical and moral critique using an ecofeminist ethics to show how the Third World, women and nature are all being fed into the global economy where a privileged minority is passing on the costs of its extravagant lifestyle to the rest of the world. Ecofeminists emphasize the need to revalue women's roles, responsibilities, tasks, all that is associated with the feminine, pay due respect to nature and develop a non-exploitative attitude toward the Third World as a genuine alternative to the current model of neo-liberal globalization. Finally, it provides us with an epistemological critique where women's indigenous knowledges are being marginalized and face extinction and need to be revived.

Thus, there is abundant literature developed by materialist ecofeminist authors that focuses on just how the state, capitalism and patriarchy have come together, in the modern era, to the detriment of women and nature in the form of globalization. This capitalist globalization is largely engineered by, and benefits predominantly, a rich, white, male elite of the developed world and has entailed, largely, the globalization of poverty, greed, exploitation, a profit-seeking motivation, alienation from nature and fellow beings, environmental pollution and degradation. Its hardest-hit victims, clearly, are the poor women in the Third World and nature (Shiva 2000, 2001, 2005a; Sydee and Beder 2001; Eaton and Lorentzen 2003).

Ecofeminism in the developing countries often manifests itself as women's struggles against state-guided 'development' or state-abetted 'globalization' or market 'reforms' in a bid to save nature and in the process secure their own survival and that of their families. Here, women use a gendered perspective in the light of their own experiences as agents situated in a complex web of relationships with humans and non-humans. Guided by their critical and self-reflexive subjectivity, these women have developed nuanced critiques and practical struggles. Women in the Third World are the active link between nature and men. The woman forms the backbone of a self-sustaining organic, rural economy in less-developed countries. Women play the larger role in agriculture, animal husbandry, provision of fodder and soil rejuvenation in Third World societies. However, their work is largely 'invisible' because national economic statistics such as gross national product make no record of work hours or subsistence production which lies outside the formal economy. Much of women's work is actually involved in subsistence and sustenance and involves considerable skill and knowledge to manage a self-sufficient micro-economy of the household under acute resource constraints. It is indeed worth quoting that more than two-thirds of the world's unpaid work is done by women, the equivalent of 11 trillion dollars (approximately half of the world's gross domestic product) (Salleh 2009, 20). Thus, despite the fact that women in the Third World are responsible for the survival of families, their work heralds no formal recognition. In fact, even socially, it is devalued because it is regarded as the mundane backdrop to 'real' work done by men who produce for the commercial economy and bring in cash. It is worth noting that women in Africa account for 80% of the agricultural sector in Africa (Denton 2002, 10), but the mechanization of agriculture and cash-cropping has resulted in the devaluing of the subsistence farming that their work involves (Tickner 1992). Rural women, mainly farmers, are at least 1.6 billion and represent more than a quarter of the total population. Women produce on average more than half of all the food that is grown up to 80% in Africa, 60% in Asia and between 30% and 40% in Latin America and

Western countries. It is also worth noting that the number of rural women living in poverty has doubled since 1970 (International Federation of Agricultural Producers document, available online http://rural-women's-day.org/).

Ecofeminist resistance and regeneration: in practice

The focus of ecofeminist resistance is food and nutritional security, protection of biodiversity and forests, and cultural diversity based on women's indigenous knowledges. As a consequence of the imposition of the neo-liberal economic reforms, food security in the Third World is seriously compromised and subsistence farming peasant women and their families have been the worst affected.

An important fallout of the monopoly by agri-business empires is the loss of biodiversity due to the introduction of mono-cropping for cash and the market. In the course of the author's field research, it was learnt that the traditional method of farming in the Garhwal region has highly evolved techniques of maintenance of soil fertility and biodiversity through special fallowing practices and crop rotations, pest and weed management, genetic resource management, etc. For instance, the practice of 'barahnaja' which literally means '12 foodgrains' involves cropping 12 grains together in each plot of land. This helps to maintain soil nutrition, water levels and alkalinity, and such a multi-cropping pattern means food and nutritional security among the Garhwalis. It also meant the conservation and growth of biodiversity. The farmers used to exchange seeds with each other and never relied on the market. All of these practices have nearly been made extinct with the introduction of the market economy and economic reforms. However, they are now being revived in order to get over the dependence on the market. Once again, it is important to stress that Garhwal is a region where farming is exclusively in the hands of women who provide for their families through subsistence farming. Increasing commercialization of agriculture has meant a dire threat to the food security of the region because the farmer is now forced to produce for the market and a new pattern of mono-cropping for cash crops is visible. This has meant increasing poverty and hunger in the region as well as the loss of its traditional biodiversity. Similarly, even the nutritional security of the region is greatly compromised because of changing dietary patterns with the introduction of cash crops into the economy. Only about two decades ago, the most popular crops were *Mandua, Jhangora* and *Sanwa* – all of which are extremely nutritious millets that provided adequate nourishment for the labor-intensive lifestyle of the agricultural labor. However, once this self-sufficient economy was penetrated, the favored crops were wheat, rice, maize, soybean, potatoes, etc., because the Garhwalis felt that they would have a better market for it in the plains. It has meant the near extinction of indigenous, local crops. The introduction of high-yielding variety (HYV) seeds by has meant the end of a self-sufficient traditional system of agriculture. Earlier, the farmer spent nothing on seeds or fertilizers, but the introduction of the HYV seeds has meant that the cropping pattern has changed globally to monoculture, cash crops and a dependence on the market for seeds that need high quantities of fertilizers. The introduction of SAPs in various parts of the Third World has meant the entry of agri-business MNCs which have further increased the vulnerability of the small farmer by gaining control over the seed sector (Shiva 1993, 2005a, 2005b, 2013; Kothari 1997). In response to these harmful changes, a campaign called 'Beej Bachao' (BBA) or 'save the seeds' began in the Hemvalghati region of Tehri Garhwal where only two to three indigenous rice varieties were left, and most of the *barahnaja* fields had been converted to new soybean. Today, some 126 varieties of rice, 8 of wheat, 40 of finger millet, 6 of barnyard millet, 110 of kidney beans, 7 of horsegram, 8 of traditional soybean and 10 of French beans are being grown. No chemical inputs are being provided. The characteristics of each – growth, resistance, special properties and so on – are being carefully observed.

Varieties with desirable properties, such as high productivity and resistance, are being propagated among other farmers. Seeds are bartered and exchanged. Practices like *barahnaja* are being revived and encouraged in place of the new soybean (Kothari 1997; Shiva 2005a). For farmers, seeds do not just mean future crops and the source of food. Seeds are about culture and the storage of history. Protecting seeds is to protect biodiversity and cultural diversity which involves festivals, ceremonies and community-based activity.

Furthermore, the women of Garhwal have resorted to organic farming in order to rejuvenate an ancient practice of farming which is increasingly being lost to younger generations due to the breakdown of the traditional system of a closed and self-sufficient economy in the mountains. With the support of an non-governmental organization (NGO), called Mahila Samakhya (MS), 50 villages in Tehri Garhwal took up organic farming in order to reverse the trend of using ever-increasing volumes of fertilizers in their farming methods.[2] Women farmers complained that the more quantity of fertilizers they used, the more they needed; this was proving to be entirely financially destabilizing for an economy that is based primarily on barter and exchange with little or no access to the market. Therefore, they decided to make organic manure and since then have been reducing the quantity of chemical fertilizers steadily. Simultaneously, a decision to ban the use of polyethylene bags was taken because of their non-biodegradable nature (Rawat 2004). The women farmers of these 50 villages have resorted to preparing special organic manures that have insecticide and pesticide properties by using recycled kitchen waste, cow dung and other biodegradable garbage, humus, grasses and leaves and earthworms. Since the introduction of organic farming, the women report a highly increased fertility in soil and better produce, the usage of much less quantity of manure and greater moisture retention in the field and are pleased that waste matter is being disposed off in a highly constructive and productive manner (MS unpublished document on *Organic Farming and SAWERA*, n.d.).

Women and afforestation in Garhwal

A materialist ecofeminist explanation is the key to understanding women's afforestation activism throughout the world. Examples of ecofeminist activism contributing to planetary survival can be seen in the Chipko movement of a peaceful Gandhian protest of hugging trees in defiance of axe-wielding contractors in the Himalayan regions in India (Shiva 1987). Yet another example of women-led afforestation movement is that of 'Maiti' in the Himalayan ranges, which shall be discussed in more detail below.

Garhwali women have had a tradition and history of a very close bond with their forests. That their survival is dependent on the flourishing of their forests is abundantly clear to them. Thus, in numerous parts of the region they have taken on the responsibility of the welfare of their forests. Such measures have included massive tree plantation, and forest conservation and protection against forest fires, illegal logging and encroachments. Women have been active participants and leaders in the struggle to preserve their lands, knowledges and resources. While women have often risen to the defense of their forests in rather heroic actions, a more common observation is the simple practice of planting trees and creating new forests. Afforestation is an integral part of the women's struggle to rejuvenate their forests because it translates into a direct attempt to revivify their own lives. For instance, in many villages in Tehri Garhwal, women had to trudge as much as 10 km to fetch grass and wood. There are numerous instances where women collaborated with other villages and created their own oak forests. Oak is the most popular choice in trees for afforestation since it is the best source of fodder and fuel in a self-sustaining subsistence economy (Unpublished MS document, *Our Traditional Forest*

Management Techniques: Some Success Stories from Village Sanghas, Tehri Garhwal, Mahila Samakhya Office, 2004).

Maiti is yet another recent innovation in an ancient tradition of tree plantation by women in the state of Uttaranchal in Garhwal. Maiti has become a movement that is spanning 5000–6000 villages in the state itself and is now spreading across many other states within India. The word Maiti is derived from the word 'mait', which means 'mother's home' in Garhwali language. It stands for the forests, which are regarded by women as their mother's home once they are married and sent off to live and adjust in their husband's families. The forest is regarded as a place of refuge by the women of Garhwal and consequently as not just a resource but a deep emotional anchor and source of emotional strength and spiritual guidance. Essentially, Maiti is, in its present form, a movement where young unmarried girls of each village have taken on the responsibility of planting trees that provide shade, fruit, fodder and fuelwood for the village. The girls plant the trees and nurture them until the day of their marriage. Each tree is blessed by the priest performing the marriage rites and the parents are asked to not only regard it as a memory of their daughter, but look after it as their daughter herself. What this has meant in real terms is massive afforestation in Garhwal. Due to the emotional aspect highlighting the bond between the daughters of the village and these trees, they are at much less risk of being cut down (Kalyan Singh Rawat. Originator of Maiti movement. 2004. Interview by author, 11 June. Tape recording. Interviewee's residence. Dehradun).

An ecofeminist ethics and alternate way of life

Much of the Third World is simply not equipped to participate in this globalized economy on an equal footing, and is instead being plundered by Northern capital that has colonized its human and natural resources and knowledge base accrued over centuries. Indigenous natural resources with which people have fostered organic relationships and deep attachments are used wastefully by MNCs. Needless to say, the worst affected by this mindless destruction of nature and indigenous knowledges are those who are dependent on it for their very subsistence. With their livelihoods taken over by modern mechanized technology, their knowledge bases and means of survival rendered redundant or usurped by capital, the poor, especially the women, are rendered powerless. The fundamental point that a Southern materialist ecofeminism makes is that the question of the survival of people in the South simply cannot be separated from nature.

While the West makes an issue of reclaiming or waiving the Third World debt, ecofeminists such as Salleh (2009) bring to notice the largely ignored issue of 'ecological and embodied debt'. The concept is based on the argument that reparations are due to the Third World by the developed world due to the simple fact that the latter is built on the depletion of the ecological resources and labor power of the former, which takes us back to ecofeminist Maria Mies's thesis that the First World is built on the backs of nature, women and colonies (1986).

Ecofeminism offers a choice – a choice of an alternate way of life that situates itself within the organic whole and finds its fulfillment in its spiritual and material union with nature. It offers a world where the prosperity of one would not be built on the exploitation of the weak and the voiceless but instead on caring, nurturing and symbiotic relationships. Other than practical considerations of planetary survival and well-being, the chief reason for adopting an ecofeminist approach is the desperate need for ethics and the need to examine carefully what should be the relationship between the self and the other in a bid to formulate relationships between different sexes, races, nations and species. It is the overcoming of the self/other dualism which is key in the construction of an ecofeminist ethics (Plumwood 2002, 2000, 1993). The self/other dichotomy itself is a reflection of the central dualism of reason/nature wherein reason tends to exclude and other all that it regards as 'nature'. It takes on an instrumental attitude toward nature which in turn, involves hyper separation between the self and the other so as to highlight the differences rather than acknowledge the similarities or the bonds and connections between them.

In these globalized times, it would mean trying to find an alternative to the current relationship of absolute domination and hierarchy between those who stand to gain the most from it and those on whose backs this prosperity is created. Therefore, what we have, essentially, is a minority of the world's populations and nations – specifically a white dominated, predominantly male population of the First World (and also women, though to a lesser extent), exploiting the natural resources and peoples of the former colonies in the Third and Fourth Worlds. It is in this context that ecofeminism makes an invaluable contribution to the relationship between the self and the other by postulating a relationship of symbiosis, trust and care without conflating one's identity with that of the other. In the words of Plumwood:

> We need a concept of the other as interconnected with self, but as also a separate being in their own right, accepting the 'uncontrollable tenacious otherness' of the world as a condition of freedom and identity for both self and other. (Plumwood 2002, 201)

Thus, Plumwood emphasizes the fact that it is possible to display a sense of political solidarity with the other (in this case, nature) without conflating/dissolving one's identity with that of the other (Mallory 2009). However, I would argue that the relationship between nature and women in the Third World is even more complex and nuanced than that. Although it is very much based on this respect for 'difference' that Plumwood espoused, it goes beyond it, wherein there exists a deeper sense of unity and bonding because in the Third World, it is impossible to separate the spiritual identity of the woman agent from her material bases (Mies and Shiva 1993, 16–20; Sydee and Beder 2001, 288). In an ecofeminist ethic, the concept of possession and ownership, as in property ownership in capitalism, is replaced by a sense of belonging. 'Belonging is the bond of love and respect that grows in the course of the seasons' (Stephens 2009, 64). The justificatory support deploys care rather than will to power as legitimator and resonates with the forms of attachment that grow through adjusting oneself to a place and its inhabitants (Stephens 2009, 64). He denounces the zero-sum game of continuous accumulation (Stephens 2009, 65).

That globalization is guided by market forces has meant a complete abandonment of ethics in the actual procedural implementation of neo-liberal economics in the countries where it has been introduced. The neo-liberal economy is dangerously bereft of morals and, therefore, takes no responsibility for the other. It is this perverse individualism that endangers human security as well as moral existence that demands immediate redressal. This is only possible by introducing ethics into the underpinning philosophy as well as procedural and substantive aspects of globalization. It is in this context that ecofeminism has a key role to play in the revitalization of ethics in the era of globalization.

A Southern materialist ecofeminism helps in providing an alternate perspective on globalization and development, which is not a replica of the Western bourgeoisie model. It offers an indigenous version of development where human beings exist in symbiotic relationships with nature and each other, where economic indicators do feature but are not the only means of calculating levels of development. It would involve a more holistic attitude to development challenging Western individualism and taking into account the well-being of the entire community of humans and non-humans.

A materialist ecofeminism is premised on its ability to care for the other based on taking due cognizance of already existing relationships and bonds between the carer and the caree and recognizes individuals as real, concrete individuals embroiled in a network of relationships. It is a way of life that boldly acknowledges dependence on the other and is unafraid to assume responsibility for the same. On the other hand, the globalized economy sees nature as well as human lives as nothing more than a resource to be exploited, used or, at best, 'managed'. In striking contrast, ecofeminism is based on its ability to care for those on whom we depend for our very survival and flourishing. This endeavor to reject the tendency to other is at the very heart of an ecofeminist ethics of care. It broadens the scope of human social relations to situate them within the context of nature. It is premised on the need to derive ethics from ties, bonds, attachments and relationships that grow out of the moral agent's relationships to others around herself. A materialist ecofeminism bases itself in the recognition of the fact that human beings are both social *and* natural beings and, therefore, situates human beings within a specific context of relationships within society and nature.

Ecofeminism is characterized by an ethics of diversity as evidenced in the work of leading Southern ecofeminist Vandana Shiva, who argues for the preservation of a diversity of livelihoods, social roles and species and equality in diversity (Shiva 1989, 1993). The origins of the need to preserve diversity can be seen clearly in the recognition of the interconnections of the complex biotic web and interdependencies among all species. Ecofeminism is based on an analysis of how nature is systematically backgrounded and reduced to an instrument in the neo-liberal discourse especially with respect to the market economy where it is taken for granted as the backdrop to market activities, as an absorber of wastes and provider of limitless resources, noticed only when it threatens to fail to perform as required (Plumwood 1993, 283, 2000). Ecofeminist ethics condemns such an instrumental attitude toward nature and all that qualifies as nature.

In fulfilling our moral responsibility toward nature, we are only recognizing all that makes us human, i.e. our relationships with others within a complex web of society and ecology that make us what we are. It is through these bonds that we formulate principles of ethics in the first place. In realizing our ethical responsibilities toward the interests of human and 'non-human' others, we are securing our own material and emotional needs.

The critical point that a materialist ecofeminism is making with respect to globalization is that it is not anthropocentric practices but practices of *certain* humans that are the cause of environmental degradation. Cuomo (1998) names corporate greed, militarism, nationalism and ethnocentrism to be some such questionable practices. To this, I would like to add capitalist globalization and the processes associated with it as the biggest culprits responsible for jeopardizing nature as well as human existence because issues of social justice cannot be separated from ecological issues.

Conclusion

This article has striven to show how a Southern materialist ecofeminism is responsible for the practical survival of the Third World and how there is a global pattern of localized as well as global resistance against the injustices of globalization. Thus, in Bolivia, women's peasant organizations led the national campaign against genetically modified organisms (Potter and Zurita 2009, 231); in Brazil, women of the Via Campesina attacked eucalyptus plantations of a pulp mill to protest against the impact of monoculture (*Rainforest Movement Bulletin* 2006); in Honduras and El Salvador where the highest rates of environmental degradation are visible, women have put up stiff resistance to the coffee export-oriented model of development (Lorentzen 1995, 57); in Argentina, native Wichi and Guarani women have raised their voices against the commercially lucrative soybean production because their traditional crops of sugarcane, tobacco, citrus and kidney beans have been removed, resulting in deforestation (*World Rainforest Movement Bulletin* 2009). Similarly, in the preservation of biodiversity, women have taken on a huge role through seed conservation whether in India through Navdanya, or Korea through Korean Peasant Women's Association or Thailand where indigenous rice varieties are fast being made extinct due to the entry of the MNCs (Seed Forum document 2008, 6).

A Southern materialist ecofeminism can be a vital tool in resisting the excesses of globalization because it is the only resort of the most marginalized of sections of human society – the poor, illiterate women of developing countries who have no recourse but to depend on nature for their very survival and that of their families. Moreover, it argues that all relationships in this globalized world need not be zero-sum games and that our material/physical and spiritual/emotional/ideological needs cannot be divorced from each other. In more practical terms, it is an argument that suggests the need to situate human beings within their material, social and ecological context in order to resolve the environmental crisis as well as the crisis of human relations since both are mutually constitutive. A materialist ecofeminism helps us understand the very roots of oppression and the whole process of othering and exploitation (whether in the context of globalization or any other) and the solution lies in replacing humanity within nature. Ecofeminist ethics point to the need to look beyond one's own rights to see that individual rights, interests and identity are completely interlinked with those of others – whether human or non-humans. Ecofeminist ethics can be a vital aid in reversing the trend of desensitization, instrumentalization and fear of responsibility in globalization and hold the promise of a meaningful and real stability and flourishing of humans and non-human others.

Notes

1. A case in point is that of the resistance put up by local population and their Gandhian agitation against the 'Narmada Bachao Andolan' (save the River Narmada movement) in the state of Gujarat in India. The chief tactics of resistance involve civil disobedience, non-payment of taxes, hunger strikes (fast unto death) and peaceful protest marches. As a mark of protest against their displacement from their ancestral lands by the Government of India's big dam project, in January 1991, June 1993, and more recently as well, the villagers and their leaders decided to submerge themselves with the rising waters of the river (a protest called *atma-jal samarpan*), but were forcibly removed by the police apparatus of the state (Peterson 2010; 12–13). The movement has completed 25 years of struggle in 2010 and its chief proponents are winners of the Right Livelihood Award/Alternate Nobel (Friends of the River Narmada, http://www.narmada.org/index.html; Bisht 2011).
2. This project is called sustainable agriculture and women's empowerment through rural approach (SAWERA) and is supported by United Nations Development Program which, in turn, relies on an NGO called MS for facilitating the project at the grassroots level. The word SAWERA itself means 'dawn' in Hindi. The main aims of this project, that started in 2000, are to provide food security and self-sufficiency, protection of biodiversity, finding alternative and better means of food grain production and distribution and helping the woman farmer find her identity as a farmer and the 'main worker' in the field (MS unpublished document, n.d.).

References

Agarwal, Bina. 1992. "The Gender and Environment Debate: Lessons from India." *Feminist Studies* 18 (1): 119–158.

Agarwal, Bina. 2007. "Gender Inequality, Cooperation and Environmental Sustainability." In *Inequality, Cooperation and Environmental Sustainability,* edited by Jean-Marie Baland, Pranab Bardhan, and Samuel Bowles, 274–313. Princeton: Princeton University Press.

Bisht, Medha. 2011. "Conceptualising Movements against Large Dams Case Study Analysis of NBA Strategies, Linkages and State Response." *Social Change* 41 (3): 397–411.

Brownhill, Leigh. 2007. "Gendered Struggles for the Commons: Food Sovereignty, Tree-Planting and Climate Change." *Women and Environments* 74/75 (Spring/Summer): 34–37.

Conference Board of Canada. 2013. "The Conference Board of Canada Document, 2003 World Income Inequality: Is the World Becoming More Unequal?" Accessed October 2. http://www.conferenceboard.ca/hcp/hot-topics/worldinequality.aspx

Cuomo, Chris. 1998. *Feminism and Ecological Communities: An Ethic of Flourishing.* London: Routledge.

Denton, Fatma. 2002. Climate Change, Vulnerability, Impacts and Adaptation: Why does Gender Matter. *Gender and Development* 10 (2): 10–20.

Eaton, Heather, and Lois Ann Lorentzen. 2003. *Ecofeminism and Globalization: Exploring Culture, Context and Religion.* Oxford: Rowman & Littlefield.

Escobar, Arturo. 1995. *Encountering Development: The Making and Unmaking of the Third World.* Princeton, NJ: Princeton University Press.

Firebaugh, G., and B. Goesling. 2004. "Accounting for the Recent Decline in Global Income Inequality." *American Journal of Sociology* 110 (2): 283–312.

Guha, Ramachandra. 1989. *The Unquiet Woods: Ecological Change and Peasant Resistance in the Himalaya.* Berkeley: University of California Press/Oxford: Oxford University Press.

Guha, Ramachandra, and Madhav Gadgil. 1992. *This Fissured Land: An Ecological History of India.* Berkeley: University of California Press.

Jackson, Cecile. 1993. "Woman/Nature or Gender/History? A Critique of Ecofeminist 'Development'." *Journal of Peasant Studies* 20 (3): 389–419.

Jackson, Cecile. 1996. "Still Stirred by the Promise of Modernity." *New Left Review* 217 (May/June): 148–154.

Kothari, Ashish. 1997. *Conserving India's Agro-biodiversity: Prospects and Policy Implications.* Gatekeeper Series no. 65. London: International Institute of Environment and Development.

Lorentzen, Lois Ann. 1995. "Bread and Soil of Our Dreams: Women, the Environment and Sustainable Development – Case Studies from Central America." In *Ecological Resistance Movements: The Global Emergence of Radical and Popular Environmentalism*, edited by Bron Raymond Taylor, 56–69. Albany: State University Press of New York.

Mallory, Chaone. 2009. "Val Plumwood and Ecofeminist Solidarity: Standing With the Natural Other." *Ethics and the Environment* 14 (2): 3–21.

Martinez-Allier, Joan. 2002. *The Environmentalism of the Poor: A Study of Ecological Conflicts and Valuations.* Cheltenham: Edward Elgar Publishing.

Mathaai, Wangari. 2008. "An Unbreakable Link: Peace, Environment and Democracy." *Harvard International Review* 29 (4): 24–27.

Mellor, Mary. 1996. "Myths and Realities: A Reply to Cecile Jackson." *New Left Review* 217 (May/June): 132–137.

Mellor, Mary. 1997. *Feminism and Ecology.* New York: New York University Press.

Mies, Maria. 1986. *Patriarchy and Capitalist Accumulation on a World Scale.* London: Zed Books.

Mies, Maria, and Vandana Shiva. 1993. *Ecofeminism.* London: Zed Books.

Mies, Maria, and Veronika Bennholdt-Thomsen. 2000. *The Subsistence Perspective: Beyond the Globalised Economy.* London: Zed Books.

Milanovic, Branko. 2012. "Evolution of Global Inequality: From Class to Location, from Proletarians to Migrants." *Global Policy* 3 (2): 124–133.

Nanda, Neeru. 1991. *Forests for Whom? Destruction and Restoration in the U.P Himalayas.* New Delhi: Har-Anand Publications.

Pandey, Anupam. 2010. "Greening Garhwal Through Stakeholder Engagement: The Role of Ecofeminism, Community and the State in Sustainable Development." *Sustainable Development* 18 (1): 12–19.

Peterson, M. J. 2010. "Narmada Dams Controversy." International Dimensions of Ethics Education in Science and Engineering. Accessed October 8, 2013. http://www.umass.edu/sts/ethics.

Plumwood, Val. 1993. *Feminism and the Mastery of Nature.* London: Routledge.

Plumwood, Val. 2000. "Integrating Ethical Frameworks for Animals, Humans and Nature: A Critical Feminist Eco-Socialist Analysis." *Ethics and the Environment* 5 (2): 285–322.

Plumwood, Val. 2002. *Environmental Culture: The Ecological Crisis of Reason.* London: Routledge.

Potter, George Ann, and Leonida Zurita. 2009. "The Peasant Women's Movement in Bolivia: 'Bartolina Sisa' and COCAMTROP." In *Rural Social Movements in Latin America: Organizing for Sustainable Livelihoods*, edited by Deere Carmen Diana and Fredrick S. Royce, 229–247. Gainesville: University of Press of Florida.

Rainforest Movement Bulletin. 2006. "Brazil: Peasant Women's Action Against Monoculture Eucalyptus Plantations on International Women's Day." *WRM's Bulletin* N° 104, March 2006. Accessed October 25, 2013. http://www.wrm.org.uy/oldsite/bulletin/104/viewpoint.html

Rawat, Sudha. 2004. NGO worker at *Mahila Samakhya* in Bhilangana block of Tehri Garhwal. Interview by author, 3 July, 2004; New Tehri, capital of Tehri Garhwal. Tape recording. *Mahila Samakhya* (NGO) office, New Tehri.

Salleh, Ariel. 2004. "Globalisation and the Meta-Industrial Alternative." In *New Socialisms: Futures Beyond Globalisation*, edited by Robert Albritton, 201–211. London: Routledge.

Salleh, Ariel. 2009. *Eco-sufficiency and Global Justice: Women Write Political Ecology*. London: Pluto Press.

Seed Forum Document. 2008. "Seed Heritage of the People for the Good of Humanity: From the Women Seed Forum of South Korea, 28th January, 2008." Accessed September 9, 2009. http://www.viacampesina.net.

Shiva, Vandana. 1987. "People's Ecology: The Chipko Movement." In *Towards a Just World Peace: Perspectives from Social Movements*, edited by Saul Mendlovitz and R. B. J Walker, 253–270. London: Butterworth.

Shiva, Vandana. 1989. *Staying Alive: Women, Ecology and Development*. London: Zed Books.

Shiva, Vandana. 1993. *Monocultures of the Mind*. London: Zed Press.

Shiva, Vandana. 2000. "Ecological Balance in an Era of Globalisation." In *Principled World Politics: The Challenge of Normative International Relation*, edited by Paul Wapner and Lester Ruiz, 130–149. Oxford: Rowman & Littlefield.

Shiva, Vandana. 2001. *Myths and Patents*. New Delhi: Penguin India.

Shiva, Vandana. 2005a. *Globalization's New Wars: Seed, Water and Life Forms*. New Delhi: Women Unlimited.

Shiva, Vandana. 2005b. *India Divided: Diversity and Democracy Under Attack*. New York: Seven Stories Press.

Shiva, Vandana. 2013. "The Law of the Seed." Accessed April 5. http://www.navdanya.org/attachments/Latest_Publications1.pdf

Stephens, Piers H. G. 2009. "Plumwood, Property, Selfhood and Sustainability." *Ethics and the Environment* 14 (2): 57–73.

Sydee, Jasmine, and Sharon Beder. 2001. "Ecofeminism and Globalisation: A Critical Appraisal." *Democracy and Nature* 7 (2): 281–302.

Tickner, Ann. 1992. *Gender in International Relations: Feminist Perspectives on Achieving Global Security*. New York: Columbia University Press.

Wade, R. 2004. "Is Globalization Reducing Poverty and Inequality?" *World Development* 32 (4): 567–589.

Warren, Karen. 1990. "The Power and the Promise of Ecological Feminism." *Environmental Ethics* 12 (2): 121–146.

Warren, Karen. 1993. "A Philosophical Perspective on Ecofeminist Spiritualities." In *Ecofeminism and the Sacred*, edited by, C. J. Adams, 119–132. Bloomington: Indiana University Press.

WILPF, Women and Human Rights Seminar. 2008. Online. Accessed November 10, 2013. http://www.wilpf.int.ch/events/2008IWDseminar.html

World Rainforest Movement Bulletin. 2009. Argentina: Wichi and Guarani Women Raise Their Voices Against Deforestation Linked to Soyabean Expansion, Iss. No. 145. Accessed May 4, 2013. http://www.wrm.org.uy

Truly humanitarian intervention: considering just causes and methods in a feminist cosmopolitan frame

Ann E. Cudd

Department of Philosophy, University of Kansas, Lawrence, KS, USA

In international law, 'humanitarian intervention' refers to the use of military force by one nation or group of nations to stop genocide or other gross human rights violations in another sovereign nation. If humanitarian intervention is conceived as military in nature, it makes sense that only the most horrible, massive, and violent violations of human rights can justify intervention. Yet, that leaves many serious evils beyond the scope of legal intervention. In particular, violations of women's rights and freedoms often go unchecked. To address this problem, I begin from two basic questions: When are violations of human rights sufficiently serious to require an international response of some sort? What should that response be? By re-orienting the aim and justification of international law to focus on individual autonomy rather than on peace between nations, I argue that women's rights violations other than genocide and mass rape can warrant intervention. Military intervention is often counter-productive to the aim of achieving autonomy, however. I suggest a range of responses to human rights violations that includes military intervention as one end of the spectrum, and combine this with a greater understanding of the scope of human rights violations that require international response.

1. Introduction

The end of the Cold War ushered in a new climate for political philosophy as well as global politics. With one military superpower in the world today, regional and intra-state conflicts have become the focus of humanitarian concern. International law governing humanitarian intervention and human rights has ascended to prominence in political philosophy after a long period of focus on domestic justice and internal political legitimacy. It is of paramount importance now to investigate what duties and obligations come with this new world order. When are violations of human rights sufficient to require an international response? What should that response be? Under what conditions may one country justly wield military or economic power to force other countries to respect human rights? What other means of intervening should international law provide or allow?

These questions raise the danger of ethnocentric and nationalistic bias as well as imperialism (Berman 1999). Perhaps less noticed, they also risk androcentric or sexist bias.[1] For, the conduct of war is among the most gendered of all human activities, yet its consequences are universal and profound. This paper investigates the gendered nature of a part of this emerging political philosophy, namely that portion that concerns intervention for humanitarian ends. I will argue that the scope of philosophical discourse surrounding humanitarian intervention is too narrow to lead to progressive, humanitarian outcomes that serve peace and justice. More specifically, I will argue that political philosophy needs to reinterpret the aims and justification of humanitarian intervention from a feminist cosmopolitan perspective in order to influence international law to serve real human needs.

International law includes two main bodies of codes concerning human rights and intervention, including military intervention: international humanitarian law, which concerns justice in the conduct of war and armed conflict, and human rights law, which applies at all times. International humanitarian law specifies the conditions under which one nation is justified in waging war on or militarily intervening in the affairs of another. Situations in which war is justified include: to repel aggression, to come to aid of countries being aggressed upon, and to intervene in severe human rights violations. Aggressive wars motivated by self-interest are never justified, although leaders often appeal to national self-interest in justifying a war to their own people. Humanitarian intervention is conceived in international law as a part of the laws of war and conflict.

Military humanitarian intervention is permitted by the international community and international law to stop genocide, aggressive wars by states on weaker neighbors, or massive human rights violations. However, there is no internationally recognized doctrine concerning the full range of options for non-military intervention. This is unfortunate both because non-military, social, or economic interventions may often be more effective and because when non-military options are ignored in the humanitarian intervention debate, the debate does not consider some of the harms women suffer at the hands of their own societies, harms which, while real, may not rise to the level of *severe* human rights violations.[2]

The past decade has seen some further clarification of the international consensus on humanitarian intervention. In 2001, the Canadian-established International Commission on Intervention and State Sovereignty issued a report entitled *The Responsibility to Protect* (R2P), in which it examined the 'right of humanitarian intervention' (The International Development Research Centre 2001). (This phrase perhaps understates its intentions because the report sets out conditions under which military intervention is not only justified, but even morally *required*.) There are five conditions under which intervention is justified or required.

1 *Just cause* – the state's inability or unwillingness to protect its people from mass terror, genocide, ethnic cleansing, mass rape, or forced expulsion.
2 *Right intention* – to prevent those forms of violent oppression.
3 Military intervention must be the *last resort*, undertaken only after other means have been attempted to prevent catastrophe.
4 *Proportional means* – the force used is to be the minimal force necessary to secure human protection.
5 There must be the *reasonable prospects* of success of halting the oppression and the expected ill consequences of the military action have to be less than that of not intervening militarily.
6 *Right authority* – the UN Security Council must authorize military intervention.

R2P remains firmly in the 'security' framework of justifying intervention, in that it allows only for military intervention, and only for the aim of protecting vulnerable populations from gross human rights violations. Yet it broadens the scope of intervention to allow interference with sovereignty when governments fail to protect their population from such violations.

None of these conditions specifically mention women, but this does not mean that they are gender-neutral. The first and fifth conditions give us a place to begin our investigation of how these rules might have differential consequences for men and women. First we can ask whether the just causes that are considered are in some sense gendered. Do they include the particular concerns of women, as well as men; does women's oppression provide a reason for intervention, or are gender-neutral human rights[3] or particularly masculine concerns the only ones that count? Second, we can ask whether the consequences to be considered in the cost–benefit analysis called for by the final condition include the consequences for women as a group.[4] Furthermore, we can ask whether the entire framework of the 'responsibility to protect' has a gendered connotation or disrespectful attitude that should be subjected to critique.

2. Women, sex, and gender in international law

Until quite recently, international law took account of women specifically only in its requirements on how an occupying force was to provide for the protection of civilians. The Geneva Convention (IV) article 27, states:

> Women shall be especially protected against any attack on their honour, in particular against rape, enforced prostitution, or any form of indecent assault. Without prejudice to the provisions relating to their state of health, age and sex, all protected persons shall be treated with the same consideration by the Party to the conflict in whose power they are, without any adverse distinction based, in particular, on race, religion or political opinion. (Reisman and Antoniou 1994, 240)

While it singles out women as particularly vulnerable to sexual violence, the Convention forbids 'adverse distinction' or discrimination based on race, religion, or political opinion, but not sex. By not including sex, the Convention in effect permits (or at least excludes as a cause for complaint) adverse distinctions or discrimination that are based on sex or gender,[5] including religiously justified gender apartheid and discrimination, and repression of sexual minorities. Of course the Geneva Convention concerns situations of war, and while sex discrimination or gender apartheid may be wrong, they are not acts of war. Violations of the Geneva Convention are taken to be violations of *jus cogens* – the pre-emptory norms taken to be the fundamental principles of international law. Given that these norms, and not norms against violence against women, sex discrimination, or gender apartheid were taken to be the fundamental norms of international law, this sends the message that sex discrimination or gender apartheid are lesser wrongs than other forms of discrimination (Charlesworth and Chinkin 1993, 66). Since gender apartheid and discrimination was nearly universally accepted at the time the Geneva Convention was written, it seems likely that its authors intended that.

Much progress has been made for women in UN treaties and resolutions since that time. Two are particularly worth mentioning here. First the Convention on the Elimination of All Forms of Discrimination Against Women (CEDAW), adopted in 1979, defines what constitutes discrimination against women and sets up an agenda for national action to foster greater equality. As of 2013, 187 (of 194) countries had ratified it (the USA not among them). CEDAW is certainly a comprehensive, progressive statement of and demand for gender equality on behalf of women. It sets a standard for gender equality that no nation in the world yet achieves.

However, there are two important limits on its applicability in international law. First, it is rarely used to criticize nations that do not live up to its standards. Article 29 provides for the means of resolving disputes, which is through the International Court of Justice, a provision that has never been used. In 1999, the UN adopted an Optional Protocol for the treaty that allows for additional means of investigation and protest against violations of CEDAW, but these means have been implemented less than a dozen times (Sokhi-Bulley 2006). Second, it allows for nations to opt out of any of the articles. Now countries are not supposed to opt out of those provisions that go against the very idea of fighting discrimination against women, but that has not stopped many countries from opting out of very basic aspects of gender equality. Many nations opt out of Article 29, which is the provision for bringing complaints against states at the International Court of Justice, and at present only 103 States are parties to the Optional Protocols.[6]

Nonetheless, CEDAW remains an aspirational statement of gender equality, and gives substance to women's human rights claims. The second advance relevant to my topic here is Security Council Resolution 1325 on women, peace, and security, adopted in 2000, which calls for greater participation of women in peacekeeping missions and for raising concern for women and gender-based violence in post-conflict situations. It is important progress that full and equal participation of men and women in these post-conflict situations is at least on the agenda of the UN.

Despite this progress, however, international law and political philosophy still conceive humanitarian intervention too narrowly to assist in achieving the progressive goals of CEDAW. Although treaties permit some forms of dialog with and critique of states that are parties to them, coercive measures are not permitted except those permitted by the Geneva Conventions and the growing international consensus around R2P.[7] As I argued above, however, the Geneva Convention treats race and religion differently from sex or gender, and R2P focuses on the same severe human rights violations, so does not modify the differential treatment of gender groups that is found in the existing international law licensing humanitarian intervention. What could justify that differential treatment? To answer this question, we need to see how international law is justified.

3. Justifying international law

International law is generally regarded as morally binding on all states and organized groups who wish to be regarded as decent and respect-worthy members of the international community. Yet the force of this obligation must be provided by a moral argument, and not simply by the force of a proclamation of a self-appointed body, no matter how grand or international in scope. Furthermore, if international law is to be criticized and repaired, we need to examine the justificatory structure from which it derives.

These conventions and customs are derived primarily from a long history of discussions of just war theory and international relations, and in contemporary thought several types of justifications for its tenets can be found. One justification is natural law and its descendants' theories of human rights. Natural law has a long and varied history, and can be found in religiously based or secular varieties. A secular version of this can be found in Michael Walzer's *Just and Unjust Wars* (1977), and in the work of Terry Nardin, who writes of the implications of 'common morality' (Nardin 2002). Natural law can now be roughly described as a pragmatic, common sense approach to the idea that each person, by nature, deserves dignity and respect. Walzer calls his theory a 'doctrine of human rights', and explains that his theory is a practical morality that proceeds by the casuistic method. A second type of justification of international law comes from the social contract tradition, which can be identified in several variants, depending on whether it takes its inspiration from Hobbes or Locke or Kant. John Rawls, in his last book, *The Law of Peoples* presents the most significant contemporary argument for the binding nature of international law.

In my view, only the social contract tradition offers a reasonable comprehensive justification of international law. I will not give an extended argument for this claim here, but simply gesture toward the type of objections I have to natural law. First, natural law of the religious form cannot be appealed to in a pluralist world, since we cannot assume broad, shared agreements on religiously based assumptions. The secular natural law option seems likewise unworkable in a situation of pluralism, since it is too ad hoc. If there is disagreement at some point over what the natural law implies for humanitarian law, there is no foundation to appeal to in order to decide the issue. Such grounding could work only in a world of broadly shared values about human nature, peace, and justice. But we do not live in that world, at least not yet. Of particular relevance to my argument, disagreements over the value of individuals vs. community and over the normative implications of religious and sexual difference deeply divide the peoples of the world. Of course, all reasoned argument must begin from some shared assumptions, such as, at minimum, the normative force of principles of logic. But in my view natural law assumes too much, even in its secular variations.

The social contract tradition takes the principles of justice to be the subject of agreement among equal, rational agents representing their own interests.[8] When this theory is extended to international law, some social contract theorists conceive of the principles of international law as an agreement between state parties, while others have continued to view individuals as the parties to the social contract. While Rawls takes the first approach, I will later argue for the second approach. Feminists, among others, raise a serious concern about this tradition of argument (Pateman 1988). If equality is in fact lacking prior to the contract, inequality in the agreed upon norms or laws will be the result of the contract. Yet, the contract tradition, on some interpretations, offers a solution: it appeals to ideal conditions of equality and ideal actors to specify principles under which persons or nations should interact, then applies those principles to the actual world. Inequality can thus be rectified through the principles derived from reasoning from equality (see Hampton 2001; Sample 2002). The problem is that the inequalities have to be recognized in advance so that the idealizations can be specified to eliminate the inequality. Unrecognized or unquestioned inequality will result in preserving the status quo inequality. Those who are considered to be of lesser worth will be left out of the contract altogether. Contractarians of the modern period, for example, failed to recognize the injustices done by their political theories to slaves, native peoples, and women.

We can correct those wrongs, and address others that become apparent, but that means that contract theory must be continually interrogated and modified. Unlike natural law theory, though, contract theory points in the direction to look for injustice in the very foundation. One of the great insights of social contract theory that can be put to use to feminist ends is to see social connections as prior to, and necessitating, morality and political institutions. Because we interact and have the ability to harm or benefit each other, we have reason to formulate agreements and norms to guide our behavior in positive ways, and to abide by our agreements. Thus, Iris Young argues, social connections can be seen as a ground of political responsibility (Young 2003, 2006; Young and Archibugi 2003).

Feminists have only begun to critically examine the ways in which women's inequalities have been allowed to remain in the very idealizations of the contract as applied to international justice.[9] As a result, the international rules of just war, just intervention, and just occupation remain gendered in concealed ways, and this gendered nature of the contract produces principles unjust to women. Thus, that what looks like justified military interventions and subsequent occupations may unequally affect women in both the near and long term. Although Security Council resolution 1325 addresses this point in the practice of conflict and post-conflict peacebuilding, it does nothing to realign the fundamental justification of humanitarian intervention, and thus to reform our thinking about when and how to intervene to address human rights violations directed at women. To rectify this, I argue, international humanitarian law needs to be realigned from a feminist perspective.

3.1 The Law of Peoples: *contractarian derivation and justification of international law*

In this section, I examine Rawls's *The Law of Peoples*, the most influential contemporary contractarian justification of international law. My aim is to show how gendered assumptions about human rights and just war restrict the meaning and legitimate uses of humanitarian intervention. Although Rawls's work provides a comprehensive philosophical treatment of international principles of justice, I confine my discussion to the portion concerned with intervention and humanitarian law.

Rawls sets out conditions under which societies (Rawls's word is 'peoples')[10] can live peaceably with each other (ideal theory), and those conditions under which war is justified (non-ideal theory). The goal of the theory is to avoid the great evils of the world – unjust war, oppression, religious persecution, genocide, mass murder, starvation, and poverty (Rawls 1999, 7) – by building just institutions to secure a peaceful world, in which nations do not wage war against each other and human rights are respected throughout the world. Rawls argues that we cannot legitimately require that all states be liberal democratic ones, merely that they meet a standard of decency requiring respect of human rights and allowing some voice for internal political dissent and change. In an ideal world consisting of only such decent nations, the basic principles of international justice – the Law of Peoples – would be determined by a hypothetical contract situation, a second original position,[11] of suitable representatives of these peoples, behind a veil of ignorance about their nation's particular features, concerned to secure peace and human rights though rational reflection on reasonable principles (Rawls 1999, 32). Rawls enumerates eight general principles, among them a duty of non-intervention, a right to wage war only in self-defense and only under specified conditions and limitations, and a duty of assistance to nations living under unfavorable conditions (Rawls 1999, 37).

We do not live in an ideal world in which there are only these tolerable, decent societies, however. Some nations wage unjust wars on others. Some nations pose a serious, credible threat to do so. And some nations violate the human rights of their people. In these cases, the right to self-defense may lead a nation to go to war, or the duty of assistance may override that of non-intervention. Without going into the main line of argument for all these justifications of war, let us consider just the case under which military intervention in the internal affairs of another country can be justified, namely severe human rights violations. What constitutes human rights violations, and in particular, the severe ones that justify intervention? Rawls argues that the human rights that are to be singled out by the Law of Peoples ought not be the same as those rights guaranteed to citizens in a liberal democratic society, since the Law of Peoples is to apply to decent non-liberal societies as well. He writes that these rights:

> express a special class of urgent rights, such as freedom from slavery and serfdom, liberty (but not equal liberty) of conscience, and security of ethnic groups from mass murder and genocide. The violation of this class of rights is equally condemned by both reasonable liberal peoples and decent hierarchical peoples. (Rawls 1999, 79)

Why this list of urgent rights? Because additional rights would not be supported by the decent non-liberal societies, societies which Rawls thinks should be tolerated by the Law of Peoples. Hence we have to either condemn those societies, or accept their illiberal practices as not falling afoul of human rights.[12]

In order to bring about the ideal Society of Peoples, who co-exist peaceably and can be seen to honor human rights, we must restrict the list of human rights to this subset of 'urgent' rights. The point of the social contract is to *construct*, not to discover, the principles that, when enforced, secure peace among the contractors. Thus they must appeal to each, so that each wills them as reasonable grounds for peaceable coexistence. While some societies will be excluded from the contract, it is important that as many societies be included as possible, so that those outlaw states are isolated and their threat to the Society of Peoples rendered impotent.

Rawls sketches a type of society that he argues would fit the description of such a decent hierarchical, non-liberal society: a Muslim society he names 'Kazanistan'. Its principal deviation from liberal democratic societies, in Rawls's description, is that it does not fully respect religious freedom, in the sense that non-Muslims are not permitted to participate in the highest levels of

government. We can presume, however, that another significant deviation from liberal democratic rights would be a society that does not respect the rights of women to participate on an
equal basis with men in all aspects of social life. Rawls's invention of a Muslim society as
his idea of a possible, decent, non-liberal society, and his failure to even mention the problem
of women's rights under such a regime are, I think, telling.[13]

The list of human rights, together with the general principles of international law, implies a specification of the conditions under which military intervention and subsequent occupation may be
waged. From the list of human rights recognized by the Law of Peoples[14] we may derive two important conditions for feminist consideration: war may not generally be waged to eliminate gender hierarchy, nor may any occupation be extended or force applied in order to secure gender equality.
Feminists, then, must be concerned about the content of international law derived from Rawls's
contractarian argument in *The Law of Peoples*. As I suggested earlier, whenever a contractarian
argument begins with an inequality in the specification of the contract situation, it is likely not to
imply rules of justice that will eliminate that inequality. But Rawls has assumed nothing about
gender in his specification of the contract.[15] Given that Rawls's discussion of Kazanistan does
not mention the problems of women's rights under existing Islamic rule, we must infer that sanc-
tioning a custom of gender apartheid does not amount to human rights violations. One might infer
from the absence of the word 'gender' from the list noted above that women do not even constitute a
group. If not, however, the violations of their rights that are inherent in the practice of religion in the
society, at least as they see it, will surely not count as 'grave' human rights violations. In short,
Rawls evinces no urgency or extreme caution to secure women's rights.

Martha Nussbaum offers a related critique of Rawls on the question of women's rights under
the Law of Peoples (Nussbaum 2002, 293). Nussbaum argues that women's rights are sacrificed
because the individuals who are party to the contract are not persons but peoples, and thus it is
the *peoples as groups* who are offered equal respect and dignity. However, she points out, if the
group has a tradition of ignoring women's equal dignity, through such things as unequal divorce
and inheritance laws, the Law of Peoples will have no recourse against that group. In effect, then,
the Law of Peoples will permit the oppression of women. Now this could happen to men or other
social groups if a society that is considered decent by Rawls' criteria still oppresses them in ways
that fall below the threshold of severe human rights violations. But as it happens, the list of
severe human rights violations that Rawls offers seems to cover most oppression of social
groups that include men.[16] Thus, oppression of women seems not to be one of the justifying conditions for intervention, unless that oppression amounts to a kind of oppression that is typically
suffered by men.

Well, most feminists are not keen to see military interventions, either.[17] However, these constraints on war are also the constraints on the limits of assistance under occupation. Once the
violations of (what the Law of Peoples regards as) human rights have ended, there is no duty
nor is it permissible to continue occupation. Rawls argues specifically against liberal societies
making any intervention or provision of incentives for non-liberal societies to become more
liberal, on the grounds that this fails to adequately respect those societies. Such intervention
or incentive provision is likely, he argues, to cause resentment and thus disturb international
peace. Rawls insists that societies must equally respect all societies that meet the minimal standards of decency. Against the notion that liberal rights must be urged on others, he writes that 'if
liberal peoples require that all societies be liberal and subject those that are not to politically
enforced sanctions, then decent non-liberal peoples – if there are such – will be denied a due
measure of respect by liberal peoples' (Rawls 1999, 61). Rawls opposes any form of political
pressure to liberalize decent, hierarchical societies. Hence, women's specific concerns that do
not rise to the level of urgent human rights violations are not recognized by Rawls as a legitimate
reason for any form of intervention.

To summarize, we can raise two criticisms of Rawls's account of humanitarian intervention. First, Rawls sets the bar for any intervention at the level of the urgent rights violation that justifies military intervention. He does this because the goal is to secure peace among Peoples, and to include among those Peoples as many societies as possible consistent with that aim. This poses a general problem for agents seeking to promote humanitarian ends across national borders, since any such promotion can be seen as a unjustified intervention. Second, human rights violations that are seen as meeting this standard are not those associated with women (or men) as a group, but rather with ethnic and religious groups. Yet such groups often themselves harbor norms and customs that discriminate against women.[18] Feminist political philosophy, therefore, must offer an alternative account of intervention that can truly be called 'humanitarian'.

3.2 *An alternative justification for humanitarian intervention*

Constructing an alternative account requires us to examine where the justification of intervention goes wrong and to seek to repair or replace that justification. There are two basic problems with Rawls's construction of the contract situation. First in taking 'Peoples' to be the parties to the contract that determines the principles of international justice, he begins with nations, rather than individuals, as the politically primary units. This beginning is expedient, but mistaken.[19] It is human individuals who live, experience, suffer, and die. Peoples can only be said to experience anything through their individuals. A People may cease to exist when the individual persons who compose a People abandon that way of life to live what they consider to be better ones among other groups. While it is true that individual human beings find meaning only in and through their communities, there would be no meaning-providing institutions or norms without the actions and intentions of individual human beings. Finally, if we had to choose between saving an individual human being and saving other aspects of a People, it would be monstrous to say that we should opt to save the latter. If we grant that individuals are morally primary, and if we accept the equality of individuals regardless of their national identity, then the principle of non-intervention, even as a *prima facie* duty, is open to question.[20]

The other main problem with Rawls's view is that he assumes that the goal to be attained through the law of peoples is peace. While peace appeals to both nations and individuals, I want to suggest that there is a more primary aim for individuals, and that is autonomy. By autonomy I mean the ability to plan one's life and live according to a moral code that one can see reasons for in recognition of our inescapable human interdependency. Feminist work on relational autonomy has shown us the importance of recognizing our non-voluntary ties to others that make human life rich and meaningful (see Friedman 2003; Mackenzie and Stoljar 2000). Autonomous persons live their own lives in the recognition that they are social beings among others also striving to live their own lives. Persons' autonomy can be compromised by their social circumstances, however. Social circumstances can be so constraining that they rule out a rich and meaningful life, and oppression or war are prime examples of such circumstances. Autonomy is both a social and an individual achievement. Thus, if the parties to the social contract that determines the principles of international justice represent individual persons rather than Peoples, it would be reasonable to expect them to aim for autonomy for themselves and to expect others to do so as well. Peace and security, of course, are still very important instrumentally to individuals. If we take this moral cosmopolitan[21] perspective of adopting individual autonomy as the primary goal of international justice, we can see that its achievement will be enhanced by global peace.

Cosmopolitanism does not deny that individuals find communities and community life meaningful (Appiah 2006). Collective self-determination of the community's norms and rules is valuable to individuals, and hence it has instrumental moral value. But the instrumental value of collective self-determination cannot ground a strict principle of non-intervention when individual moral rights are threatened (a point that Rawls also acknowledges). The principle of non-intervention must be weighed against other instrumental values for individuals, including rights and other goods as well.

I propose a contractarian approach to the international law governing humanitarian intervention that takes human individuals to be the parties to the contract and thus adopts as its aim maximizing individual autonomy, understood in the relational sense of the ability of each to live their own lives in the recognition that they are social beings essentially connected to others also striving to live their own lives. Given autonomy as the aim, when would intervention ever be justified? In the individual case, intervention might be justified when an individual's life is so constrained or disordered that autonomy is not achievable without intervention. The aim of achieving autonomy also sets limits on the kinds and methods of intervention that are justifiable. So, I shall argue, in the intercultural or international case, when individuals are systematically constrained or unable to achieve autonomy, intervention will be warranted, if the intervention itself does not constrain autonomy to an even greater degree. Thus, the aim of achieving autonomy will again set the limit on the kinds and methods of intervention that are justifiable.

Steven Lee argues for a similar justificatory structure for military humanitarian intervention (Lee 2008). I will adopt his balancing procedure, but argue that there is no reason to restrict it to the realm of *military* humanitarian intervention. Lee's structure allows us to justify other forms of coercive humanitarian intervention that fall short of military force. Furthermore, this structure allows us to consider all human rights violations, including those of particular concern to women, as possibly licensing intervention of some sort.

On Lee's view, coercion in the international sphere should be justified in the same way as it is in the national domestic sphere, namely to protect rights. But the scope of permissible military humanitarian intervention turns out on Lee's analysis to be just as limited as it is on standard international law by the kind of cost–benefit analysis that the potential intervener should engage in. Specifically, Lee thinks that such considerations lead to two types of limitations. *Efficiency limitations* consider the ability of the intervening power to succeed in protecting human rights and the material costs of intervening. *Rights-balancing limitations* consider the need of the intervening power to violate rights in order to succeed in protecting human rights and the tendency of the intervening power to become oppressive even when promoting some human rights. These limitations on military intervention turn out to be so restrictive that it is justified only in those cases where there are massive human rights violations by a state that is so disordered as to be incapable of mounting a serious defense of its national sovereignty. Lee summarizes his general view as follows:

> Given the grim consequences of war and the risk that a general rule might be misused or abused by powerful states to rationalize military adventures it may be appropriate to accept a defeasible rule that [military humanitarian intervention] is justified only when severe and widespread rights violations are in progress. (Lee 2008, 188)

I agree with Lee's cosmopolitanism and his balancing of efficiency and rights limitations in justifying humanitarian intervention. However, he does not go far enough in the direction of measuring either the potential benefits of humanitarian interventions or the costs of military interventions. To accurately assess both the benefits and the costs, we need to frame the analysis with a feminist cosmopolitan lens. By this I mean, we need to take into account the effects of war on women as well as on men, from the perspective of autonomy as the essential goal. Instead of asking as Lee does, 'when should coercive force be used to protect human rights?' I shall ask 'when should intervention (of some sort) be used to promote autonomy?'

3.3 *Intervention to support autonomy: military vs. humanitarian*

Consider the costs of military humanitarian interventions. These include the killed and wounded on all sides, as well as the damage to the environment and economy of the invaded country; these are the only costs that Lee considers. We should also consider additional or new types of rights and autonomy violations that are introduced or facilitated by the intervention. Interventions often upset the social balance of power among social groups. Of course this is often the aim of an intervention: to remove or disempower a group that is oppressing another group in the society. However, there are also unintended effects in this regard. The kinds of examples I have in mind are between men and women, although in specific cases it may be between different religious sects, economic classes, or perhaps other groups. I would categorize such changes in the balance of power as important considerations, but they are not included among the rights-balancing considerations raised by Lee, where the intervening power infringes on rights. Interventions may intentionally or unintentionally give one part of the society unfair additional power or privilege. Consider the interventions in Iraq or Afghanistan, where women have clearly suffered great losses of power vis-à-vis men as a result of the military conflicts, which in turn have caused human rights violations and the imposition of laws that are opposed to the equality of women. I will call these *autonomy considerations*, because they involve compromises of the autonomy of members of social groups.

Moreover, this suggests that there needs to be greater attention to the results of military action in itself. Militarization tends to hyper-masculinize a society and may lead to greater death and oppression from that fact itself (Orford 2003, 12–13). Military intervention makes violent, lethal force the typical response to disagreement in a society, at least for some time. Since men have a near monopoly on lethal force in most societies (by possessing and wielding, whether legally or illegally, the vast majority of weapons), they tend to strengthen their power and hold on social and political power when lethal force is the currency of power.

Women are generally made more vulnerable to rape as a result of the unrest caused by military intervention. Furthermore, military defeat constitutes an affront to the honor of the defeated men, who then feel that their honor must be proven and upheld in other ways, such as through commanding absolute obedience from their women. As we have learned from the wars in Bosnia and Croatia (to mention only recent examples), rape is a means of *conducting* civil war/ethnic conflict, and it seems to be a means employed in Iraq now by ethnic gangs who wish to sully the honor of their rivals by raping 'their' women. Finally, women's ill treatment is exacerbated by the presence of male soldiers. The situation of Iraqi women is worse than it was before the US humanitarian intervention, and the intervention is in large part responsible for their worsened situation (see also Chew 2010).

This loss of women's rights and power, and therefore in many cases their autonomy, in conflict and post-conflict situations should be considered among the costs in weighing the costs and benefits of interventions. These considerations weigh heavily against military force as a legitimate means of intervening. But we need not, therefore, conclude that this is where the considerations of international law cease. Since all aspects of human rights are legitimately a concern of international law, and since we have rejected the non-intervention principle, we can now consider non-military state interventions as a legitimate subject for international law. A continuum of coercive force may be considered in humanitarian intervention, where military force is only one end point of this continuum, as well as a continuum of rights violations as justifying conditions for interventions. As Catherine Lu has argued,

> we should be careful not to conflate the problem of intervention with the problem of the use of force . . . . The conflation of these two issues in international theory and practice has meant that governments have been able to claim a much stronger social convention against all types of intervention

than is supported even in international law .... Many situations may justify some kind of interventionary international response that violates or restricts some aspect of a state's sovereign authority while ruling out a full-scale military assault. (Lu 2005, 190)

Given the serious costs of military intervention, non-military humanitarian interventions must be prioritized in most cases of even the most severe human rights violations. For state actors[22], the following might be a reasonable start on a list of intervention strategies from least to most coercive:

(1) diplomatic persuasion
(2) support for non-violent internal resistance groups
(3) diplomatic criticism
(4) propaganda
(5) economic incentives (targeted subsidies or grants in return for progressive reforms)
(6) economic sanctions (trade restrictions etc.)
(7) total embargoes
(8) support for violent internal resistance
(9) military intervention aimed at preventing killing
(10) military intervention aimed at removing governmental authority

In this way, the different levels of cost and risk can be weighed against the benefits foreseen by the intervention. Many of the gender injustices that I am most concerned with are probably best responded to with intervention strategies of type 2, support for non-violent internal resistance groups. This is also the kind of intervention that non-state actors will be most likely to be able to (and to legitimately) engage in. Where there are such internal groups, supporting their autonomous resistance has the benefit of not only combating oppressors, but also of building autonomy of survivors, and is likely to progressively transform a society rather than simply prevent current oppressions. More needs to be said about what it means to provide that kind of support, but that is beyond the scope of the present essay. My concern here is to argue for the recognition of this sort of preventive non-violent intervention in international law itself.[23] It must be noted that the second half of this continuum, beginning with economic sanctions, all involve lethal force and so must be considered as types of violent intervention, with all of the autonomy considerations that follow from that, particularly for women. Furthermore, as Laura Sjoberg has argued, economic sanctions have serious, gendered consequences for the targeted population (Sjoberg 2006, chap. 9). Such lethal interventions can only be justified by equally serious causes to intervene. Hence, a full assessment of which sort of intervention is warranted must include consideration of the benefits of these potential interventions.[24]

4. Justifying causes for intervention: oppressive social norms

Social norms and customs that inhibit women's autonomy can, under my proposal, justify intervention in cases where international law would now prohibit it. If autonomy is the legitimate goal for intervention, then a respectful, hands-off approach to the mythical Kazanistan needs to be reconsidered, if, as I supposed, the women of Kazanistan are confined to the domestic sphere or treated unequally, whether by custom or by law. Such customs or laws amount to gender apartheid if women are prohibited from moving about freely and taking up occupations and social positions among men.[25] This and other forms of gender discrimination and gender violence – many practiced or permitted in the West and by fundamentalist Christian groups, as well – are serious violations of human rights. Fundamentalist versions of many world religions privilege men as a group and constrain women's autonomy. They may portray women as seductive temptresses, or weaker, inferior beings to be protected and confined, and so harm women by giving them an inferior self-image and making it difficult to move confidently in the world. The patronizing connotation of the language of protection is reason to avoid that terminology, but not to avoid supporting the autonomy and empowerment of those who are vulnerable to such religiously based oppression.

One might object that the kind of harm done to women by religion in this way is not severe: psychological oppression in the form of internalized inferiority and acceptance of norms that continue their oppression are not as serious as death. It certainly does not rise to the level of genocide; and may not generate serious human rights violations if the norms are not violently resisted by the women themselves. But we must consider that such oppression is passed on through generations of humanity, and there is, therefore, a kind of compound interest involved in the disutility of this harm over the generations. Women under sexist regimes may not get out from under this oppression for 10–20 generations. In that case, many generations live stunted, restricted lives, and that may begin to sound comparable to the cutting short of the lives of a single generation. And this is only to count the psychological harm to the women themselves. Since the material well-being of societies in which women are subject to gender apartheid (and therefore lowered education and ability to affect the public sphere) is also much lower, this underestimates the actual harm done. But more to the point of the present paper, a human rights violation need not rise to the level of genocide if non-military intervention strategies are also under consideration.

The situation of women in the Iraq and Afghanistan occupations shows that the practical application of humanitarian law in actual occupations of outlaw societies that seriously oppress women can make the situation of women even worse than before occupation. But the lesson of Kazanistan and the many real-world societies that resemble it in the way that women are confined is that we tend to be blind to the kinds of human rights violations that rob women of full autonomy under the guise of custom or religion. Furthermore, liberal ideology considers those to be private choices by individuals, and, therefore, not a concern of an intervening force charged with helping to devise public institutions to achieve internal security. Family, community, religion are values to men and women alike, and so seem to be the kinds of things that human rights law should aim to protect. Yet, they are also both the sites of women's daily lives, and the sites in which they are most often violated and abused. When women must choose from a bargaining position that is unequal, their choices are between bad and worse: choose this traditional religion/family structure, or none. This is the case not only in war and occupation, but also in times and places of so-called peace. While it seems that interventions should not interfere in those valuable traditional institutions, on a deeper analysis that apparent truth gives way.

Kazanistan is a mythical state, and so a full assessment of the potential benefits of humanitarian intervention would be speculative at best. I am not arguing that military humanitarian intervention is warranted wherever there is gender apartheid, of course, since militarization is likely to make matters even worse for the women who are already suffering human rights violations. I am suggesting that the violation of autonomy in a state in which gender apartheid is practiced for generations is massive and may warrant some form of intervention.

The idea that intervention should aim to support autonomy may seem paradoxical. Intervention by its nature disrupts a process, often one that has been voluntarily embarked upon. Intervention in collective decision-making or collective self-determination would itself seem to be a violation of autonomy. However, when some individuals are prevented from freely participating in collective decision-making, then the paradox of intervening in collective decisions to achieve autonomy dissolves. The collective decision process itself is the violation of autonomy, and intervention in that process may reinstate the individuals' autonomy. Collective processes that deny autonomy should be subject to intervention. Autonomy-inhibiting social norms and traditions may be supported by some and resisted by others. Deciding how to intervene to support autonomy in these situations without violating it is a difficult question, and beyond the scope of this essay.[26]

I propose alternative conditions on intervention to the ones proposed by the International Commission on Intervention and State Sovereignty, which might be proposed by a mythical 'International Commission on Intervention and Cosmopolitan Autonomy'. These would be conditions that any group must meet if it intervenes within the borders of a foreign state.

(1) *Just cause*: the state's inability or unwillingness to protect its people from mass terror, genocide, ethnic cleansing, mass rape, or forced expulsion, or systematic and serious violations of individual autonomy.

(2) The intervening group must have the *right intention*, in particular, the intention to prevent those forms of oppression and to build capacities for individual autonomy.

(3) Intervention strategies must be attempted in order, so that military intervention is the *last resort*.

(4) The force used is to be the *minimal intervention necessary* to support and defend human autonomy for all individuals.

(5) There must be the *expectation of good consequences*: there has to be a reasonable chance of halting the oppression and supporting autonomy, and the expected ill consequences of the intervention for autonomy have to be less than that of not intervening at all.

These conditions aim at halting oppression and supporting conditions of autonomy without undue respect for national sovereignty. The just cause condition includes violation of autonomy, and the right intention clause is to aim at supporting autonomy. I have argued that we should recognize the relational nature of human life and meaning, yet we must also recognize the way in which social life can seriously constrain groups of individuals for the benefit of other groups. This account of the right of intervention allows for intervention to support autonomy and aid the resistance to oppression across international borders, recognizing the great harms of longterm, non-lethal oppression.

5. Conclusion

If we were to take seriously the oppression of women, including the suppression of autonomy by ordinary social institutions, then we would see the estimation of the costs and the benefits of humanitarian intervention as more complex than those typically considered by either just war theory or political philosophy more generally. As under the standard just war view or Lee's theory, we could agree that military intervention is rarely warranted, but we would see failure to intervene at all as more costly than previously considered, as well.

Military intervention and occupation in seriously disordered states that also have a tradition of discrimination against women are likely to lead to worse consequences for women, even if peace and order are restored, if they are brokered on masculine terms. Yet, from a feminist perspective, it is also not acceptable to say that no intervention can ever be warranted. Indeed, feminists might insist that intervention is warranted in many more (or different) situations than current political thought seems to justify. The emphasis in international law on military intervention is misguided, however. International law informed by a feminist perspective requires that new means of social intervention, which disrupt traditional roles and gender hierarchies, must be considered to replace military intervention which tends to maintain the global dominance of military power over the freedom of autonomous individuals and of men over women. By putting all these forms on a single continuum, we can begin to see that there exist many options for intervention and many more situations where intervention is both required and permitted.

Acknowledgements

Earlier versions of this paper were presented at the Department of Philosophy, Texas Tech University, and the Department of Philosophy, University of Oklahoma. For helpful comments I thank the audiences of those sessions, three anonymous reviewers and the editor of this journal, as well as Emily Crookston, Lisa Fuller, and Sandra Raponi.

Notes

1. But not entirely unnoticed by feminists. See, for example, Cudd (2009), Orford (2003), Sjoberg (2008), and Sylvester (2002).
2. This is a point also highlighted by Engel (2007), who is particularly concerned about how feminist discourse has been co-opted in some cases to elevate the level of human rights violations in order to legitimate military intervention. This is the mirror image of my concern in this paper, which is to show how the focus on the military aspect of humanitarian intervention has tended to dismiss violations of women's rights (among others, such as the rights of sexual minorities or the disabled) as beneath international concern. But like her, I am arguing against human rights 'hawks' who favor military intervention for human rights abuses.
3. For a clear discussion of the problems of a 'gender-blind' human rights discourse, see Rao (1993); reprinted in Rao (2001). See also Charlesworth and Chinkin (1993).
4. Sjoberg (2006) takes up these questions in the context of just war theory more generally. See especially Chapter 5.
5. By sex I mean to refer both to biological distinctions between males and females as well as sexual behaviors. By gender I mean to refer to the social distinctions between men and women, as individuals present themselves or as they are ascribed by others.
6. Many nations opt out of Article 29, which is the provision for bringing complaints against states at the International Court of Justice, and at present only 103 States are parties to the Optional Protocols.
7. I address below the objection that the 'protection' framework of R2P licenses too much intervention and does so in a way that is disrespectful of persons on whose behalf intervention is waged. My main concern in this paper is the narrow scope of the framework, not the patronizing attitude of the term 'protection'.
8. While some feminists argue that the notion of rational agent is masculinist and exclusionary, others argue that it can be repurposed for feminist ends. For an overview of criticisms of reason see Nagl-Docekal (1999). I defend the notion of the rational agent and its use in rational choice theory for feminist ends in Witt (2002).
9. Nussbaum (2002) is an exception to this generalization. I discuss her critique of Rawls below.
10. Rawls uses the word 'Peoples' to mean a coherent group of individuals ruled by a common government, bound together by 'common sympathies', sharing a common conception of right and justice. A People is thus an idealization of shared identity and governance, and hence a moralized concept.
11. The first original position is that in which the principles of justice for a people are derived. Rawls (1971) set out this argument in *A Theory of Justice*.
12. No doubt those non-liberal decent societies will have to restrict their favored list of human rights, as well, to accommodate the liberal democracies that Rawls favors. For example, they cannot insist on egalitarian economic outcomes, as that may require liberals to give up cherished property rights.
13. It may be that differential treatment of men and women by customary or religious laws can be justified as 'separate but equal', but the argument surely has to be made in the case of gender just as much as in the case of race.
14. This list is the 'special class of urgent rights, such as freedom from slavery and serfdom, liberty (but not equal liberty) of conscience, and security of ethnic groups from mass murder and genocide' (Rawls

1999, 79). It is important to notice for my purposes here that 'ethnic groups' are singled out but gender groups are not.

15. It is worth pointing out that Rawls does not mention gender in the original specification of the first original position in *Theory of Justice*. It was only after sustained critique by feminists, particularly Okin (1989), that Rawls ultimately added gender to the list of aspects of which the first original position participants are ignorant in *Political Liberalism*. The addition is critical, since it entails that participants in the contract will seek principles of justice that are sensitive to gender inequalities. In order for this to be the case, the participants in the original position must not only be ignorant of their gender, but also aware that their gender may well be a significant determinant of their status and well-being in society.

16. Among the human rights are the right to life (to the means of subsistence and security); to liberty (to freedom from slavery, serfdom and forced occupation, and to a sufficient measure of liberty of conscience to ensure freedom of religion and thought); to property (personal property); and to formal equality as expressed by the rules of natural justice (that is, that similar cases be treated similarly). (Rawls 1999, 65).

17. Indeed, Nussbaum goes on to argue that Rawls is right about not intervening in societies because of women's rights violations. Also, Young (2005) argues for quite different reasons against military intervention.

18. Both of these criticisms are made against the idea of *jus cogens* in Charlesworth and Chinkin (1993).

19. Sjoberg (2006) criticizes seeing war as primarily a matter between states as a masculinist assumption that feminism can help to reveal and correct. She writes:
   In common usage, war is the use of military force to protect state borders or advance state interests. Security then is about state safety. Feminists reinterpret security to focus on individual lives ... Feminisms emphasize individual human safety, especially at the political margins. This refocuses security from state politics toward peoples' lives. (50).

20. Wellman (2011) makes a convincing argument that sovereignty cannot override the right to intervene to prevent human rights violations, although there may be other reasons not to, of course.

21. Reilly (2007, 182) credits Gould (2004) with the distinction between moral and political cosmopolitanism.

22. Non-state actors, including non-governmental organizations, have other means of intervention which would yield a different range of intervention strategies. But the fundamental balancing principles would remain the same.

23. Here my approach differs from that of care ethicists, such as Held (2008), who argues for a care ethics-guided approach to international aid that is entirely apart from international law, which she sees as coming into play only when force is considered. She writes: 'instead of relying on military intervention to punish violators of the norms of international law, the ethics of care would counsel preventive engagements and measures aimed at deflecting violations and undercutting the need for punishment' (14). This approach strikes me as too voluntary and lacking in force to be effective.

24. Thoughtful concerns about positions such as the one I take may be raised, such as by McCormack (2008), however space does not allow reply.

25. In Saudi Arabia, for example, women are not permitted by law to drive, nor may they leave their homes without a male chaperone; they face separate laws pertaining to marriage and divorce, giving them lesser power within families; and they have different and lesser rights to their guidance and custody of children. They do not yet have the right to vote. Furthermore, they are forced to engage separate forms of education and religious worship (Husain 2011). Women in Saudi Arabia resist these rules, but so far have not been successful in eliminating them. Regardless of the purported justification, the 'separate but equal' claim rings as hollow in this case as in the case of Blacks in the USA.

26. An important recent attempt to address this question is Khader (2011). See also my review of this book at *Notre Dame Philosophical Reviews*, November 2011. Accessed September 15, 2013. http://ndpr.nd. edu/news/27280-adaptive-preferences-and-women-s-empowerment/.

References

Appiah, Kwame Anthony. 2006. *Cosmopolitanism: Ethics in a World of Strangers*. New York: WW Norton.

Berman, Nathaniel. 1999. "In the Wake of Empire." *American University International Law Review* 14 (6): 1521–1554.

Charlesworth, Hilary, and Christine Chinkin. 1993. "The Gender of Jus Cogens." *Human Rights Quarterly* 15 (1): 63–76.

Chew, Huiben Aimee. 2010. "Why the War Is Sexist." Accessed November 27, 2010. http://www.zcommunications.org/why-the-war-is-sexist-by-huibin-amee-chew-1

Cudd, Ann E. 2009. "When to Intervene: Atrocity, Inequality, and Oppression." In *Evil, Political Violence and Forgiveness: Essays in Honor of Claudia Card*, edited by Andrea Veltman and Katherine Norlock, 97–114. Lanham, MD: Rowman and Littlefield.

Engel, Karen. 2007. "'Calling in the Troops': The Uneasy Relationship among Women's Rights, Human Rights, and Humanitarian Intervention." *Harvard Human Rights Journal* 20 (1): 189–226.

Friedman, Marilyn. 2003. *Autonomy, Gender, and Politics*. New York: Oxford University Press.

Gould, Carol C. 2004. *Globalizing Democracy and Human Rights*. Cambridge: Cambridge University Press.

Hampton, Jean. 2001. "Feminist Contractarianism." In *A Mind of One's Own*, 2nd ed., edited by Louise Antony and Charlotte Witt, 337–368. Boulder: Westview Press.

Held, Virginia. 2008. "Military Intervention and the Ethics of Care." *Southern Journal of Philosophy* 46 (S1): 1–20.

Husain, Ed. 2011. "Why Women's Rights in Saudi Arabia Are Still So Bad." *The Atlantic*, September 28. Accessed February 9, 2012. http://www.theatlantic.com/international/archive/2011/09/why-womens-rights-in-saudi-arabia-are-still-so-bad/245780/

Khader, Serene J. 2011. *Adaptive Preferences and Women's Empowerment*. New York: Oxford University Press.

Lee, Steven. 2008. "Coercion Abroad to Protect Rights." In *Coercion and the State*, edited by D. A. Reidy and W. J. Riker, 177–188. Dordrecht: Springer Science and Business Media B.V.

Lu, Catherine. 2005. "Whose Principles? Whose Institutions? Legitimacy Challenges for Humanitarian Intervention." In *Humanitarian Intervention*, edited by Terry Nardin and Melissa Williams, 188–216. New York: New York University Press.

MackenzieCatriona, and Natalie Stoljar, eds. 2000. *Relational Autonomy: Feminist Perspectives on Autonomy, Agency, and the Social Self*. New York: Oxford University Press.

McCormack, Tara. 2008. "Power and Agency in the Human Security Framework." *Cambridge Review of International Affairs* 21 (1): 113–128.

Nagl-Docekal, Herta. 1999. "The Feminist Critique of Reason Revisited." *Hypatia* 14 (1): 49–76.

Nardin, Terry. 2002. "The Moral Basis of Humanitarian Intervention." *Ethics and International Affairs* 16 (1): 57–70.

Nussbaum, Martha. 2002. "Women and the Law of Peoples." *Politics, Philosophy & Economics* 1 (3): 283–306.

Okin, Susan Moller. 1989. *Justice, Gender and the Family*. New York: Basic Books.

Orford, Anne. 2003. *Reading Humanitarian Intervention*. Cambridge: Cambridge University Press.

Pateman, Carole. 1988. *The Sexual Contract*. Palo Alto: Stanford University Press.

Rao, Arati. 1993. "Right in the Home: Feminist Theoretical Perspectives on International Human Rights." *National Law School Journal* 1 (5): 62–81.

Rao, Arati. 2001. "Right in the Home: Feminist Theoretical Perspectives on International Human Rights." *The Philosophy of Human Rights*, edited by Patrick Hayden, 505–525. St. Paul: Paragon House.

Rawls, John. 1971. *A Theory of Justice*. Cambridge, MA: Harvard University Press.

Rawls, John. 1999. *The Law of Peoples*. Cambridge, MA: Harvard University Press (first paperback edition, 2001).

Reilly, Naimh. 2007. "Cosmopolitan Feminism and Human Rights." *Hypatia* 22 (4): 180–198.

Reisman, Michael, and Chris T. Antoniou, eds. 1994. *The Laws of War*. New York: Vintage Books.

Sample, Ruth. 2002. "Why Feminist Contractarianism?" *Journal of Social Philosophy* 33: 257–281.

Sjoberg, Laura. 2006. *Gender, Justice, and the Wars in Iraq*. Lanham, MD: Lexington Books.

Sjoberg, Laura. 2008. "Why Just War Needs Feminism Now More than Ever." *International Politics* 45 (1): 1–18.

Sokhi-Bulley, Bal. 2006. "The Optional Protocol to CEDAW: First Steps." *Human Rights Law Review* 6 (1): 143–159.

Sylvester, C. 2002. *Feminist International Relations: An Unfinished Journey*. Cambridge: Cambridge University Press.

The International Development Research Centre. 2001. *The Responsibility to Protect*. Ottawa: International Development Research Centre. Accessed September 15, 2013. http://www.responsibilitytoprotect.org/ICISS%20Report.pdf

Wellman, Christopher Heath. 2011. "Taking Human Rights Seriously." *Journal of Political Philosophy* 20 (1): 1–12.

Witt, Charlotte. 2002. "Rational Choice Theory and the Lessons of Feminism." In *A Mind of One's Own*, 2nd ed., edited by Louise Antony and Charlotte Witt, 398–417. Boulder: Westview Press.

Young, Iris Marion. 2003. "Violence Against Power: Critical Thoughts on Military Intervention." In *Ethics and Foreign Intervention*, edited by Deen Chatterjee, 251–273. New York: Cambridge University Press.

Young, Iris Marion. 2005. "The Logic of Masculinist Protection: Reflections on the Current Security State." In *Women and Citizenship*, edited by Marilyn Friedman, 15–34. New York: Oxford University Press.

Young, Iris Marion. 2006. "Responsibility and Social Justice: A Social Connection Model." *Social Philosophy and Policy* 23 (1): 102–130.

Young, Iris Marion, and Daniele Archibugi. 2003. "Envisioning a Global Rule of Law." In *Terrorism and International Justice*, edited by James Sterba, 158–170. New York: Oxford University Press.

Index

For Product Safety Concerns and Information please contact our EU
representative GPSR@taylorandfrancis.com Taylor & Francis Verlag GmbH,
Kaufingerstraße 24, 80331 München, Germany

Batch number: 08158490

Printed by Printforce, the Netherlands